Fisheries and the Law in Europe

Examining fisheries, Brexit, the Trade and Cooperation Agreement (TCA) and its consequences for the fishing industry in the UK and the EU, this book explores key issues within the complex topic of fisheries after Brexit. Assessing the new fishing relationship between the UK and the EU, which will continue to develop over the next decade, it provides an important study of the state of fisheries post-Brexit.

Taking a cross-cutting economic, legal and policy approach, the book outlines the social and economic impacts of Brexit on the UK and EU fishing industries. It critically analyses the provisions relevant to fisheries in the TCA, reflects on the bilateral fishing negotiations between the EU, UK and Norway, providing inferences as to what the "new and special relationship" might be in fisheries. It then focuses on the 2020 Fisheries Act and explores internal divergences in the nations of the UK because of devolution. Taking an international approach, the work offers an exploration of cooperation in fisheries enforcement, international and regional obligations in marine conservation, and the new horizons for the UK in international fisheries organizations and arrangements now it is no longer a member of the EU. It offers an overview of expert opinion on fisheries post-Brexit, highlighting lessons learned and future developments for fisheries in a post-Brexit world.

Having finally signed the Trade and Cooperation Agreement on 31 December 2020 after tense negotiations, the United Kingdom and European Union have found themselves in a new fisheries relationship. This book maps the complex social, economic, legal and policy issues of fisheries in a post-Brexit world and will be of interest to stakeholders and scholars.

Jonatan Echebarria Fernández is Associate Professor of Law at the Department of Law and Governance, BI Norwegian Business School, Oslo, Norway. He is Honorary Lecturer at The City Law School (City, University of London, UK) and a Spanish qualified lawyer.

Tafsir Matin Johansson holds a PhD in Maritime Affairs and currently serves as an Associate Research Officer at the World Maritime University-Sasakawa Global Ocean Institute.

Jon A. Skinner is a retired Commander, US Navy, and a long-time Alaskan resident. His PhD from the University of Alaska Fairbanks is Interdisciplinary – Polar Geography and Strategic Studies. He currently serves as an Adjunct at Matanuska-Susitna College, University of Alaska Anchorage, USA.

Mitchell Lennan is an Affiliate Researcher at the Strathclyde Centre for Environmental Law & Governance (SCELG), University of Strathclyde, Glasgow, Scotland. At the time of publication, Mitchell is completing his PhD at Strathclyde, examining the international legal challenges presented by shifting fish stocks due to climate change.

Legal Perspectives on Brexit

'Legal Perspectives on Brexit' is a peer-reviewed series of books which goes beyond responding to public curiosity aroused by the triggering of Article 50 to recognize the ongoing legal and political disputes Brexit has prompted. Aimed at academics and professionals it provides expert commentary on and predictions about the possible legislative and judicial implications of Brexit for each of the different sectors of regulation which have for so long been dominated by EU Law, creating a valuable one stop resource which exposes, explores and perhaps even resolves legal problems stemming from the separation of UK and EU legal systems.

Brexit and Aviation Law
Jan Walulik

Brexit and Procurement Law
Catherine Maddox

Brexit and the Car Industry
Matthew Humphreys and Doug Munro

Brexit and Competition Law
Andreas Stephan and Barry Rodger

Brexit and Agriculture
Ludivine Petetin and Mary Dobbs

Brexit and Intellectual Property Law
Janice Denoncourt

Fisheries and the Law in Europe
Regulation After Brexit
Edited by Jonatan Echebarria Fernández, Tafsir Matin Johansson, Jon A. Skinner and Mitchell Lennan

https://www.routledge.com/Legal-Perspectives-on-Brexit/book-series/BREXIT

Fisheries and the Law in Europe

Regulation After Brexit

Edited by
Jonatan Echebarria Fernández, Tafsir Matin Johansson, Jon A. Skinner and Mitchell Lennan

Routledge
Taylor & Francis Group
LONDON AND NEW YORK

First published 2022
by Routledge
4 Park Square, Milton Park, Abingdon, Oxon OX14 4RN

and by Routledge
605 Third Avenue, New York, NY 10158

Routledge is an imprint of the Taylor & Francis Group, an informa business

British Library Cataloguing-in-Publication Data
A catalogue record for this book is available from the British Library

Library of Congress Cataloging-in-Publication Data
A catalog record has been requested for this book

ISBN: 978-1-032-16823-4 (hbk)
ISBN: 978-1-032-17250-7 (pbk)
ISBN: 978-1-003-25248-1 (ebk)

DOI: 10.4324/9781003252481

Typeset in Bembo
by Taylor & Francis Books

Contents

Illustrations

Figures

Tables

The Editors

Jonatan Echebarria Fernández is Associate Professor of Law at the Department of Law and Governance, BI Norwegian Business School, Oslo, Norway. He is Honorary Lecturer at The City Law School (City, University of London, UK) and a Spanish qualified lawyer. He holds a PhD in Law from the Copenhagen Business School. His research interests span from Maritime and Commercial Law to Public and Private International Law as well as Environmental Law. Dr Echebarria's earlier professional experience includes working as the Permanent Representation of Spain to the EU (Shipping Working Party, Council of the EU), the European Investment Bank (EIB), the Trade Office of the Spanish Embassy in Brussels, the Luxembourg Maritime Administration and the Bilbao Port Authority (Spain).

Tafsir Matin Johansson holds a PhD in Maritime Affairs and currently serves as an Associate Research Officer at the World Maritime University-Sasakawa Global Ocean Institute. His duties include ocean governance and policy research (projects funded by the Government of Canada) and teaching and developing innovative statistical models to better assess drivers and indicators relevant to ocean research agenda. Dr Johansson is currently acting as a Principal Investigator in a technology-policy project titled BUGWRIGHT2 funded by the European Union Horizon 2020 Research and Innovation Programme.

Jon A. Skinner is a retired Commander, US Navy, and a long-time Alaskan resident. His PhD from the University of Alaska Fairbanks is Interdisciplinary – Polar Geography and Strategic Studies. He also holds an MS (Intelligence) and (MA) Strategic Planning from the Naval Postgraduate School, Monterey California. He currently serves as an Adjunct at Matanuska-Susitna College, University of Alaska Anchorage, USA.

Mitchell Lennan is an Affiliate Researcher at the Strathclyde Centre for Environmental Law & Governance (SCELG), University of Strathclyde, Glasgow, Scotland. At the time publication, Mitchell is completing his PhD at Strathclyde, examining the international legal challenges presented by shifting fish stocks due to climate change. Mr Lennan holds a BSc (Hons) in Marine and Freshwater Biology from the University of Glasgow, an MSc in Marine Science, Policy and Law from the University of Southampton, and an LLM in Global Environmental Law from the University of Edinburgh.

Contributors

Emeritus Professor Robin Churchill, University of Dundee
Professor Andrew Serdy, University of Southampton
Dr Mercedes Rosello, Senior Lecturer, Leeds-Beckett University
Mr Gerard van Balsfoort, President, Pelagic Freezer-Trawler Association
Professor Catherine Barnard, University of Cambridge
Professor Richard Barnes, University of Lincoln, University of Tromsø
Dr Miguel Núñez Sánchez, Civil servant (Special Services), Spanish Ministry of Transport, Mobility and Urban Agenda
Ms Elizabeth Bourke, Policy Officer, National Federation of Fishermen's Organisations
Mr Seán Marriott, University of Lincoln
Mr Rod Cappell, Director, Poseidon Aquatic Resource Management
Mr Ciarán O'Driscoll, Policy and Research Officer, European Movement Ireland
Mr Jimmy Buchan, Chief Executive Officer, Scottish Seafood Association

Acknowledgements

This publication is intended to capture and expand upon the findings of the research project "Legal challenges faced by coastal and fishing communities and the new British Fisheries Policy" (2020–2021). It aims to bring together leading fisheries experts from academia, industry and policy to share their expert views and experience pertaining to Brexit. The project is led by Dr Jonatan Echebarria Fernández (Principal Investigator; BI Norwegian Business School and The City Law School), Dr Tafsir Matin Johansson (Senior Expert Consultant; World Maritime University), Mr Mitchell Lennan (Impact Assistant; University of Strathclyde) and Dr Jon A. Skinner (University of Alaska, Matanuska-Susitna College).

The editors would like to thank the City Law School Higher Education Innovation Fund (HEIF) for their generous financial support without which this publication would not have materialised. The editors are also sincerely grateful to the scholars and the "Legal Challenges Faced by Coastal and Fishing Communities, Brexit and the New British Fisheries Policy" workshop participants (8 June 2021), which have supported the development of this publication with chapter contributions.

Finally, the editors would like to acknowledge with gratitude the support of the City Law School, the World Maritime University-Sasakawa Global Ocean Institute, Nippon Foundation, the University of Strathclyde, the University of Alaska and BI Norwegian Business School.

The editors
London, United Kingdom, 1 August 2021

1 Introduction

The UK and EU Fishing Industries in Profile

Jonatan Echebarria Fernández, Tafsir Matin Johansson, Mitchell Lennan and Jon A. Skinner

Introduction

For the purpose of context this first chapter sets the scene for the book by examining the United Kingdom (UK) and European Union (EU) fishing industries, utilising the best currently available reports and statistical information on the UK fishing industry. It is important to emphasise this data was collected prior to the end of the Brexit transition period, which ended on 31 December 2020. Therefore, this study can only provide an economic "snapshot" to enable a limited forensic projection based on the best currently available information. The first section will outline and summarise the UK fishing industry, while the second section provides a similar breakdown of the EU fishing industry as it pertains to fishing in UK waters. Finally, an outline of the subsequent nine chapters of this book is provided.

The UK Fishing Industry – an Overview

This subsection provides a short summary of the UK fishing industry based on the latest statistics at the time of writing by the UK government, the European Commission, independent scientific bodies and NGOs.

Breakdown of the UK fishing industry

The UK fishing industry is extremely diverse. This diversity lies in both the types of fishing vessels and fishing activity gear used,[1] the species fished and the markets they access. Additionally, "ownership of quota" is also a significant factor, and one that has been criticised for existing in an effectively privatised system.[2] The UK fishing industry is also distinguished by having both a

1 See Tables 1.1 and 1.2.
2 See G Carpenter, 'To really "take back control" of UK fisheries, we must treat fishing rights as a public resource' *SERA,* <https://www.sera.org.uk/to_really_take_back_control_of_uk_fisheries_we_must_treat_fishing_rights_as_a_public_resource> accessed 6 April 2021.

DOI: 10.4324/9781003252481-1

commercial and recreational (e.g., sea angling) component.[3] Though the recreational fishing industry in the UK is of significant economic value, contributing £1.5 billion per year,[4] this book focuses *only* on the commercial component. The commercial UK fishing industry employs over 31,000 people in the UK (0.04% of total UK employment).[5] The industry contributes annually 0.12% of Gross Domestic Product (GDP), with an average annual economic output of £1.4 billion.[6] Commercial UK fishing comprises three sectors:

1 The fishing industry – harvest of wild fish, crustaceans and molluscs;
2 The aquaculture sector – farming of fish, crustaceans, molluscs and seaweed;
3 The fish processing industry – preparation and preservation of fish for human and animal consumption[7]

Table 1.1 Breakdown of gear type and percentage of fish and shellfish catch (UK).

Fear Type	*Examples*	*Percentage of UK Catch*
Active – pursue the catch	Demersal trawlers Beam trawlers Dredges Sein nets	87% in 2019 99% of pelagic fish 91% of demersal fish
Passive – stay in place and catch comes to them	Pots and traps/creels Hooks Drift and fixed nets	< 50% of shellfish 13% of fish catch

Source: Statistics from Marine Management Organisation (MMO) 2019.[8]

3 European Parliament, 2017. Report on the state of play of recreational fisheries in the European Union. 2017/2120(INI), <www.europarl.europa.eu/doceo/document/A-8-2018-0191_EN.html?redirect#title2> accessed 6 April 2021.
4 K Hyder *et al.*, 'Recreational sea fishing in Europe in a global context – participation rates, fishing effort, expenditure, and implications for monitoring and assessment' *Fish and Fisheries* 19, 225–243; D Diz, M Lennan, K Hyder, 'Assessment of governance structures and legal instruments for recreational sea fishing and its inclusion in broader fisheries governance' *Report for Cefas* (forthcoming 2022).
5 Marine Management Organization, 'UK Sea Fisheries Statistics 2018' *Office for National Statistics, Long-term trends in UK employment: 1861 to 2018.*
6 E Ares, C Rhodes, M Ward, 'The UK Fishing Industry' House of Commons Debate Pack CDP 2017/0256 (2017), <https://researchbriefings.files.parliament.uk/documents/CDP-2017-0256/CDP-2017-0256.pdf> accessed 8 April 2021, at 4.
7 E Uberoi, G Hutton, M Ward, E Ares, 'UK Fisheries Statistics' Briefing Paper Number 2788, 23 November 2020, <https://commonslibrary.parliament.uk/research-briefings/sn02788/> accessed 8 April 2021, at 4.
8 Marine Management Organisation (MMO) 'UK Sea Fisheries Statistics 2019' (2019), https://assets.publishing.service.gov.uk/government/uploads/system/uploads/attachment_data/file/920679/UK_Sea_Fisheries_Statistics_2019_-_access_checked-002.pdf accessed 10 April 2021, at 34.

Table 1.2 Breakdown of species category (UK).

Species Category	*Definition*	*Examples*
Pelagic	Fish that inhabit the water column	e.g., Mackerel, Blue whiting, Herring, Sardines
Demersal	Fish that inhabit near and the bottom of the sea	e.g., Bass, Brill, Cod, Haddock, Hake, Halibut, Lemon Sole, Monkfish, Plaice, Whiting
Shellfish	General term for several aquatic invertebrates including molluscs and crustaceans	e.g., Nephrops (Langoustines), Lobsters, Crabs, Cockles Mussels, Clams, Scallops, Shrimps and Prawns, Squid, Whelks

Economic Output

In 2019, the fishing and aquaculture sector of the UK had an economic output of £446 million as defined in terms of Gross Value Added (GVA).[9] This was 59% lower than in 1990, highlighting the fact that the UK fishing industry has been in steady decline since 1992.[10] It is important to note that fishing productivity in the UK varies regionally. For example, in 2018 Scotland contributed 61% GVA of the UK fishing industry total (this figure includes aquaculture output), whereas the South West of the UK contributed 10%, Northern Ireland contributed 6% and Wales was 3%.[11] There were 4,491 fishing vessels registered as active in the UK in 2019 (35% had an annual fishing income of under £10,000).[12] In terms of GDP, the UK fishing industry in 2019 was worth £747 million as a whole, an increase of 44% from the £520 million in 2009.[13]

Employment and Fleet Size

In 2020 alone a total of 3,705 fishing businesses were registered in the UK.[14] In terms of employment, the UK fishing industry has also been in steady decline, with the number of fishers working on UK-registered vessels decreasing from the 48,000 when records began in 1938 to 12,000 in 2019.[15] This figure of 12,000 has remained stable since 2009.[16] Presently 45% of fishers working on

9 GVA is similar to GDP, see E Uberoi *et al.* (n 7).
10 Ibid.
11 Ibid at 5.
12 Seafish, 'Economics of the UK Fishing Fleet' (2020), <https://www.seafish.org/document/?id=c0640cf9-a9c8-4d03-8c35-6f7a966ad056> accessed 10 April 2021.
13 MMO (n 8) at 54.
14 E Uberoi *et al.* (n 7) at 6.
15 MMO (n 8) at 13.
16 Ibid. at 4.

UK vessels are on English vessels, and 40% are on Scottish vessels, 7% on Welsh, and 7% on Northern Irish. In Scotland, there were 4,847 registered fishers with the Scottish port authorities.[17] Of note, 80% of the UK fishing fleet comprises vessels 10 metres or less in length.[18] Only 4% of the UK fleet are vessels over 24 metres in length. However, these vessels consist of three-fifths total fishing capacity.[19] In terms of regions, England has the largest number of vessels in the UK; however, Scottish vessels have the highest capacity (57%) and power (49%) despite compromising only 36% of the total number of vessels in the UK.[20]

Table 1.3 Size of UK fishing fleet by country.

	Vessels <10m	*Vessels >10m*	*Total*
England	2,323	496	2,819
Scotland	156	549	2,109
Wales	385	29	414
Northern Ireland	198	128	326
Crown Dependencies	168	32	200
Total	4,634	1,234	5,958

Source: Data from MMO 2019[21]

Landings and Efforts

Between 2018 and 2019, fishing effort by the UK fleet over 10 metres decreased by 3%, with overall fishing effort by this section of the UK fleet decreasing by 35% since 2003.[22] The UK Marine Management Organisation (MMO) indicates that most of the decline of overall fishing effort has been driven by a 36% reduction in effort in the demersal trawl and seine sector of the UK fleet from 2004 to 2019.[23] The majority of fish caught by the UK fishing industry is landed in UK ports. That being said, a 'substantial proportion is landed in foreign ports. In 2019, the total weight of fish landed by UK vessels in the UK and abroad was 621,900 tonnes, of which 230,700 tonnes (37%) were landed abroad.'[24] All of the top three ports for landings of fish and shellfish in the UK are located in the north of Scotland (Peterhead, Lerwick, Fraserburgh), totalling 180,600 tonnes worth £260.3 million in 2019.[25]

17 Ibid.
18 Ibid. at 10.
19 Ibid. at 10.
20 Ibid. at 8.
21 Ibid.
22 Ibid. at 42.
23 Ibid. at 43.
24 E Uberoi *et al.* (n 7) at 16.
25 MMO (n 8) at 30.

The UK fleet catches over 150,000 tonnes of mackerel per year constituting 24% of the total UK sea fisheries catch, and of this 60% of the mackerel catch is landed outside of the UK.[26] Turning attention to shellfish, the MMO has indicated that since 1996, 'the quantity and value of key shellfish species landed by the UK fleet has increased'.[27] Two-thirds of all shellfish landed in the UK are nephrops, (i.e., langoustine or Norway lobster), scallops and crabs; the largest quantity and highest value of shellfish species are caught closest to the UK coast.[28] The total catch for shellfish by UK vessels was 146,800 tonnes, representing 25% of the total landed catch by weight.[29] In 2019, £393 million worth of shellfish was landed by the UK fleet. Pelagic fish landings were worth £247 million, and demersal fish landings were worth £347 million.[30]

Trade

As mentioned in the introduction, seafood is a globally traded commodity. Globally, the UK imports more fish than it exports. The MMO has estimated that the UK's "trade gap" is 270,000 tonnes of fish.[31] However in 2019, the UK exported more seafood to the EU than it imported from the EU.[32] The UK's imports and exports of fish and fish products are broken down in Table 1.4. It is important to bear in mind that these statistics are from 2019, prior to the UK formally leaving the EU, and thus it is difficult to gauge the true economic impact on the trade of seafood between the two trade partners at this time.

Imports

The UK is a net importer of seafood (see Table 1.4). In terms of fish imports into the UK, demersal (so-called groundfish, e.g., cod, haddock and flatfish, see

Table 1.4 Imports and exports of fish and fish products into and out of the UK by tonnage and value in GBP.

	Tonnage	*Value*
Import	854,300 tonnes	£3.6 billion
Export	496,300 tonnes	£1.9 billion
Deficit	–358,000 tonnes	–£1.7 billion

Source: Figures from 2019[33]

26 Ibid. at 24.
27 Ibid. at 27.
28 Ibid. at 27–29.
29 E Uberoi *et al.* (n 7) at 16.
30 Ibid.
31 MMO (n 8) at 4.
32 E Uberoi *et al.* (n 7) at 12.
33 Ibid. at 11.

Table 1.4) and pelagic (e.g., herring and mackerel) fish comprised 82% by weight.[34] The remaining 18% by weight were shellfish (e.g., shrimp and prawns); this is primarily due to the higher price of shellfish species.[35] In terms of fish products, 133,000 tonnes of fish products (e.g., fish meal and oils) were imported into the UK in 2019. The total imports for 2019 were 854,000 tonnes (see Table 1.4).[36] During 2019, the UK was a net importer of cod (106,000 tonnes), tuna (110,000 tonnes), and prawns (78,000 tonnes).[37] This can be explained by the fact that "UK consumers are extremely conservative in their seafood tastes and this trend is increasing over time".[38] Consumers prefer the "big five" species: cod, salmon, tuna, haddock and shrimp, which account for 80% of the market share.[39] In 2019, the UK's fish imports from the EU were worth £1.2 billion – this comprises 35% of all fish imports into the UK by value.[40] The UK's imports from non-EU countries were worth £2.2 billion.[41]

Exports

The UK exports around 80% of its catch, with the key markets being France, the United States, Spain and Ireland. In terms of exports, demersal and pelagic fish comprised 82% of fish exports from the UK by weight, while shellfish comprised 18%.[42] Total tonnage of fish products exported out of the UK was 44,000 tonnes in 2019, meaning the total exports of sea fish, fish products and freshwater fish were 500,000 tonnes.[43] The UK exported 62,000 tonnes of mackerel in 2019 and remains a net exporter of this species.[44] By value, in 2019, the UK's fish exports to the EU were worth approximately £1.4 billion, representing 67% of all fish exports from the UK by value.[45]

Preliminary Conclusions

Based on the statistics presented above, the general picture painted of the fishing industry in the UK, in at least some aspects, is an industry trending in a steady decline prior to Brexit. Indeed, the UK fishing industry is proportionally a small national industry, contributing a very small portion of total GDP. The

34 MMO (n 8) at 50.
35 Ibid.
36 Ibid. at 50.
37 Ibid. at 51–52.
38 *Fisheries and Brexit, UK in a Changing Europe Report* (2020), <https://ukandeu.ac.uk/research-papers/fisheries-and-brexit-3/> at 8.
39 Ibid. at 8.
40 E Uberoi *et al.* (n 7) at 12.
41 Ibid.
42 MMO (n 8) at 53.
43 Ibid. at 53.
44 Ibid. at 53.
45 E Uberoi *et al.* (n 7) at 12.

industry, moreover, relies heavily on exports to EU markets to stay afloat. Consumer preferences in the UK drive higher imports of fish from the EU than corresponding exports to the EU. Further, statics argue that fishing activity is not distributed evenly across the four nations of the UK – Scotland has larger vessels and lands a significantly greater tonnage of catch while England has larger vessels and employs a greater number of people. Fishing, at least in the UK public's imagination, appears to be a largely romanticised image of itself as an island nation rather than a currently accurate statistical fact. This, in conjunction with the fact that UK waters are a major source of fish for EU vessels, appeared to have given confidence to UK government negotiators that they had the upper hand when finalising the Trade and Cooperation Agreement (TCA) with their EU counterparts. An overview of the EU fishing industry as it relates to access of UK waters is outlined below.

The EU Fishing Industry in UK Waters – an Overview

This smaller section provides a snapshot of the EU fishing industry, as it pertains to vessels that fish in UK waters. This overview is based on the latest statistics available from the UK government, the European Commission, independent scientific bodies and NGOs. Globally, the EU is not a large fishing entity; like the UK the EU fishing industry does not make up a large part of the EU economy accounting for only 6% of global EU trade and 4% of fish production.[46] Most EU Member States, barring its landlocked members, have a fishing industry. Spain, Denmark and France are the big players and account for over 50% of total catch within the EU-27.[47] Prior to Brexit, the UK was between Denmark and France in terms of average catches.[48] In contrast to the previous section, it is worth emphasising that the EU is a bloc of States, some whose vessels fish UK waters only some of the time, and some whose vessels do not fish in UK waters at all. A consequence of this is that it is challenging to find disaggregated data on topics such as number of individuals employed in the EU on vessels who fish in UK waters. As such, this section groups together subsections that were presented individually in the previous section.

Breakdown of the EU Fishing Industry in UK Waters

It is estimated that in the past decade, an average of 42% of fish catches (by volume) by EU Member States were caught in UK waters. This statistic can rise to 60% depending on species or fleet.[49] EU fishers rely heavily on the

46 Fisheries and Brexit, UK in a Changing Europe Report (n 38) at 9; fishing as a percentage of EU economies for every Member State in 2017 can also be viewed here and at *Eurostat*, <ec.europa.eu/eurostat/web/national-accounts/data/database> accessed 12 April 2021.

47 Ibid. Fisheries and Brexit, UK in a Changing Europe Report at 9.

48 Ibid. at 9–10.

49 M Minarik, 'All in The Same Boat: Free Markets and Fishing Grounds – European Fisheries Alliance EUFA' *European Fisheries Alliance EUFA*, 2021, <https://fish

north-east Atlantic, which includes a substantial portion of UK waters. For example, EU-27 vessels operating in UK waters landed 656,000 tonnes of fish in 2012–2014.[50] More detail and catch breakdown by EU Member State fleets in UK waters is given here.[51] Five EU Member States historically catch 90% of the catch by weight in UK waters. These States are Demark (32%), the Netherlands (24%), France (16%), Ireland (12%) and Germany (10%).[52] These Member States rely rather heavily on access to UK waters, especially around the north-east Atlantic. For example, the Netherlands fish catch is greater than half from this area.[53]

Economic Output, Employment, Landings

The value of catches by EU vessels in UK waters was estimated to be around €524 million for the years 2013–2015.[54] Additionally, fish processing is a greater industry than in the UK. France, for example, employs twice as many individuals in fish processing compared with fish catch; Germany employs 85% of the entire fishing sector; while in Spain, one-third of jobs in the fishing industry are in fish processing.[55] These processing industries rely on the export of UK catch to maintain a steady supply of fish to process. In terms of target species, species caught by EU vessels are very different to those caught by the UK. For example, French vessels catch the greatest share of monkfish, whiting and hake, while Irish vessels catch the largest share of horse mackerel.[56] Dutch fisheries catch 80% of North Sea sole, and Danish fishers catch 90% of North Sea sprats.[57] By contrast, only 13% of UK catch comes from EU waters.[58]

Trade, Import and Exports

As discussed above the EU exports more fish to the UK than the EU imports from the UK (see also Table 1.4). This constitutes the so-called "fish swap" where France, Spain and Ireland import langoustines, scallops, crab and

eriesalliance.eu/key-issues/all-in-the-same-boat-free-markets-and-fishing-grounds/> accessed 12 April 2021.

50 J M Sobrino Heredia, 'Research for PECH Committee – Common Fisheries Policy and BREXIT – Legal Framework for Governance' *Policy Department for Structural and Cohesion Policies* (European Parliament, 2017), <https://www.europarl.europa.eu/RegData/etudes/STUD/2017/601981/IPOL_STU(2017)601981_EN.pdf> accessed 13 April 2021 at 61.

51 Ibid.

52 Fisheries and Brexit, UK in a Changing Europe Report (n 38) at 11; J M Sobrino Heredia (n 50) at 61–62.

53 Ibid. Fisheries and Brexit, UK in a Changing Europe Report.

54 J M Sobrino Heredia (n 50) at 63.

55 Fisheries and Brexit, UK in a Changing Europe Report (n 38) at 11.

56 Ibid.

57 Ibid.

58 Ibid. at 10.

mackerel from the UK. Farmed salmon is also largely imported into the EU from the UK. The greatest importers of fish and fish products from the UK, and exports from the EU to the UK were covered above.

Preliminary Conclusions

In comparison with the UK fishing industry profiled in 'The UK Fishing Industry – An Overview', it is apparent that the northern EU Member States are reliant on access to UK waters for fisheries. Vessels fish particularly in the north-east Atlantic and catch different species than UK vessels. However, the EU exports a greater value and tonnage of fish to the UK. Certain EU Member States rely on catches from UK waters to maintain their large fish processing industries.

Covid-19

In addition to the uncertainties for the UK and EU fishing industries brought about by Brexit, the unprecedented Covid-19 pandemic has seen the UK fishing industry impacted badly in its key local and international markets, including export of valuable seafood to European markets, and the closure of restaurants in the UK and abroad who source UK seafood. However, compensation schemes were created for fishers by the UK government; for example,[59] it remains to be seen how the seascape of the UK fishing industry will look when the pandemic subsides. It is important to mention the pandemic here to indicate another prominent cause of harm to the UK and EU fishing industries, which has compounded the impacts of Brexit.

For the purpose of introduction, both the UK and EU fishing industries, respectively, have been profiled with a focus on EU vessels that have access to UK waters for their catch. It can be said that the EU relies more on access to UK waters than vice versa while the UK imports a greater volume of fish from the EU, and the UK industry relies heavily on exporting catch to the EU. Brexit has brought about huge challenges in this regard. The rest of the book will address the following topics.

Chapter 2 by Robin Churchill outlines the fisheries management position of the UK up until 2020, and then analyses the constraints placed on UK fisheries management as a result of the TCA, and outlines the changes the TCA has made to fisheries management in the UK from the previous status quo. Andrew Serdy analyses the fisheries provisions of the TCA (Articles 493–511) in Chapter 3, and the imbalance of negotiating power between the parties, as well as issues with the dispute settlement provisions and the potential for

59 Marine Management Organisation, COVID Pandemic: COVID Financial Support Guide for Fishing and Seafood Businesses (2021), <https://assets.publishing.service.gov.uk/government/uploads/system/uploads/attachment_data/file/970524/One_Stop_Shop_Covid_v9-2.pdf> accessed 5 April 2021.

overcatch. Chapter 4 analyses the recent trilateral and bilateral fishing negotiations between the UK and EU, and the UK, EU and Norway to glean an initial picture of the UK's new role as an "independent" fisheries player in the North Atlantic.

Chapter 5 then examines the Fisheries Act 2020 vis-à-vis devolution in the UK, and makes inferences on how this new key piece of UK fisheries legislation empowers the devolved powers in the UK to manage fisheries in their respective waters. In keeping with the national approach, Chapter 6 by Mercedes Rosello and the editors illustrates, using the case study of Rockall, the complex framework of international legal commitments in fisheries enforcement that still apply to the UK. Continuing with international legal obligations, Chapter 7 elaborates on the UK's commitments under international environmental law applicable to fisheries, while Chapter 8 explores the UK's participation in regional fisheries management organisations after Brexit.

Chapter 9 offers multiple expert perspectives on Brexit and the new British fishing policy, based on the outcome of the workshop titled "Legal Challenges Faced by Coastal and Fishing Communities, Brexit and the New British Fisheries Policy" jointly organized by the City Law School, the International Law and Affairs Group, the Institute for the Study of European Law, the London Universities Maritime Law and Policy Research Group and the World Maritime University held on 8 June 2021. Finally, Chapter 10 offers some conclusions and summarises the key points of the book.

2 Fisheries Management in United Kingdom Waters after Brexit

An Assessment of the Changes Made by the Trade and Cooperation Agreement

Robin Churchill[*]

Introduction

Before it joined what was then the European Economic Community (EEC) in 1973, the United Kingdom (UK) had exclusive fisheries management authority over those waters to which international law accorded it jurisdiction. From 1973 to 1983 that authority was tempered by certain obligations of EEC law. However, from the beginning of 1983 the EEC, having become exclusively competent for fisheries management in the waters (i.e., the territorial sea and exclusive economic zone (EEZ)) of its Member States, adopted a comprehensive system of fisheries management for those waters under its Common Fisheries Policy (CFP). For almost 40 years, until the end of 2020, UK waters were included in that system. At the beginning of 2021, however, the UK regained its former fisheries management autonomy as a consequence of having left the European Union (EU), as the EEC had by that time become. Nevertheless, that autonomy is subject to considerable constraints under the Trade and Cooperation Agreement (TCA), the main treaty governing post-Brexit relations between the UK and the EU.[1]

The following three sections of this chapter outline in more detail the developments briefly described above. They are followed by a section analysing the constraints on the UK's regained fisheries regulatory autonomy that result from the TCA. The chapter ends with some concluding observations, briefly assessing the changes made by the TCA.[2]

* This chapter draws on the author's article, 'Fisheries Management in European Union and United Kingdom Waters after Brexit – A Change for the Better?' (2022) 36 *Ocean Yearbook* (forthcoming).

1 Trade and Cooperation Agreement between the European Union and the European Atomic Energy Community, of the one part, and the United Kingdom of Great Britain and Northern Ireland, of the other part, December 30, 2020 (entered into force provisionally on 1 January 2021 and definitively on 1 May 2021) UKTS 2021 No. 8; OJ 2021 L149/10 (TCA).

2 The provisions of the TCA relating to the waters of the Channel Islands and the Isle of Man are not discussed in this chapter as the islands are not part of the UK,

DOI: 10.4324/9781003252481-2

Fisheries Management in UK Waters before 2021

Until 1965, the UK's jurisdiction to manage fisheries was limited to its territorial sea, which at that time was no more than three miles in breadth.[3] In that year the UK extended its fisheries jurisdiction to 12 miles in accordance with the European Fisheries Convention, which, with 11 other States, it had concluded the previous year.[4] Under the Convention a State party was permitted to establish a 12-mile fisheries zone off its coasts within which it had the exclusive right to regulate fisheries. However, vessels from other parties that had traditionally fished in the outer six miles of the new zone were permitted to continue to fish there indefinitely. Importantly, Article 10 of the Convention stipulated that its provisions did not prevent the establishment of a 'special regime in matters of fisheries' between Member States of the EEC.

In June 1970, the then six members of the EEC took the first steps towards such a 'special regime', and the CFP, with the adoption of two regulations, one on 'structural' issues, the other on the common organisation of the market in fishery products.[5] The former included the so-called 'equal access' principle, according to which the vessels of one EEC Member State had the right to fish in the waters of any other Member State on the same conditions as the vessels of that other Member State. At that time, the UK had already applied to become a member of the EEC, as had Denmark, Ireland and Norway. These four applicant States were dismayed that after years of difficult negotiations, the EEC had reached agreement on the two regulations just before membership negotiations were due to begin, so that the applicant States would have to accept them as part of the *acquis communautaire*. They were particularly opposed to the equal access principle, which they feared would lead to large numbers of EEC vessels coming to fish in their waters. That fear was undoubtedly an important reason why there was a majority against Norwegian membership in the subsequent referendum. The other applicant States, however, became members of the EEC at the beginning of 1973, after having succeeded in negotiating a ten-year derogation to the equal access principle, under which fishing was reserved to the vessels of an EEC Member State in a six-mile zone off its coasts. In certain specified regions where the local population was heavily dependent on fishing, including considerable stretches of the UK's coast, access to the 6–12-mile zone was reserved for local fishing vessels, subject to any rights that the vessels of other Member States enjoyed under the European Fisheries Convention.[6]

but British Crown Dependencies. For such discussion, see Chapter 3 by Andrew Serdy in this book.

3 In this chapter, all references to 'miles' are to nautical miles.

4 Fisheries Convention, March 9, 1964 (entered into force 15 March 1966) 581 *United Nations Treaty Series* 57. The 12 parties were: Belgium, Denmark, France, Germany, Ireland, Italy, Netherlands, Poland, Portugal, Spain, Sweden and the UK.

5 Regs 2141/70 and 2142/70, OJ Special Edition 1970 (III) 707.

6 Act of Accession 1972, Arts. 100–103, OJ 1972 L73.

By the mid to late 1970s, there was a world-wide move, encouraged by the progress made in negotiations on a new coastal State maritime zone, the EEZ, at the Third UN Conference on the Law of the Sea, unilaterally to establish 200-mile EEZs or exclusive fishing zones (EFZs), without waiting for the Conference to end and the adoption of a new treaty on the law of the sea. In the north-east Atlantic, Iceland established a 200-mile EFZ in 1975, while the Faroe Islands, Greenland and Norway made it clear during 1976 that they would establish 200-mile EFZs or EEZs from the beginning of the following year. Those developments had significant implications for EEC fishing vessels, many of which (including UK vessels) had traditionally fished in the waters embraced by the new zones. They also led the EEC Commission to put forward a package of proposals under which EEC Member States in the north-east Atlantic would extend their fisheries jurisdiction to 200 miles in concert from the beginning of 1977; management of the fish stocks found within the new limits would become the exclusive responsibility of the EEC, and not individual Member States; and the EEC, rather than individual Member States, would negotiate agreements on the access of EEC fishing vessels to the waters of third States. The first of those proposed measures was successfully implemented, all the Member States concerned establishing a 200-mile EEZ or EFZ at the beginning of 1977 or shortly thereafter.[7] The EEC also successfully negotiated agreements with the Faroe Islands and Norway permitting EEC vessels to continue to fish in Faroese and Norwegian waters, albeit at a reduced level of activity.[8] No agreement could be reached with Iceland, however.[9]

There was considerable resistance, particularly from the UK, to the Commission's proposal that the EEC should become responsible for fisheries management in its Member States' waters, and negotiations on the matter in the Council of Ministers made little progress. However, the Commission received considerable support for its proposal from a ruling of the European Court of Justice in 1981 that as from the beginning of 1979 the 'power to adopt, as part of the common fisheries policy, measures relating to the conservation of the resources of the sea has belonged fully and definitively to the Community'.[10]

7 The UK established a 200-mile EFZ from the beginning of 1977 by means of the Fishery Limits Act, 1976. C. 86, <www.legislation.gov.uk/ukpga/1976/86/contents> accessed 1 July 2021; the EFZ was not converted into an EEZ until 2014.

8 Agreement on Fisheries between the European Economic Community, of the one part, and the Government of Denmark and the Home Government of the Faroe Islands, of the other part, 15 March 1977 (entered into force provisionally 1 January 1977) OJ 1980 L226/12; and Agreement on Fisheries between the European Economic Community and the Kingdom of Norway, 27 February 1980 (entered into force 16 June 1981) OJ 1980 L226/48.

9 An agreement was eventually reached in 1992. See further R Churchill and D Owen, *The EC Common Fisheries Policy* (Oxford: Oxford University Press, 2010), p. 340. See also pp. 333–338 on the EEC's Agreements with the Faroe Islands and Norway, <https://ec.europa.eu/oceans-and-fisheries/fisheries/international-agreements/northern-agreements_en> accessed 2 July 2021.

10 Case 804/79, *Commission v. United Kingdom* [1981] ECR 1045, para 17. The Court's ruling was subsequently codified in Art. 3(1)(d) of the Treaty on the

Nevertheless, it was not until January 1983 that the Council was able to agree on a community system of fisheries management.[11]

Although that system has been reviewed and modified at ten-year intervals (in 1992, 2002 and 2012/2013),[12] its basic features, as far as EU waters in the north-east Atlantic Ocean are concerned, have remained largely unchanged. Thus, each year the Council, acting on a proposal from the Commission, which in turn bases its proposals on scientific advice received from the International Council for the Exploration of the Sea (ICES), adopts total allowable catches (TAC) for most stocks of commercial interest found in EU waters. Most TACs are divided into quotas, allocated to individual Member States. The basis of allocation is the principle of 'relative stability'. The principle combines three elements – past catches, preferential treatment for regions particularly dependent on fishing, and the loss of catches resulting from the exclusion of EU vessels following the extension of fisheries jurisdiction to 200 miles – to give each Member State a percentage share of the TAC. Those percentages were negotiated and fixed in 1983,[13] and have remained largely unchanged since.

TACs and quotas are set in terms of ICES Statistical Areas, not the zones of individual Member States. The principle of equal access means that the vessels of a Member State that holds a quota for a particular ICES Statistical Area may fish for that quota anywhere in that Area, regardless of which Member States' waters come within the Area. There is one qualification to that principle: a vessel may not fish within the 12-mile zone off any Member State unless a vessel has the nationality of a Member State that enjoys historic rights to fish in the outer six miles of the zone. Those rights are set out in an annex to the basic regulation. Essentially, they are the rights that derive from the European Fisheries Convention (see above).

Although the second and third elements of the principle of relative stability tended to favour the UK, the principle as a whole, together with the equal access principle, have proved very unpopular with the UK fishing industry and many UK politicians. The two principles are seen as the reason why vessels

Functioning of the European Union (TFEU) (OJ 2016 C202/47), which provides that the EU has 'exclusive competence' in relation to 'the conservation of marine biological resources under the common fisheries policy'. This phrase has never been defined either by the Court or the EU legislature. In practice it has been interpreted widely to include most kinds of fisheries management measures. In relation to other kinds of fisheries' measures, competence is shared between the EU and its Member States: TFEU Art. 4(2)(d). However, where the EU exercises its shared competence in respect of a particular matter, the Member States lose their competence in respect of that matter: TFEU, Art. 2(2).

11 Council Regulation (EEC) 170/83, OJ 1983 L24/1.

12 See, successively, Reg. 3760/92, OJ 1992 L389/1; Reg. 2371/2002, OJ 2002 L358/59; and Reg. 1380/2013, OJ 2013 L354/22. Collectively, they are known as the basic regulations.

13 See Regs 170/83 (n 11) and 172/73, OJ 1983 L24/30. See further R Churchill and D Owen (n 9), at 149–154.

from EU Member States have taken what many in the UK have regarded as a disproportionate proportion of the catch in UK waters in recent years. Thus, during the period 2015–2018 (inclusive) that proportion has been calculated to average 46 per cent by weight (35.5 per cent by value), compared with the proportion taken by UK vessels of 33 per cent by weight (51 per cent by value).[14] By contrast, the waters of EU Member States have been far less important for UK vessels, accounting over the same period for 13.5 per cent of the UK catch by weight (10.5 per cent by value), compared with figures of 80 and 82 per cent for UK waters.[15] The catch by UK vessels in EU waters was only about one-eighth by weight (one-sixth by value) of that by EU vessels in UK waters.[16]

TACs and quotas are the central elements of management under the CFP. They are supplemented by a number of other measures. These include: technical conservation measures, such as closed areas and seasons, gear regulations, minimum fish sizes and so on;[17] multiannual plans for some stocks;[18] the landing obligation, which requires EU vessels to land all the fish that they catch rather than, as was previously often the case, discarding fish at sea that were over quota or undersized;[19] and some input controls, such as effort limitation. Although the adoption of conservation and management measures (i.e., legislative jurisdiction) lies with the EU (subject to some limited powers delegated to Member States to adopt emergency or local measures[20]), the enforcement of those measures is largely the responsibility of Member States, subject to a degree of oversight and coordination by the EU,[21] as the EU lacks more than a rudimentary competence to exercise enforcement jurisdiction.

14 See I R Napier, *Fish Landings from the UK EEZ 2015–2018* (Scalloway: NAFC Marine Centre, University of the Highlands and Islands, 2020), p. 8, <https://www.nafc.uhi.ac.uk/t4-media/one-web/nafc/research/statistics/eez-reports/EEZ-Report-2020-07-01.pdf> accessed 1 July 2021, at 8. The remaining share of the catch was taken by vessels from Norway and the Faroe Islands. Popescu and Scholaert give similar figures for the period 2012–2019: see I Popescu and F Scholaert, *EU-UK Relations in Fisheries* (European Parliament, 2021), <www.europarl.europa.eu/RegData/etudes/IDAN/2021/689341/EPRS_IDA(2021)689341_EN.pdf> accessed 1 July 2021, at 4. All website references in this chapter were correct as at 1 July 2021.

15 Ibid., at 61. Most of the catch came from Irish waters: ibid., at 69.

16 Ibid., at 113.

17 On which, see Reg. 1380/2013, (n 12), Arts. 6 and 7 and Reg. 2019/1241, OJ 2019 L198/205.

18 On which, see ibid., Arts. 9 and 10. Two such plans, those for the North Sea and Western Waters, are of particular interest to the UK. For those plans, see Regs 2018/973 and 2019/472, OJ 2018 L179/1 and Reg. 2019/472 OJ 2019 L83/2.

19 The landing obligation was introduced by Art. 15 of Reg. 1380/2013 (n 12) with effect from 2015, but did not become fully operational until 2019.

20 On which, see Reg. 1380/2013 (n 12), Arts. 13, 19 and 20.

21 On which, see ibid., Arts. 36–39 and Reg. 1224/2009, OJ 2009 L343/1.

From the EU Referendum to the Trade and Cooperation Treaty: A Fisheries Perspective

Following its success in the 2015 UK General Election, the new Conservative government decided to hold a referendum in June 2016 on whether the UK should remain within the EU or leave. The referendum resulted in a 52–48 majority in favour of 'leave'. Much of the UK fishing industry had campaigned enthusiastically in favour of 'leave', seeing it as an opportunity to throw off the shackles of the CFP, with its principles of relative stability and equal access, and obtain a much greater share of the catch in UK waters. Salmon farmers and shellfish producers, however, were much less enthusiastic, fearing that the UK's departure from the EU would mean the loss of obstacle-free access for the then sizeable export of their products to other EU Member States.[22]

The withdrawal of a Member State from the EU is governed by Article 50 of the Treaty on the European Union (TEU).[23] The 27 members of the EU other than the UK (EU-27) interpreted its somewhat ambiguous provisions to mean that an agreement on the terms of withdrawal, such as the division of EU assets and liabilities, should be negotiated first. Only when such an agreement had been concluded could negotiations begin on an agreement on the UK's future relationship with the EU. Accordingly, negotiations began on a withdrawal agreement, eventually resulting in the conclusion, in November 2018, of the Agreement on the Withdrawal of the United Kingdom from the European Union, together with an accompanying Political Declaration setting out the Framework for the Future Relationship between the European Union and the United Kingdom.[24] However, despite three attempts to do so, the then Prime Minister, Theresa May, failed to persuade the House of Commons to approve the Agreement and Declaration. That led May to resign. She was succeeded as Prime Minister by Boris Johnson. He engaged in fresh negotiations with the EU, those negotiations resulting in October 2019 in the conclusion of a revised Withdrawal Agreement and Political Declaration.[25] The main difference between Johnson's Agreement and May's concerns arrangements for Northern

22 In 2018 such exports were worth around £870 million: see Marine Management Organisation, *Sea Fisheries Statistics 2019*, Section 4: Trade, <www.gov.uk/government/statistics/uk-sea-fisheries-annual-statistics-report-2019> accessed 1 July 2021; see further Chap. 1.

23 Treaty on the European Union (2007), OJ 2016 C202/1.

24 The Agreement on the Withdrawal of the United Kingdom from the European Union, together with an accompanying Political Declaration setting out the Framework for the Future Relationship between the European Union and the United Kingdom, <www.gov.uk/government/publications/withdrawal-agreement-and-political-declaration> accessed 1 July 2021.

25 Agreement on the Withdrawal of the United Kingdom from the European Union and the European Atomic Energy Community, 24 January 2020, United Kingdom Treaty Series 2020 No. 3; and Political Declaration setting out the Framework for the Future Relationship between the European Union and the United Kingdom, <https://assets.publishing.service.gov.uk/government/uploads/system/uploads/attachment_data/file/840656/Political_Declaration_setting_out_the_framework_for_

Ireland. The House of Commons approved the revised Withdrawal Agreement by a large majority on 9 January 2020, and the UK formally left the EU on 31 January 2020.

Articles 126 and 127 of the 2019 Withdrawal Agreement established a transition period following the UK's departure from the EU, which was due to end on 31 December 2020 unless extended for one or two years by mutual agreement. During that period, the UK would remain generally subject to EU law, including that relating to the CFP. Article 130 of the Agreement provided that the UK would be consulted over any TACs adopted during the transition period and that allocation of those TACs would continue to be determined by the principle of relative stability. Paragraphs 71–74 of the Political Declaration on the framework of the future relationship stated that while 'preserving regulatory autonomy', the EU and UK should cooperate with each other, and other States, to ensure fishing at sustainable levels and to develop non-discriminatory measures for the conservation, rational management and regulation of fisheries, including shared stocks. Furthermore, the EU and UK would 'use their best endeavours' to conclude and ratify 'a new fisheries agreement on, *inter alia*, access to waters and quota shares' by 1 July 2020 in order for it to be in place in time to be used for determining TACs and quotas for the first year after the transition period.

While negotiations on the first Withdrawal Agreement had been taking place, the UK government published a White Paper on *Sustainable Fisheries for Future Generations* in July 2018.[26] This set out the government's vision as to how fisheries in UK waters would be managed after the UK had left the EU. The core principles of management would be sustainability and an ecosystem approach. In addition, the White Paper outlined the proposed form that future fisheries relations between the UK and the EU should take.[27]

Following the UK's departure from the EU, negotiations began on an agreement on future relations between the UK and the EU. Each party published its proposals for the form that such relations should take as far as fisheries were concerned. The UK's proposals were set out in a draft agreement published in May 2020,[28] which reflects and builds on the proposals in the government's 2018 White Paper. Under the draft agreement, the parties would conduct negotiations each year over TACs for fish stocks that were 'shared', defined as stocks that are found in the waters of both the UK and EU. Very

the_future_relationship_between_the_European_Union_and_the_United_Kingdom.pdf> accessed 1 July 2021.

26 *Sustainable Fisheries for Future Generations* (The White Paper) July 2018, Cm. 9660 (2018), <https://assets.publishing.service.gov.uk/government/uploads/system/uploads/attachment_data/file/722074/fisheries-wp-consult-document.pdf> accessed 1 July 2021.

27 Ibid., at 8 and 18–19.

28 UK government, Draft Working Text for a Fisheries Framework Agreement between the UK and EU, <https://assets.publishing.service.gov.uk/government/uploads/system/uploads/attachment_data/file/886009/DRAFT_Fisheries_Framework_Agreement.pdf> accessed 2 July 2021.

many of the stocks of chief commercial interest found in UK waters are of this character. Annual negotiations would also cover the allocation of TACs between the parties, based on the principle of zonal attachment,[29] and access to each other's waters. The draft agreement is broadly similar to the EU's agreement with Norway,[30] which the UK government saw as a suitable model.[31]

The EU, however, had very different ideas about its future fisheries relations with the UK. The negotiating directives adopted by the Council of Ministers in February 2020 to direct the European Commission in its negotiations with the UK stated that the EU should seek to maintain the status quo on allocation and access, while proposing cooperation over the sustainable management of stocks that had now become shared between the EU and the UK.[32] In March 2020 the European Commission added further detail to the EU's proposals in the section of fisheries in its Draft Agreement on the New Partnership with the UK.[33]

Not surprisingly, given how far apart the parties' initial negotiating positions were, fisheries proved to be one of the thorniest issues in the negotiations on the future relationship agreement.[34] Negotiations became so protracted that it proved impossible to conclude the separate fisheries agreement envisaged by the Political Declaration by the deadline specified. Eventually, however, with both sides making considerable concessions, agreement was reached on the fisheries elements, along with all the other elements, of the future relationship agreement on Christmas Eve 2020, just one week before the expiry of the transition period. The agreement, the Trade and Cooperation Agreement (TCA) as it is formally entitled,[35] was signed on 30 December1, and entered provisionally into force on 1 January 2020.

The Regaining of Fisheries Management Autonomy by the UK

The TCA provides that in principle the EU and UK each has regulatory autonomy for the management of the fish stocks found in its waters.[36] It was

29 The principle of zonal attachment is not defined in the draft agreement. It is often considered to mean that each party's share of the TAC of a shared fish stock should correspond to the proportion of that stock found in its waters. See also Annex C of the government's White Paper (n 26), where the concept of zonal attachment is discussed.

30 See (n 8).

31 See White Paper (n 26), at 8 and 18.

32 Council of the EU, doc. 5870/20 ADD 1 REV 3 of 25 February 2020, paras 86–91, <www.consilium.europa.eu/media/42736/st05870-ad01re03-en20.pdf> accessed 1 July 2021.

33 Draft Agreement on the New Partnership with the UK, <https://ec.europa.eu/info/sites/default/files/200318-draft-agreement-gen.pdf> accessed 1 July 2021; the fisheries provisions are at 93–98.

34 For a detailed account of the fisheries negotiations, see R Churchill at * at the beginning of this chapter.

35 See (n 1).

36 Ibid., Art. 496(1).

politically important for the UK government to have this principle recognised explicitly in the TCA, given its attachment to the idea of Brexit as representing the regaining of lost sovereignty by the UK and once again becoming an 'independent coastal State'. This phrase is both a tautology, as States are by definition independent, and misleading, as it implies that the United Kingdom was not an 'independent State' while a member of the EU. While there were certainly greater limitations on its sovereignty while a member compared with the position before and since, it did not cease to be 'independent'.[37] Nevertheless, the phrase has been widely used in official UK publications and is even found in the TCA itself.[38]

The regaining of its fisheries management autonomy represents a significant challenge for the UK. Prior to 2021, it had not engaged in fisheries management for nearly 40 years, apart from the enforcement of EU measures and the adoption of some local measures permitted by the basic regulations of the CFP. Its principal fisheries legislation dated from the period 1966–1981 and was unsuitable for the new world of sustainable, precautionary and ecosystem-based management. Once it became clear that it would be leaving the EU, the UK had to set about creating the necessary administrative and legislative framework to enable it to exercise its new powers of fisheries management. The legislative framework is now provided by the Fisheries Act 2020.[39] The Act sets out the objectives of UK fisheries management, and confers a duty on ministers to implement those objectives and the powers necessary to do so. Day-to-day management is carried out by the Marine Management Organisation, an executive non-departmental public body, sponsored by the government ministry responsible for fisheries, the Department for Environment, Food and Rural Affairs. In exercising its fisheries management responsibilities, the Organisation works closely with the relevant bodies of the devolved administrations in Northern Ireland, Scotland and Wales, fisheries being a devolved matter.[40]

37 See further A Serdy, 'The 2018 Fisheries White Paper, the Fisheries Act 2020 and Their International Legal Dimension' (2021) 10(1) *Cambridge International Law Journal* 73 at 76–77. He suggests that the reference to 'coastal' in the phrase reflects the change in the position of the UK from having had significant distant-water fishing interests up to the mid-1970s to the position today, where UK vessels fish predominantly in UK waters.

38 See (n 1), for example, Preamble, recital 19; Art. 494(1); and Annex 38, preamble.

39 Fisheries Act 2020, <www.legislation.gov.uk/ukpga/2020/22/contents/enacted> accessed 1 July 2021; for commentary on the Act, see E Ares, *Fisheries Act 2020*, House of Commons Library Briefing Paper No. 8994 (2020), <https://researchbriefings.files.parliament.uk/documents/CBP-8994/CBP-8994.pdf> accessed 2 July 2021.

40 Further details on how management responsibilities are shared between the constituent parts of the UK are beyond the scope of this chapter. For discussion of this issue, see chap. 5 of this book and the White Paper, (n. 26), pp. 21–2 and 26–8.

Constraints on the UK's Fisheries Management Autonomy Resulting from the Trade and Cooperation Treaty

Although the UK has regained regulatory autonomy for fisheries management in its waters, that autonomy is subject to a number of wide-ranging constraints laid down by the TCA. The principal constraints concern the objectives and principles of fisheries management; obligations of non-discrimination, proportionality and prior notification; the joint management of many stocks; and the access of EU vessels to UK waters. The details of these constraints, which also apply to the EU *mutatis mutandis*, will be examined in turn.

Objectives and Principles of Fisheries Management

Article 494 of the TCA sets out various objectives and principles of fisheries management. There is a degree of ambiguity in the TCA about both the normativity of these objectives and principles and the fish stocks to which they apply. As regards the latter, Article 494(1) and (2) state that the objectives apply to 'shared stocks', whereas according to Article 494(3), only two of the nine principles listed there explicitly apply to 'shared stocks', the remainder applying to stocks generally. Article 496 also refers to the objectives and principles set out in Article 494 in the context of 'any [fisheries management] measures', without limiting such measures to those applicable only to shared stocks. In practice, the ambiguity over whether the TCA's objectives and principles apply only to the management of shared stocks is of limited significance because of the TCA's definition of 'shared stocks'. According to that definition, '"shared stocks" means fish, including shellfish, of any kind that are found in the waters of the Parties, which includes molluscs and crustaceans'.[41] This is a somewhat odd, and grammatically cumbersome, definition. It does not state explicitly that a shared stock has to be found in the waters of *both* parties, as is generally understood to be necessary under international fisheries law.[42] In any case, most stocks found in UK waters (with the exception of most stocks of shellfish) are also found in the waters of the EU (and in some cases Norway) and are therefore 'shared' as that term is generally used in international fisheries discourse.

As mentioned, the TCA is also ambiguous about the normativity of the objectives and principles set out in Article 494. As regards objectives, Article 494(1) provides that the parties (i.e., the UK and EU) 'shall cooperate with a view to ensuring that fishing activities for shared stocks in their waters are environmentally sustainable in the long term and contribute to achieving economic and social benefits'. Article 494(2) goes on to provide that the parties 'share the objective of exploiting shared stocks at rates intended to maintain and progressively restore populations of harvested species above biomass levels

41 TCA (n 1), Art. 495(1)(c).

42 D R Rothwell and T Stephens, *The International Law of the Sea* (Oxford: Hart, second edition, 2016) 327.

that can produce the maximum sustainable yield'. Article 496 also addresses the objectives in Article 494, paragraph 1 stipulating that 'each Party shall decide on any measures applicable to its waters in pursuit of the objectives set out in Article 494(1) and (2)'. None of the three provisions actually lays down an *obligation* to give effect to a particular objective: they are all essentially hortatory. In substantive terms, there is also some potential inconsistency between the objectives of environmental sustainability and the achievement of 'economic and social benefits' if the latter means that measures may be adopted in order to allow fishers to take increased catches for short-term economic gain, even if that impacts negatively on the sustainability of stocks.

Normatively, the position with the principles of management listed in Articles 494(3) is more straightforward, both that provision and Article 496(1) stipulating that the parties are required to do no more than 'have regard' to them. However, even that stipulation is a little misleading, as closer inspection of the TCA reveals that three of the principles in Article 494 – those providing that conservation and management measures should be based on the best scientific advice, principally that of ICES (principle (c)), that fisheries management measures should be non-discriminatory (principle (f)) and that fisheries data should be shared (principle (g)) – are made legally binding by later provisions of the TCA.[43] Moreover, the principle of ensuring compliance with fisheries management measures (principle (h)) is effectively legally binding, as any non-compliance by one party entitles the other party to take remedial measures under Article 506.[44] There is also a specific, if limited, obligation to ensure compliance in Article 497(2).[45] The remaining five principles that are not otherwise made legally binding include: (a) 'applying the precautionary approach to fisheries management';[46] (b) 'promoting long-term sustainability (environmental, social and economic) and optimum utilisation of shared stocks', which largely repeats the objective in Article 494(1); (d) 'ensuring selectivity in fisheries to protect juvenile and spawning aggregations of fish and to avoid and reduce unwanted bycatch'; (e) 'taking due account of and minimising harmful impacts of fishing on the marine ecosystem and taking due account of the need to preserve marine biological diversity'; and (i) 'ensuring the timely implementation of any agreed measures into the Parties' regulatory frameworks'.

In practice, the objectives and principles in Article 494 provide quite limited constraints on the UK's fisheries management autonomy. Indeed, from an environmental perspective, one might wish that they placed rather greater constraints on that autonomy. In any case, the TCA's provisions on objectives and principles do not go beyond the fisheries management objectives of the Fisheries Act 2020.[47] Indeed, the Act goes further in some respects, notably in

43 TCA (n 1), see Arts. 496(2) and 507.
44 For discussion of this provision, see Serdy (n 2).
45 See TCA (n 1). See further the text following note 69 .
46 For comment on this principle, see Serdy (n 2).
47 See Fisheries Act 2020 (n 39), c. 22, s. 1.

requiring an ecosystem-based approach to management,[48] something that is not explicitly called for by the TCA, although it is to some extent covered by principle (e) above.

Obligations of Non-discrimination, Proportionality and Prior Notification

A more significant restriction on the UK's fisheries management autonomy are certain obligations of form and procedure. First, Article 496(2) lays down an obligation on each party not to apply measures to the fishing vessels of the other party in its waters unless it also applies the same measures to its own vessels. Second, Article 494(3)(f) provides that a party's measures must be 'proportionate', a term that the TCA does not define or explain. The term may well be intended to have the meaning that it has in EU and UK administrative law, where the concept of proportionality refers to a requirement that no stricter means be used than are necessary to achieve the particular end desired; or as Lord Diplock, a former senior British judge once graphically put it: 'you must not use a sledgehammer to crack a nut when a nutcracker will do'. Strictly speaking, proportionality under the TCA is a principle rather than an obligation, but in practice the victim of an allegedly disproportionate fisheries measure could invoke EU or UK administrative law to challenge it before an appropriate court. Third, Article 496(3) of the TCA provides that the measures of one party that 'are likely to affect the vessels' of the other party must be notified to the other party before they are applied, 'allowing sufficient time for the other Party to provide comments or seek clarification'.

Joint Management of Stocks

A far-reaching constraint on the UK's fisheries management autonomy are various obligations of joint management for many stocks, most importantly the 76 stocks listed in Annex 35. Although these stocks are nowhere identified or described in the TCA as 'shared stocks', it is likely that they are, both as that term is used in international fisheries discourse and as defined in the TCA.

The main tool for joint UK–EU management of Annex 35 stocks is the setting each year of total allowable catches (TACs). Under Article 498 TACs are to be based on 'the best available scientific advice, as well as other relevant factors, including socio-economic aspects'. The reference to 'socio-economic aspects' suggests that the scientific advice, which is primarily to be provided by ICES, may be departed from to set larger TACs than recommended by ICES in order to obtain short-term economic gain for the fishing industry. If that happens in practice to any degree, as it has in the past,[49] stocks will be fished above safe biological levels and the TCA's objective of sustainability ignored. If the parties have failed to agree on TACs by 20 December preceding the year to

48 See ibid., s. 1(4) and (10).
49 See infra (n 77).

which TACs are intended to apply, each party must set 'a provisional TAC corresponding to the level advised by ICES, applying from 1 January'.[50] Provisional TACs continue to apply until the parties reach agreement on definitive TACs.

Given that the TCA did not come into force provisionally until 1 January 2021, it was too late for the timetable envisaged for the setting of agreed TACs for 2021 to apply. Nevertheless, the parties held talks to agree TACs for 2021, although agreement was not reached until June 2021.[51] In the meantime, each party had set provisional TACs, as required by Article 499 of the TCA.[52]

The setting of TACs is the only management measure prescribed by the TCA for Annex 35 stocks. In the case of the EU, those TACs will be supplemented by the measures outlined earlier in this chapter, such as technical conservation measures, the landing obligation and so on. Those measures will apply to EU waters and, to some degree, to EU vessels fishing in UK waters. However, the TCA does not oblige the UK to adopt any comparable measures for its vessels fishing in its waters. Nevertheless, the UK has done so, in the first instance by rolling over into UK law those EU fisheries measures that were in force on the date that it left the EU.[53] Amendments may subsequently be made to those measures: that has already been done to a degree,[54] and no doubt will happen further as time goes by. The TCA imposes no constraints on the non-TAC measures for Annex 35 stocks that the UK may decide to adopt other than the general constraints on the UK's management authority identified above. One might have thought that a degree of harmonisation of EU and UK measures would be desirable in order to avoid the risk of one party's conservation and management measures undermining the other party's measures. However, the TCA does no more than provide that the parties' annual consultations on TACs 'may also cover … measures for fisheries management, including, where appropriate, fishing effort limits'.[55] Such measures were in fact discussed during the 2021 consultations.[56]

50 TCA (n 1), Art. 499(2).

51 Written Record of Fisheries Consultations between the United Kingdom and European Union for 2021, 11 June 2021 (hereafter EU–UK Written Record 2021), <https://ec.europa.eu/oceans-and-fisheries/news/sustainable-fisheries-commission-signs-first-ever-annual-agreement-fishing-united-kingdom-2021_en> accessed 1 July 2021.

52 EU Regs 2021/91 and 2021/92, OJ 2021 L31/20 and 31, as amended by Regs 2021/406 and 2021/703, OJ 2021 L81/1 and L146/1. The Regs cover the period from 1 January to 31 July 2021. The UK does not appear to have published provisional TACs. Instead, it has published the UK's share of provisional TACs, <www.gov.uk/government/publications/fishing-opportunities-for-british-fishing-boats-in-2021> accessed 2 July 2021.

53 Under the European Union (Withdrawal) Act 2018, c. 16, <www.legislation.gov.uk/ukpga/2018/16/contents/enacted> accessed 2 July 2021, s. 3.

54 See, for example, Fisheries Act 2020 (n. 39), Schedule 11, para. 11.

55 TCA (n 1) Article 498(4). Such measures are also among the matters that the Specialised Committee on Fisheries, established by Art. 8(1)(q) of the TCA (n 1), may discuss: see Art. 508(1)(d).

56 See EU–UK Written Record 2021 (n 51), para. 12.

The UK and the EU together share a number of commercially important stocks in the North Sea with Norway. They are listed in table A of Annex 36. The management of those stocks is obviously not directly addressed by the TCA as Norway is not a party to it. Instead, it is envisaged that such management will take place under a new trilateral agreement to be negotiated.[57] Pending the conclusion of such an agreement, the three parties reached an ad hoc agreement in March 2021, which establishes TACs for the stocks concerned for 2021 and each party's share of those TACs.[58] Although the management of such stocks is not in principle governed by the TCA, the latter is not without some relevance. First, Article 505(5) provides that the UK and EU 'shall approach the management of those stocks … in accordance with objectives and principles set out in Article 494'. Second, Article 499(2) provides that should the three parties be unable to agree on TACs for any future year, the EU and UK are to set provisional TACs in the way described above. These two articles also apply to certain stocks of mackerel and blue whiting listed in table B of Annex 36, which the UK and EU together share with a number of third countries, including the Faroe Islands, Iceland and Norway.

Access of EU Vessels to UK Waters

A further constraint on the UK's fisheries management autonomy concerns its competence to determine how many and which EU vessels may fish in its waters. Where the parties have agreed on TACs for Annex 35 stocks, the TAC for each stock is shared between the UK and the EU according to the percentage shares set out in Annex 35, which vary from stock to stock.[59] Where the parties have been unable to agree on TACs and thus have unilaterally set provisional TACs (as explained above), each of them must also set its share of the provisional TAC, which must not exceed its share as set out in Annex 35.[60]

The EU will allocate its share of agreed (or provisional) TACs for Annex 35 stocks between its Member States in the form of quotas, according to the principle of relative stability. Those States will in turn distribute their quotas to vessels having their nationality. That raises the question of what access a vessel holding such a quota in respect of an ICES Statistical Area that includes UK waters will have to those waters. During the period 2021–2026 inclusive, that access will essentially be the same as it was under the CFP before Brexit (as outlined earlier in this chapter), except that in those parts of the 6–12-mile zone around the coasts of Scotland and the north of England where vessels from some EU Member States had access before Brexit, they no longer have

57 Agreed Record of Fisheries Consultations between the European Union, Norway and the United Kingdom for 2021, 16 March 2021, <https://ec.europa.eu/oceans-and-fisheries/fisheries/international-agreements/northern-agreements_en> accessed 2 July 2021, para. 8. See also Chapters 3 and 4 in this book.

58 Ibid., Table 1.

59 TCA (n 1), Art. 498(3).

60 Ibid., Art. 499(7).

such access.[61] From 2027 onwards the terms of access are to be discussed in the annual consultations between the UK and EU on TACs. Where agreement has been reached on TACs for Annex 35 stocks, each party must grant the vessels of the other party access to fish in its waters in the relevant ICES areas 'at a level and on conditions determined in' those consultations with the aim of 'ensuring a mutually satisfactory balance between the interests of both Parties … In particular, the outcome of the consultations should normally result in each Party granting access at a level that is reasonably commensurate with the Parties' respective shares of the TACs.'[62] EU vessels will also have access on the same basis for any quotas they hold under arrangements between the UK, EU and third countries such as Norway.[63] Where the parties have not been able to agree on TACs, the TCA contains complex provisions on provisional access, the details of which are beyond the scope of this chapter.[64]

In addition to access to fish for Annex 35 stocks, EU vessels will be able to fish in UK waters 'for non-quota stocks … at a level that at least equates to the average tonnage fished by' EU vessels in UK waters during the period 2012–2016.[65] 'Non quota stocks' are defined in Article 495(1)(e) as 'stocks which are not managed through TACs'. Instead, they are stocks that are managed by other means, such as limitations on effort. Such stocks include most species of shellfish, sardines, red mullet and lemon sole. The TCA has little to say about such stocks. Apart from the provisions on access and the definition section, the only other reference is to the Specialised Committee on Fisheries developing 'multi-year strategies for the conservation and management of non-quota stocks'.[66]

The TCA also provides that each party shall grant access to vessels of the other party to fish for the 12 stocks listed in table F of Annex 36 'at a level that is reasonably commensurate with the Parties' respective shares of the TACs'.[67] The stocks listed in table F are ones 'that are only present in one Party's waters', for which TACs are set unilaterally by the party concerned. Nevertheless, table F, reflecting past practice, provides for a fixed percentage share of these stocks for the other party.[68]

61 Ibid., Annex 38.
62 Ibid., Art. 500(3) and (4).
63 Ibid., Annex 38, Art. 2(1)(a), for the period 2021–27; and Art. 500(4)(a), for the period thereafter.
64 Ibid., Art. 500(5) and (6); for a detailed discussion of these provisions, see Serdy (n 2).
65 Ibid. (n 1) Annex 38, Art. 2(1)(b), for the period 2021–2027; and Art. 500(4)(b), for the period thereafter.
66 Ibid., Art. 508(1)(c). In their discussions on TACs for 2021, the parties confirmed their commitment to developing such strategies: see EU–UK Written Record 2021 (n 51), para. 13.
67 Ibid. (n 1), Annex 38, Art. 2(1)(a), for the period 2021–2027; and Art. 500(4)(a), for the period thereafter.
68 See also EU–UK Written Record 2021 (n 51), para. 7 and table 2.

Where EU vessels have access to UK waters in the ways described above, the EU must send the UK a list of vessels for which it seeks authorisations or licences to fish, and the UK 'shall issue' such authorisations or licences, seemingly without any discretion.[69] Under Article 497(2) the EU must 'take all necessary measures to ensure compliance by its vessels with the rules applicable to those vessels' in the UK's waters. When granting access to its waters from 2027 onwards, the UK will be able to take into account the compliance of individual or groups of EU vessels with its rules during the previous year, and the measures taken by the EU to address any non-compliance.[70] Also from 2027 onwards, the parties may agree 'further specific access conditions' during their annual consultations on access.[71]

An Assessment of the Changes Made by the Trade and Cooperation Agreement

This chapter will conclude by attempting to assess the changes made by the TCA. This will be done from two perspectives: that of fisheries management in UK waters, and that of the UK fishing industry. As regards the former, the UK's departure from the EU and CFP means that it has in principle become responsible for the management of the fish stocks found in its waters. However, that newly regained fisheries management autonomy is subject to a number of significant constraints prescribed by the TCA. Thus, the UK is required to: pursue the objectives and principles of fisheries management set out in the TCA; ensure that any fisheries management measures that it may adopt are non-discriminatory vis-à-vis EU vessels, proportionate and notified to the EU before their adoption; set TACs for the 76 stocks listed in Annex 35 jointly with the EU; and allow EU fishing vessels much the same access to its waters as they enjoyed before Brexit, at least until 2027.

It remains to be seen whether the UK's management of the fish stocks found in its waters, both when undertaken alone and when exercised together with the EU, or with the EU and Norway, will meet the goal of sustainability prescribed both by the TCA and the Fisheries Act 2020. The TACs for Annex 35 stocks agreed by the UK and EU for 2021 will need to be studied carefully to assess how far they conform to ICES scientific advice – an exercise that is beyond the scope of this chapter – and thus what kind of pointer that they offer to the future. For comparison, it appears that the TACs agreed by the UK, EU and Norway in 2021 for the six most commercially important North Sea stocks are in line with ICES' advice.[72]

There is certainly scope for the new post-Brexit management regime to improve on the EU's past record of fisheries management in UK waters.

69 TCA (n 1), Art. 497(1).
70 Ibid., Art. 500(7).
71 Ibid., Art. 500(2).
72 Agreed Record (n 57), paras 12–17.

According to a report by the environmental NGO, Oceana, published in January 2021, of 104 stocks audited (of which 82 are shared by the EU and the UK, or by the EU, the UK and Norway), only 35.6 per cent (43.9 per cent of shared stocks) were healthy in terms of stock size; 20.2 per cent (15.9 per cent of shared stocks) were in a critical condition, and there was insufficient data to make a judgement about the remainder, 'leaving them at greater risk of unsuitable management decisions'.[73] In terms of exploitation status, 37.5 per cent (42.7 per cent of shared stocks) were exploited sustainably, while 28.8 per cent (25.6 per cent of shared stocks) were overfished: in relation to the remainder, there was insufficient data to reach a conclusion.[74] It is noteworthy that the record for shared stocks is a little better than for stocks found only in UK waters. Of the ten most commercially important stocks for UK fishers (eight of which are shared), three (north-east Atlantic mackerel, North Sea haddock and west of Scotland nephrops) were in a healthy state and sustainably exploited. Of the remainder, two (North Sea whiting and north-east Atlantic blue whiting) had a healthy stock size but were being overfished; one (North Sea herring) was in a critical condition but being sustainably exploited; two (North Sea cod and southern North Sea crab) were overexploited and consequently their biomass was below safe biological reference points; and for two of the ten stocks (North Sea monkfish and English Channel scallops), there was inadequate data.[75] Similar findings have also been made by the Marine Management Organisation for 13 'key' stocks found in UK waters.[76]

It has been argued that the main reason why the EU does not have a better record of management for the fish stocks in the north-east Atlantic (including those found in UK waters) is because it has frequently set TACs for some stocks in excess of scientific advice,[77] although in recent years the degree to which it has done so has declined.[78] It remains to be seen whether that trend will continue under the TCA, or whether there will be a reversion to greater departure from the scientific advice. The fact that it took the EU and the UK

73 Oceana, *UK Fisheries Audit* (2021), <https://europe.oceana.org/sites/default/files/oceana_uk_fisheries_audit.pdf> accessed 2 July 2021, pp. 7, 27 and 30–31.

74 Ibid.

75 Ibid., at 45. Commercial importance was based on landings by UK vessels. Thus, not all the stocks are found exclusively in UK waters. This is especially the case with blue whiting – see Chapter 4.

76 Marine Management Organisation, *Stocks and their Level of Exploitation* (2020), 9–23, <https://assets.publishing.service.gov.uk/government/uploads/system/uploads/attachment_data/file/920035/2019_Main_stocks_and_their_level_of_exploitation.pdf> accessed 2 July 2021. 'Key' stocks are not defined. In places they are referred to as the 'main' stocks in UK waters. There is a fair degree of overlap between these stocks and Oceana's ten stocks.

77 Oceana (n 73), *passim*; and the New Economics Foundation, *Landing the Blame: Overfishing in the North-East Atlantic 2020*, <https://neweconomics.org/uploads/files/LtB_NE_Atlantic_2020.pdf> accessed 2 July 2021. The latter estimates that between 2001 and 2019 60 per cent of TACs, on average, exceeded ICES advice: see pp.1–2.

78 Oceana (n 73), at 10 and 71–73.

five months to agree on TACs for 2021 may simply be a sign of teething problems, exacerbated by the fact that the TCA was not concluded until almost the end of 2020 so that the envisaged timetable for agreeing TACs could not be followed, or it may be an indication that the EU and the UK will find it more difficult to agree on TACs than the Council of the EU on its own has done in the past. It is concerning that while it was a member of the EU, the UK is said to have been one of the Member States that regularly pushed for TACs to exceed ICES advice.[79]

Other reasons for the EU's inadequate management record in the north-east Atlantic include poor compliance with its measures, driven in part by excess capacity in EU fishing fleets. Following Brexit, the UK is in a position to improve compliance both by better enforcement and by eliminating excess capacity from its fishing fleet. Whether it will do so remains to be seen.

Turning now to an assessment of the changes made by the TCA from the perspective of the UK fishing industry, the latter is not a monolithic entity with a single set of interests.[80] The focus here will be on the marine capture side of the industry rather than on processing and mariculture. The TCA confers two significant benefits on UK fishers. First, there will be a gradual increase during the period 2021–2026 in the UK's share of TACs for 53 of the 76 Annex 35 stocks and of the stocks listed in tables A and B of Annex 36 (those shared with Norway and other north-east Atlantic countries), compared with its pre-Brexit shares under the CFP. Most of those increases are slight and will be distributed unevenly between different sectors of the industry.[81] Stocks where there are significant increases include Celtic Sea haddock, North Sea haddock, hake, herring, sole and whiting, and nephrops in ICES Area 7.[82]

According to the UK government, the increase in quotas equates to a transfer of 25 per cent by value of the EU's pre-Brexit catch in UK waters to the UK, which is worth £146m, and the share of the total catch taken in UK waters taken by UK vessels rising to around two-thirds.[83] Nevertheless, that increase is significantly less than the UK fishing industry had been hoping for.

The second benefit of the TCA for UK fishers is the ending of the access of some EU vessels to the 6–12-mile zone around Scotland and the north of England. That means that inshore fishermen in those areas will no longer face competition from EU vessels. That change is in theory balanced by the loss of

79 New Economics Foundation (n 77), p. 2.

80 See further Chapter 1 of this book.

81 See further B Stewart, 'What does the Trade Deal mean for Fisheries', <https://ukandeu.ac.uk/fisheries-trade-deal/> accessed 2 July 2021.

82 See further ABPmer, *EU–UK Trade and Cooperation Agreement: Thoughts on Fisheries from a UK Perspective* (2021), <www.abpmer.co.uk/blog/white-paper-eu-uk-trade-and-cooperation-agreement-thoughts-on-fisheries-from-a-uk-perspective/> accessed 2 July 2021, at 2–5.

83 UK government, *UK–EU Trade and Cooperation Agreement: Summary* (2020), <https://assets.publishing.service.gov.uk/government/uploads/system/uploads/attachment_data/file/962125/TCA_SUMMARY_PDF_V1-.pdf> accessed 2 July 2021, para 125.

access of UK fishers to two of the five areas of the 6–12-mile zone off the coasts of EU Member States where previously they had the right to fish. However, it appears that in practice those rights were little exercised, so that the changes made by the TCA in access to the 6–12-mile zone represent an overall gain for UK fishers. However, that gain is less than the UK industry had been hoping for, and indeed had been led by the UK government to expect, which was an end to fishing by EU vessels in the whole of the UK's 6–12-mile zone.

While UK fishers have obtained some modest benefit from the TCA in terms of increased quotas and reduced access to the 6–12-mile zone, they have also suffered a major setback. That setback results, not from the fisheries provisions of the TCA, but from its trade provisions. Because consumer demand for fish in the UK is concentrated on a limited number of species (principally white fish), UK fishers have traditionally exported a significant proportion of their catch, around half of it going to the EU.[84] Before Brexit, such exports were free of tariffs, quantitative restrictions and other non-tariff barriers under the rules of the EU's internal market. However, following the 2016 referendum on EU membership, the UK government decided that the UK would leave the internal market. That was not an inevitable consequence of Brexit: it is possible for a State to be within the internal market even though it is not a member of the EU, as shown by the examples of Iceland, Liechtenstein and Norway. Instead of continuing UK participation in the internal market, the TCA has replaced it with a free trade area between the UK and the EU. That means that goods, including fishery products, may continue to be exported from the UK to the EU free of tariffs and quantitative restrictions. However, they are now subject to the EU's non-tariff trade measures. In the case of fisheries, those measures include a requirement to provide documentation showing that the fishery product in question complies with the rules of origin prescribed by the TCA and is not the product of illegal, unreported or unregulated fishing. Exports must also comply with the EU's sanitary and phytosanitary regulations, and such compliance must be certified and documented.[85] Completing the required documentation and obtaining the necessary veterinary certification represent considerable extra costs for UK exporters of fishery products.

When introduced at the beginning of 2021, the EU's non-tariff measures had a dramatic, and adverse, impact on UK exports of fishery products to the

84 Marine Management Organisation, *Sea Fisheries Statistics 2019, Section 4: Trade*, <www.gov.uk/government/statistics/uk-sea-fisheries-annual-statistics-report-2019> accessed 2 July 2021. See also Popescu and Scholaert (n 14), pp. 8–9 and Chapter 1 of this book.

85 For a summary of these measures, see Popescu and Scholaert (n 14), pp. 11–12. The Marine Management Organisation has produced guidance to UK exporters on these matters: Exporting or Moving Fish from the UK, <www.gov.uk/guidance/exporting-or-moving-fish-from-the-uk> accessed 2 July 2021. See also Chapter 1 of this book.

EU. There were considerable delays at UK/EU border ports while the requisite documentation was inspected, causing much fresh fish to deteriorate and no longer be marketable.[86] In addition, in early 2021 the EU introduced a ban on the import of live bivalve molluscs (including mussels and oysters) from most parts of the UK because the waters where they were produced did not meet EU water quality standards.[87] These developments caused a decline of 79 per cent in exports of fishery products to the EU during January 2021, compared with the position 12 months earlier,[88] and a decline of 52 per cent for the first quarter of 2021.[89] That led the UK government to establish a fund of £23 million to compensate exporters who had suffered losses.[90] At the time of writing (July 2021), it remained to be seen how much of the decline in UK exports has been caused by teething problems while exporters and customs officials adjust to the new documentary requirements, and possibly also by the Covid-19 pandemic, and how much of the decline is long-term.

Finally, there is one change for the UK fishing industry as a result of Brexit that it was not possible to evaluate at the time of writing. Before Brexit, the UK fishing industry was eligible for, and received, significant financial assistance from the European Maritime and Fisheries Fund (EMFF). With the departure of the UK from the EU, the eligibility of the UK fishing industry for such funding ceased. The UK government announced in February 2021 that it would be 'bringing forward details of a … £100 million package to help the industry to maximise the opportunities for growth' post Brexit.[91] Until the details of that package have been revealed, it is impossible to know how it will compare with the funding that the industry formerly received from the EMFF.

There is little doubt that overall the UK fishing industry is worse off after Brexit, very much contrary to what it had been led to expect by the UK government. The disappointment at what the TCA means for the industry has

86 For example, journey times, by lorry and ferry, from the exporting UK seller to the importing EU buyer that had previously taken around 16 hours were now taking two to three days: see *Channel 4 News*, 4 February 2021, <www.channel4.com/programmes/channel-4-news> accessed 2 July 2021; and *The Guardian*, 14 January 2021, <www.theguardian.com/theguardian/2021/jan/14> accessed 2 July 2021.

87 *The Fishing Daily*, 3 February 2021, <https://thefishingdaily.com/latest-news/eu-bans-the-importing-of-live-class-b-bivalve-molluscs-from-uk/> accessed 2 July 2021. See also UK government, 'Export of Live Bivalve Molluscs', <https://deframedia.blog.gov.uk/2021/03/26/export-of-live-bivalve-molluscs/>.

88 *The Guardian*, 5 February 2021, quoting a report from the Office for National Statistics.

89 BBC, 'UK food and drink exports to the EU almost halve in first quarter', <www.bbc.co.uk/news/business-57518910> accessed 2 July 2021.

90 Department for Environment, Food and Rural Affairs, Press Release, 19 January 2021, <www.gov.uk/government/news/new-financial-support-for-the-uks-fishing-businesses-that-export-to-the-eu> accessed 2 July 2021.

91 Department for Environment, Food and Rural Affairs, Press Release, 25 February 2021, <www.gov.uk/government/news/additional-support-for-uk-fish-and-shellfish-exporters-to-the-eu> accessed 2 July 2021.

been expressed in no uncertain terms by the leaders of various fisher organisations in the UK.[92] In the longer term, the UK government could improve the situation for the industry if, through careful management, both on its own and in collaboration with the EU, it restored those fish stocks in UK waters with an unsatisfactory status to a level that would support the maximum sustainable yield, a goal that is stipulated not only by the TCA,[93] but also by both UK and EU law.[94]

92 For samples of such views, see Stewart (n 81); *Fishing News*, 11 January 2021, <https://fishingnews.co.uk/news/boris-brexit-betrayal/> accessed 2 July 2021; Press Releases of the National Federation of Fishermen's Organisations (the main organisation representing English fishers) of 26 December 2020 and 4 and 15 January 2021, <www.nffo.org.uk/category/news/?tag=brexit> accessed 2 July 2021; and Press Releases of the Scottish Fishermen's Federation (the main organisation representing Scottish fishers) of 24 and 29 December 2020 and 15 January 2021, <www.sff.co.uk/news/> accessed 2 July 2021.

93 TCA (n 1), See Art. 494(2).

94 See, respectively, the Fisheries Act 2020 (n 39), s. 1(3) and Reg. 1380/2013 (n 12), Art. 2(2). According to the latter, the goal should have been achieved by 2020 at the latest. As is evident from what was said above (see text at notes 74–77), that did not happen.

3 The Fisheries Provisions of the Trade and Cooperation Agreement

An Analytical Conspectus

Andrew Serdy

Introduction

Despite its formal departure from the European Union (EU) on 31 January 2020, the United Kingdom (UK) remained until 31 December 2020 under the EU's Common Fisheries Policy (CFP) pursuant to the Agreement on the Withdrawal of the United Kingdom of Great Britain and Northern Ireland from the European Union and the European Atomic Energy Community,[1] the future fisheries relationship beyond the latter date becoming the subject of a dedicated set of provisions in the Trade and Cooperation Agreement concluded at the end of that year.[2] What the UK hoped to achieve as regards fisheries was set out in a 2018 White Paper.[3] The UK's preference was for annual quota negotiations rather than a longer-term agreement.[4] In these it wished to secure a much larger share of the fish stocks in its surrounding seas than had long been the case under the CFP, a source of great discontent to the UK fishing industry that motivated its strong support for Brexit; accordingly it espoused the principle of zonal attachment, whereby the UK and EU shares of the quota for each stock would reflect how much of it is present in the UK's and EU Member States' exclusive economic zones (EEZs) averaged over a year.[5] This was to be kept separate from the issue of continued unhindered access of UK-caught fish to the EU market, a point of vulnerability for the UK, since an increase in its share of the catch would be of little use if it could

1 Agreement on the Withdrawal of the United Kingdom of Great Britain and Northern Ireland from the European Union and the European Atomic Energy Community, Brussels and London, 24 January 2020, UKTS No 3 (2020), Art 126.
2 Trade and Cooperation Agreement between the European Union and the European Atomic Energy Community, of the one part, and the United Kingdom of Great Britain and Northern Ireland, of the other part, Brussels and London, December 30, 2020 (entered into force provisionally on 1 January 2021 and definitively on 1 May 2021) UKTS 2021 No. 8; OJ 2021 L149/10 (TCA).
3 Department for Environment, Food and Rural Affairs, "Sustainable Fisheries for Future Generations" (Cm 9660, 2018).
4 Ibid., at 18 ("on an annual basis").
5 Ibid., at 12 and 26; see also 44–56, "Annex C: Zonal Attachment Evidence", on different ways to measure this.

DOI: 10.4324/9781003252481-3

be sold only on the UK market or outside Europe, where it would fetch lower prices. For this reason, fisheries was all but excluded from the UK's draft of a trade agreement, mentioned solely in the context of subsidies, and was instead the subject of a separate draft treaty published in May 2020.[6] This was noteworthy chiefly for a clause by which either of the parties could unilaterally suspend the treaty if a dispute were to arise between them about it, the allegation by one party of breach by the other party of its obligations being sufficient for this, independently of any dispute settlement process being invoked to determine whether the allegation was made out, and of its outcome.[7]

The bulk of this chapter is devoted to an examination of the 19 articles of Heading Five of Part Two (Trade, Transport, Fisheries and Other Arrangements) of the Trade and Cooperation Agreement, dealing with fisheries, with commentary, followed by a concluding evaluation of the extent to which the UK's goals were achieved.

Contents of the Fisheries Provisions

The 19 articles are grouped into four chapters, supplemented by four annexes. Perhaps the most remarkable feature of the architecture of these provisions is that they attempt to fit what is substantively a cooperation agreement in relation to shared fish stocks of two adjacent EEZs,[8] entered into by the parties in discharge of their obligation to seek to cooperate, found in Article 63(1) of the United Nations Convention on the Law of the Sea (UNCLOS),[9] into the legal framework of what is primarily a free-trade agreement within the meaning of Article XXIV of the General Agreement on Tariffs and Trade (GATT) annexed to the Agreement Establishing the World Trade Organization.[10] Combining trade, fisheries and many other matters into a single treaty was the EU's choice; the UK, as noted above, would have preferred to keep non-trade aspects of its relationship with the EU in a series of distinct agreements. At least

6 Draft Working Text for a Fisheries Framework Agreement between the United Kingdom of Great Britain and Northern Ireland and the European Union, <https://assets.publishing.service.gov.uk/government/uploads/system/uploads/attachment_data/file/886009/DRAFT_Fisheries_Framework_Agreement.pdf> accessed 29 May 2021.

7 Ibid., Art 9.

8 For present purposes the EEZs of the EU Member States facing the UK across the North and Irish Seas can be treated as a single EEZ under the control of a single regulatory authority, reflecting the fact that fisheries is one of the few areas of exclusive EU competence vis-à-vis its Member States: Treaty on the Functioning of the European Union, in Consolidated Texts of the EU Treaties as Amended by the Treaty of Lisbon, January 2008, Cm 7310, <https://assets.publishing.service.gov.uk/government/uploads/system/uploads/attachment_data/file/228848/7310.pdf> accessed 29 May 2021, Art 3(1)(d).

9 United Nations Convention on the Law of the Sea (UNCLOS), Montego Bay, 10 December 1982, 1833 UNTS 3.

10 Agreement establishing the World Trade Organization, Marrakesh, 15 April 1994, 1867 UNTS 3.

as far as fisheries are concerned, initially the UK did seem to get its way: the Political Declaration accompanying the Withdrawal Agreement did in fact call for the parties' "best endeavours to conclude and ratify by 1 July 2020" a separate treaty "on, inter alia, access to waters and quota shares", a target date that would have allowed it to settle these matters for 2021 as well as subsequent years.[11] It is not clear why this plan was abandoned.

Chapter One (Initial provisions)

Chapter One runs from Article 493 to Article 495. The latter, which defines certain terms, is not given separate treatment below, but where necessary the definitions are discussed piecemeal in association with the other articles in which the defined terms appear.

Without explicitly mentioning their EEZs (instead, it is "their waters"), Article 493 affirms that the parties' sovereign rights to explore, exploit, conserve and manage the living resources, a phrase taken from Article 56 of UNCLOS relating to that zone, "should be conducted pursuant to and in accordance with the principles of international law", an unhelpfully broad and vague formulation somewhat tempered by an express reference to UNCLOS as included in this. Those waters are defined in Article 495(1)(a), (f) and (g) to comprise not just their EEZs but also their territorial seas, in a way that, if it were the complete definition, would lack symmetry: for the EU only the EEZs and territorial seas "established by its Member States adjacent to their European territories" are within scope, whereas for the UK, which has numerous territorial possessions and thus territorial seas and EEZs all around the world, the parallel expression is "its territorial sea, excluding for the purposes of Articles 500 and 501 and Annex 38 the territorial sea adjacent to the Bailiwick of Guernsey, the Bailiwick of Jersey and the Isle of Man". The lopsidedness is counteracted, however, by Article 774(3) and (4), which set the geographical scope of the Agreement as a whole and remove from it both Gibraltar and all of the UK's territories outside Europe, narrowing accordingly the reach of the definition.

Article 494 sets out the objectives and principles underlying the relevant provisions. Again without referring to UNCLOS Article 63(1), paragraph 1 imposes an obligation "to cooperate with a view to ensuring that fishing activities for shared stocks in their waters are environmentally sustainable in the long term and contribute to achieving economic and social benefits, while fully respecting the rights and obligations of independent coastal States as exercised by the Parties." The reason for the omission may be that "shared stocks" is

11 Political Declaration setting out the framework for the future relationship between the European Union and the United Kingdom, 19 October 2019, <https://assets.publishing.service.gov.uk/government/uploads/system/uploads/attachment_data/file/840656/Political_Declaration_setting_out_the_framework_for_the_future_relationship_between_the_European_Union_and_the_United_Kingdom.pdf> accessed 28 June 2021, at paragraphs 73 and 74.

given by Article 495(1)(c) a definition that does not require the range or migratory path of the stocks concerned to have any transboundary element, speaking simply of "fish, including shellfish of any kind that are found in the waters of the Parties, which includes molluscs and crustaceans". The effect of this is that the access arrangements detailed further in Article 500 permit fishing vessels of the parties access not just to each other's EEZs, but also to certain parts of their territorial seas, a result not contemplated by UNCLOS Article 63, but not incompatible with it either.

Paragraph 2 is more disturbing. Whereas the obligation for managing stocks in the EEZ under Article 61 of UNCLOS is for them to be maintained at, or restored to, biomass levels that can produce the maximum sustainable yield, this reduces it in status to an "objective" that the parties share, intimating that they are unlikely to have much interest in holding each other to account for any departures from this standard. Despite the potentially helpful commitment in Article 404(2)(a) to complying or acting in accordance with UNCLOS and several other fisheries treaties and non-binding instruments, any allegation of breach of Article 61 cannot be pursued without the other party's consent under the otherwise compulsory UNCLOS dispute settlement mechanism because of the exclusion of EEZ fisheries disputes by Article 297(3) of UNCLOS, and the radically different parallel mechanism for this Agreement in Article 506 discussed below[12] does nothing to fill that gap.

The subtle undermining of international fisheries law norms continues into paragraph 3, which lists nine "principles", discussed in detail in the companion chapter by Churchill in this volume,[13] to which the parties "shall have regard", again as opposed to making them enforceable obligations. As a consequence, if the parties find themselves in future in stark disagreement about stock management, the Article 506 dispute settlement mechanism will be closed to them,[14] nor is a claim of breach of UNCLOS Article 63(1) likely to succeed if it rests merely on a failure to apply vague principles, as opposed to breach of concrete obligations. Space does not permit their enumeration, but while the principles are unobjectionable in themselves, it is notable that the first of them, "applying the precautionary approach to fisheries management", is a backward step because of the definition of the latter term in Article 495(1)(b): "an approach according to which the absence of adequate scientific information does not justify postponing or failing to take management measures to conserve target species, associated or dependent species and non-target species and their environment". This is a great deal less onerous than the preferable conception found in Annex II to the UN Fish Stocks Agreement,[15] one of the treaties

12 Infra, text following (n 50).
13 See R Churchill (Chapter 2).
14 Infra, text between (nn 47 and 50).
15 Agreement for the Implementation of the Provisions of the United Nations Convention on the Law of the Sea of 10 December 1982 relating to the Conservation and Management of Straddling Fish Stocks and Highly Migratory Fish Stocks, New York, 4 August 1995; 2167 UNTS 3.

listed in Article 404(2)(a), to which the UK and the EU as well as all its Member States are party, centring on the identification of target and limit reference points and the automatic imposition of pre-agreed measures to restore stocks to those points if their biomass approaches or falls below the limit. True it is that strictly this Agreement is applicable only to fish stocks also found on the high seas, but the regression in policy terms hardly inspires confidence in the parties' willingness to resist political pressure from their fishing interests to allow overexploitation that risks the stocks' collapse.

Chapter Two (Conservation and sustainable exploitation)

Chapter Two consists of Articles 496 and 497. The first sentence of Article 496(2) partially compensates for the downgrading by Article 494(3)(c) of basing conservation and management decisions for fisheries on the best available scientific advice to a principle to which regard needs to be had, by re-elevating this to an obligation. The second sentence is a non-discrimination rule; it permits each party to apply only those management measures to vessels of the other party in its waters that it also applies to its own vessels, although this is subject to any contrary obligation under the Port State Measures Agreement,[16] the North-East Atlantic Fisheries Commission (NEAFC) Scheme of Control and Enforcement,[17] the Northwest Atlantic Fisheries Organization (NAFO) Conservation and Enforcement Measures[18] and Recommendation 18–09 of the International Commission for the Conservation of Atlantic Tunas,[19] a list that can be amended by the Specialised Committee on Fisheries created by Article 508 considered below.[20] To this paragraph 3 usefully adds a requirement to notify the other party of "new measures … that are likely to affect the vessels of the other Party before those measures are applied, allowing sufficient time for the other Party to provide comments or seek clarification".

Article 497 reveals that the right of vessels of one party to fish in the other's waters pursuant to Articles 500 and 502 is not automatic; rather, paragraph 1 contemplates that each party must communicate to the other "in sufficient time", a phrase it might have been better not to leave undefined, a list of

16 Agreement on Port State Measures to Prevent, Deter and Eliminate Illegal, Unreported and Unregulated Fishing, Rome, 22 November 2009, <www.fao.org/fileadmin/user_upload/legal/docs/037t-e.pdf> accessed 5 July 2021.

17 NEAFC Scheme of Control and Enforcement, the version dated 11 February 2021 can be downloaded from <https://www.neafc.org/system/files/NEAFC_Scheme-2021-a4Dbl_sided.pdf> accessed 22 May 2021.

18 These are updated every year; for the 2021 consolidation, see NAFO doc NAFO/COM Doc. 21–01, *Northwest Atlantic Fisheries Organization Conservation and Enforcement Measures 2021*, <www.nafo.int/Portals/0/PDFs/COM/2021/comdoc21-01.pdf> accessed 22 May 2021.

19 Recommendation by ICCAT on Port State Measures to Prevent, Deter and Eliminate Illegal, Unreported and Unregulated Fishing, <www.iccat.int/Documents/Recs/compendiopdf-e/2018-09-e.pdf> accessed 22 May 2021.

20 See infra, text at (n 55).

vessels for which it seeks authorisations or licences to fish, which the second party must then issue. In this way each party should know precisely which vessels of the other are permitted to fish in its waters at any given time, thus exposing fishing by any other unlisted vessels to the standard penalties for illegal fishing. Paragraph 2 requires each party to "take all necessary measures to ensure compliance by its vessels with the rules applicable to those vessels in the other Party's waters, including authorisation or licence conditions". This does not appear to encompass patrolling their vessels in each other's waters, which would be sufficiently unusual to merit express provision if that were the parties' intention. Although the sovereign rights of coastal States under UNCLOS include full enforcement powers subject only to the requirement to release fishing vessels and their crews promptly on payment of a reasonable bond, and the prohibition of imprisonment and other forms of corporal punishment without the flag State's consent,[21] that does not render paragraph 2 superfluous. It is easily conceivable that vessels of one party will fish illegally in the other party's waters and either escape detection altogether in the short term or flee to their own territorial sea or that of a third State, where, by UNCLOS Article 111(3), any hot pursuit by the authorities of the first party must cease as the right to conduct it is exhausted, and it would not be desirable for this to remain without consequences. On the other hand, there is equally nothing to suggest that hot pursuit of fleeing vessels into each other's EEZs is impermissible, a conclusion supported *a contrario* by the last-mentioned provision.

Chapter Three (Access)

Chapter Three (Articles 498–505) is the longest of the four and establishes the arrangements on access by vessels of each party to the waters of the other for fishing.

The lengthy Article 498 governs the apportionment between the parties of the total allowable catch (TAC) or effort for the stocks the parties share, utilising the term "Fishing opportunities", drawn from CFP terminology.[22] Paragraph 1 is a procedural opening to the annual process for setting TACs for the following year for 76 stocks listed in Annex 35, directing the parties to set a schedule for consultations to this end. By paragraph 2 agreement is to be achieved by 10 December of each year on the TACs for the following year, on the basis of the best available scientific advice, as well as other relevant factors, which may be socio-economic in nature, and complying with any applicable multi-year strategies for conservation and management they may have agreed. Although paragraph 1 contemplates that the agreement may be for more than

21 UNCLOS (n 9) Art 73(2) and (3).

22 See Regulation (EU) No 1380/2013 of the European Parliament and of the Council of 11 December 2013 on the Common Fisheries Policy, Amending Council Regulations (EC) No 1954/2003 and (EC) No 1224/2009 and Repealing Council Regulations (EC) No 2371/2002 and (EC) No 639/2004 and Council Decision 2004/585/EC, [2013] OJ L354/22, Arts 16 and 17.

one year, paragraph 2 does not relieve the parties of its annual requirement in that event, possibly on the reasonable assumption that it would be unlikely for there to be nothing at all to discuss because there is not even one listed stock without an agreed limit for the following year, and none of the non-exhaustive list of other matters that may be discussed in these annual consultations, appearing in paragraph 4,[23] are of sufficient moment to warrant holding the consultations. At least initially, there is no need to negotiate on their respective shares of the catch limits, because these are already fixed according to paragraph 3 by Annex 35. It cannot be gleaned from the Agreement itself to what degree the UK's aims regarding quotas were achieved, as the Annex tabulates catch shares gradually moving in the UK's favour from 2021 to 2026 (with no further adjustment thereafter), but contains no comparable figures from 2020 or earlier against which to measure them, although a UK Government document claims that ultimately shares representing 25 per cent of the value of the EU's catch in UK waters of all stocks subject to quotas will be transferred to the UK.[24]

Outside this annual cycle, by implication at any rate, at either party's request there may by paragraph 5 also be consultations aiming to amend TACs by agreement. The results of consultations under Article 498 are to be embodied in a written record signed by the heads of their delegations documenting the arrangements made: paragraph 6. For the 19 stocks listed in Annex 37 that one of the parties can set or amend, by implication unilaterally, it must under paragraph 7 give the other party sufficient prior notice. Finally, paragraph 8 mandates the Specialised Committee on Fisheries to decide on the details of a mechanism for voluntary in-year transfers of fishing opportunities between the parties, through which they must consider making available, at market value, transfers of fishing opportunities for stocks which are, or are projected to be, underfished.

The possibility of failing to reach agreement is catered for by Article 499. Paragraph 1 in essence provides that if the parties have not agreed the TAC[25] for any stock listed in Annex 35 or Tables A or B of Annex 36 by 10 December of the previous year, they must keep trying to do so as soon as

23 These are enumerated in successive subparagraphs:
(a) transfers of parts of one party's quota shares of TACs to the other;
(b) prohibiting fishing altogether for certain stocks;
(c) determination of the TAC for any stock not listed in Annexes 35 or 36 and of their respective shares of these;
(d) fisheries management measures, including limits on fishing effort;
(e) stocks of common interest to the parties other than those listed in Annexes 35–37.

24 UK Government, "UK–EU Trade and Cooperation Agreement: Summary" (December 2020), <https://assets.publishing.service.gov.uk/government/uploads/system/uploads/attachment_data/file/962125/TCA_SUMMARY_PDF_V1-.pdf> accessed 29 May 2021, at 24, paragraph 125.

25 Defined by Art 495(1)(d) as the maximum quantity of a stock (or stocks) of a particular description that may be caught over a given period.

possible. If by 20 December they have not succeeded, then the combined effect of paragraphs 2 to 5, 7 and 9 is that each party must set and notify to the other a provisional TAC equal to its share as per the relevant annex of the level advised by the International Council for the Exploration of the Sea (ICES),[26] applying from the following 1 January, except stocks for which the ICES advice is for a zero TAC, stocks caught in a mixed fishery in which that or another stock is vulnerable, or any other stocks that the parties consider require special treatment, for which the TACs are to be set in accordance with guidelines to be adopted by the Specialised Committee on Fisheries by 1 July 2021.[27] The provisional TACs and shares so derived apply until agreement is reached: paragraph 8.

An elaborate regime for reciprocal access by the parties' vessels to fish in each other's waters is contained in Article 500, which by paragraph 8 applies subject to Annex 38, whose preamble notes the "social and economic benefits of a further period of stability". Article 1 of this Annex establishes an adjustment period lasting from 1 January 2021 until 30 June 2026. Article 2 postpones the application of most of Article 500 until the end of this period,[28] during which each party must allow the other's vessels full access to its waters to fish: (a) stocks listed in Annex 35 and in Tables A, B and F of Annex 36, at a level reasonably commensurate with their respective shares of the fishing opportunities set out in those annexes; (b) non-quota stocks, at a level equating to the average tonnage fished by vessels of each party in the other party's waters during the period 2012–2016. In addition, vessels that fished in the outer six miles of the other party's territorial sea in ICES statistical areas 4c and 7d–g[29] in

26 ICES is an intergovernmental scientific organisation from which the EU and NEAFC among others obtain scientific advice on their fisheries. Originally formed in 1902 by a number of northern European States, in recent decades it has operated under the Convention for the International Council for the Exploration of the Sea, Copenhagen, 12 September 1964, 652 UNTS 237.

27 At the time of the last opportunity to update this contribution in August 2021, this had not happened. According to a UK Government press release of 11 June 2021, the Committee would not meet for the first time until later that month: "UK and EU agreement on catch levels for 2021", <www.gov.uk/government/news/uk-and-eu-agreement-on-catch-levels-for-2021> accessed 5 July 2021.

28 It does this by individually listing the paragraphs concerned, oddly omitting paragraph 2, which may be a drafting oversight, as there is little point in preserving the possibility of consultations, as paragraph 2 does, while jettisoning all the surrounding obligations, including such basic ones as conducting them in good faith (paragraph 3).

29 These are misnamed mainly as "sub-areas" in Article 500 and in a few places as "divisions". The untidiness is regrettable but probably creates only a low risk of adverse legal consequences; moreover, ICES itself is not consistent in how it refers to them, using both "statistical areas" and "fishing areas" on its website. Area 4c is the southernmost portion of the North Sea to around 53°N; areas 7d and 7e between them cover the English Channel, while 7f and 7g are the sea between southern Wales and the south coast of Ireland; see the map on the ICES website, <www.ices.dk/data/Documents/Maps/ICES_Areas_maps.zip> accessed 31 May 2021.

at least four of the years from 2012 to 2016, or their direct replacements, retain the access that they had to that zone on 31 December 2020. Each party must notify the other of any change in the level and conditions of access to waters that will apply from 1 July 2026, though this is subject to the application *mutatis mutandis* of the Article 501 compensatory measures obligation[30] for the remainder of 2026.

Different arrangements prevail depending on whether the TACs are agreed under Article 498 on one hand, or provisional under Article 499 on the other. In the former case, by paragraph 1 of Article 500 each party is obliged to grant vessels of the other party access to fish in its waters that year in the relevant sub-areas defined by ICES, at a level and on conditions determined in the annual consultations pursuant to Article 498. In doing so, however, either party may by paragraph 7 take into account the extent of compliance of vessels, individual or grouped, with the applicable rules in its waters during the preceding year, and of enforcement measures taken by the other party during that year pursuant to Article 497(2). Paragraph 2 contemplates that there may emerge from the Article 498 consultations further specific access conditions concerning the fishing opportunities agreed, any multi-year strategies for non-quota stocks[31] developed by the Specialised Committee on Fisheries under Article 508(1)(c); or technical and conservation measures. By paragraphs 3 and 4, the objective of the consultations is to ensure a mutually satisfactory balance between both parties' interests, and "should normally result" in the parties granting access at levels calculated in one of three ways. Access to fish in each other's EEZs the stocks listed in Annex 35 and Tables A, B and F of Annex 36, i.e., those subject to quotas, must be at a level "reasonably commensurate with the Parties' respective shares of the TACs", in other words each party's vessels should be able to fish their quotas largely in the other party's EEZ if they so wish. Access to fish non-quota stocks in each other's EEZs should be at a level no less than the average tonnage fished by either party in the other's waters in the period 2012–2016. For both quota and non-quota stocks, access is extended to the EEZ portion of ICES statistical areas 4c and 7d–g already mentioned if it is granted to the outer six miles of the parties' territorial seas in those areas. Such access as existed on 31 December 2020 under the CFP to that belt of water is also preserved for any vessel that had fished there in any four years between 2012 and 2016, or its direct replacement. In respect of access to that belt, the specific statement that annual consultations "may include appropriate financial commitments and quota transfers between the Parties" implies that these possibilities do not exist outside that context.

By contrast, under paragraph 5, while a provisional TAC is in force, the provisional access to fish in the relevant ICES statistical areas for stocks listed in Annex 35 and non-quota stocks runs from 1 January to 31 March at the levels provided for in paragraph 4(a) and (b), while the corresponding obligation for

30 See infra, text at (nn 32–42).
31 Those that are not managed through TACs: Art 495(1)(e).

28 stocks listed in Annex 36 runs from 1 January until 14 February at the levels provided for in paragraph 4(a), in proportion to the average percentage of the party's share of the annual TAC that its vessels fished in the other party's waters in the relevant ICES areas during the same period of the previous three calendar years. The same applies *mutatis mutandis* to access to fish non-quota stocks. In the outer six miles of the territorial sea the obligation is for access in accordance with paragraph 4(c) throughout January only, at a level equivalent to the average monthly tonnage fished there in the previous three months. By 15 January in relation to the stocks in that belt, 31 January for Annex 36 stocks and 15 March for all other stocks, each party must notify the other of the change in the level and conditions of access to its waters that will apply once the provisional access periods expire, roughly a fortnight's notice in each case, after which paragraph 6 obliges them to "seek to agree further provisional access arrangements at the appropriate geographical level with the aim of minimising disruption to fishing activities".

Arguably out of place given its relationship to dispute settlement in both the next chapter and Title 1 of Part Six of the Agreement, Article 501 is a special provision envisaging compensatory measures in case of withdrawal or reduction of access notified by one party (the "host Party") to the other under Article 500(5). If this happens, the other party (the "fishing Party") may according to paragraph 1 take compensatory measures "commensurate to the economic and societal impact of the change in the level and conditions of access to waters ... measured on the basis of reliable evidence and not merely on conjecture and remote possibility". The fishing Party may then suspend, wholly or partly, not just the host Party's access to its waters but also the preferential tariff treatment granted to fishery products under Article 21 (which prohibits imposition of customs duties on trade between the parties).[32] By paragraph 2, such measures may not take effect until at least seven days after the fishing Party has given notice of them to the host Party, identifying the date on which it intends the suspension to begin, the obligations to be suspended and the level of the intended suspension, and in any event no earlier than the day after any provisional TAC expires under Article 500(5). The parties must then consult within the Specialised Committee with a view to reaching a mutually agreeable solution, and by paragraph 4 the measures must be withdrawn immediately when the conditions that justified taking them are no longer met.

This notification opens the way in paragraph 3 for the establishment at the host Party's request of an arbitration tribunal constituted under Article 739

32 The exemption from tariffs does not, however, shield exporters from other customs formalities at the border, including significant paperwork through the need to produce a variety of certificates with every shipment, which have proved since the start of 2021 to be formidable barriers in their own right to trade in fishery products; see, e.g., R Syal, "Yorkshire lobster exporter says Brexit costs have forced it to close" (*The Guardian*, 8 February 2021), <www.theguardian.com/politics/2021/feb/08/yorkshire-lobster-exporter-baron-shellfish-brexit-costs-forced-close> accessed 1 June 2021.

without the need for prior recourse to consultations pursuant to Article 738. The arbitration tribunal's sole task is to review the conformity of the compensatory measures with paragraph 1, and the issue is deemed to be a case of urgency for the purposes of Article 744, halving in urgent proceedings the otherwise applicable time periods set out in Article 745. As set out in paragraph 5, the consequence if the arbitration tribunal finds a significant inconsistency of the fishing Party's compensatory measures with paragraph 1 is that the host Party may request the tribunal, within 30 days from its ruling, to determine a level of suspension of obligations under the Agreement "not exceeding the level equivalent to the nullification or impairment caused by the application of the compensatory measures", a formulation clearly inspired by Article 22 of the Understanding on Procedures Governing the Settlement of Disputes annexed to the WTO Agreement (DSU).[33] The request must propose an alternative level of suspension meeting the standard laid down in paragraph 1 and the principles set out in Article 761: it must not exceed the level equivalent to the nullification or impairment of benefits under this Agreement directly caused by the compensatory measures from the date of their taking effect until the date of the arbitration ruling;[34] it must be based on facts demonstrating that the nullification or impairment arises directly from the application of the compensatory measure and affects specific goods, service suppliers, investors or other economic actors and not merely on allegation, conjecture or remote possibility;[35] it must not include punitive damages, interest or hypothetical losses of profits or business opportunities, and must be reduced by any prior refunds of duties, indemnification of damages or other forms of compensation already received by the concerned operators or the host Party and by the contribution to the nullification or impairment by wilful or negligent action or omission of the host Party or any person or entity in relation to whom remedies are sought.[36] Fifteen days or more after the ruling, the host Party may then suspend part of its obligations under the Agreement up to the level determined by the arbitration tribunal.

Despite the parallel to WTO law, paragraph 6 prevents the parties from invoking the WTO Agreement or any other treaty to challenge the suspension of obligations under this Article. But what would happen if a party were nonetheless to do so? That could be made the subject of dispute settlement proceedings under the general dispute settlement provisions of the Agreement in Title 1 of Part Six, where Article 736 is a similar exclusivity provision,[37]

33 WTO Agreement (n 10), Annex 2.
34 TCA (n 2), Art 761(1).
35 Ibid., Art 761(2).
36 Ibid., Art 761(3).
37 It reads: "The Parties undertake not to submit a dispute between them regarding the interpretation or application of provisions of this Agreement … to a mechanism of settlement other than those provided for in this Agreement". Art 737 does in fact foresee the parallel availability of recourse to the WTO's dispute settlement mechanism and requires an election to be made by the complaining party, which

alone or in combination with the remedial measures available under Article 506,[38] leading to an odd situation of circularity: their application is to breaches of "all provisions" of the Agreement (Article 735(2)) or of Heading Five (Article 506(1)), thus including this one, so any attempt to have the WTO declare a suspension of tariff-free access unlawful would itself retrigger the right to do so. This at least avoids the consequence suffered by Australia when Timor-Leste instituted compulsory conciliation proceedings under Article 298(1)(a)(i) of UNCLOS over the maritime boundary between the two States, despite the preclusion under Article 4 of the Treaty between the Government of Australia and the Government of the Democratic Republic of Timor-Leste on Certain Maritime Arrangements in the Timor Sea[39] of the initiation of conciliation or any other proceedings under UNCLOS. This prompted Australia to object to the Conciliation Commission's competence; although the Commission dismissed the objection,[40] that outcome rested solely on its interpretation of Articles 280 and 281 of UNCLOS, which made it unnecessary to decide whether or not Timor-Leste had breached another treaty in bringing the proceedings. The result, however, is that the terms of Article 4 of the 2006 Treaty could have been enforced by Australia only through separate proceedings under that treaty itself, which for lack of an effective dispute settlement clause was impossible without Timor-Leste's concurrence – a situation not replicated here. What is not certain is whether a WTO panel would itself decline to rule on a challenge on the basis that Articles 501 and 736 had deprived it of the jurisdiction it would otherwise have, as a breach of the obligation to act in good faith found in Article 3.10 of the DSU.[41] On the

cannot be varied "unless the forum selected first fails to make findings for procedural or jurisdictional reasons". Paragraph 4 begins by laying down that "nothing in this Agreement … shall preclude a Party from suspending obligations authorised by the Dispute Settlement Body of the WTO or authorised under the dispute settlement procedures of another international agreement to which the Parties are party", but then repeats the substance of Art 501(6): "The WTO Agreement or any other international agreement between the Parties shall not be invoked to preclude a Party from suspending obligations under this Title".

38 See infra (text between nn 48 and 50).

39 Sydney, 12 January 2006; 2483 UNTS 359.

40 Permanent Court of Arbitration Case 2016–10, *In the Matter of a Conciliation before a Conciliation Commission Constituted under Annex V to the 1982 United Nations Convention on the Law of the Sea between the Democratic Republic of Timor-Leste and the Commonwealth of Australia, Decision on Australia's Objections to Competence, 19 September 2016*, <https://pcacases.com/web/sendAttach/10052> accessed 1 June 2021.

41 No case has to date decided this issue, but one has come close: in *Peru – Additional Duty on Imports of Certain Agricultural Products*, WTO doc WT/DS457/AB/R (20 July 2015), Peru argued that, since its free-trade agreement with Guatemala had allowed it to maintain the impugned measure, this amounted to waiver by Guatemala of the right to challenge it under the DSU. Disagreeing and upholding with modifications the panel's findings for Guatemala on the merits, the Appellate Body noted that the disputant parties were at odds over whether their free-trade agreement did in fact constitute a waiver; the relevant clause is near-identical to Art 737

other hand, under current conditions it is hard to see what benefit either party would gain from the WTO alternative, since the UK is not party to the DSU Article 25 arbitration workaround prompted by the EU to allow quasi-appeals from panel decisions while the Appellate Body remains in suspension for lack of members. This leaves the losing party able to prevent any such decision from taking effect, by the expedient of an "appeal into the void", the only alternative to automatic adoption of the report by the Dispute Settlement Body (DSB).[42]

Article 502 is another special provision relating to access of EU fishing vessels to waters around Guernsey, Jersey and the Isle of Man, overriding anything to the contrary in Articles 500(1) and (3) to (7), 501 and Annex 38. Pursuant to paragraph 1, each party must grant the other's vessels access to fish in its waters reflecting the actual extent and nature of fishing activity that was demonstrably carried out there between 1 February 2017 and 31 January 2020 by qualifying vessels of the other party in the waters and under any treaty arrangements that existed on 31 January 2020. The only such treaty appears to be the agreement with France of 2000;[43] although there also exists a voisinage arrangement between the Republic of Ireland and Northern Ireland, despite their relative proximity to the Isle of Man, the exclusion by paragraph 2 of the territorial sea off Northern Ireland from the waters concerned prevents it from being captured by paragraph 1, and the fact that it is not of treaty status leads in parallel to the same result.[44] Paragraph 2 defines "qualifying vessel" to mean any vessel

rather than to Art 501. It appeared to suggest, however, that, had the provision been of the latter type, it might have reached the opposite conclusion and decided that the panel lacked jurisdiction: ibid., at 21 (para 5.28: "we do not consider that a clear stipulation of a relinquishment of Guatemala's right to have recourse to the WTO dispute settlement system exists in this case").

42 WTO Agreement (n 10), Annex 2, Art 16(4); WTO doc JOB/DSB/1/Add.12 (30 April 2020), <https://docs.wto.org/dol2fe/Pages/FE_Search/FE_S_S009-DP.aspx?language=E&CatalogueIdList=263504> accessed 1 July 2021; "Statement on a Mechanism for Developing, Documenting and Sharing Practices and Procedures in the Conduct of WTO Disputes[,] Addendum", incorporating the Multi-Party Interim Appeal Arbitration Arrangement Pursuant to Article 25 of the DSU. Appointment of new Appellate Body members would require the United States to join a consensus to this effect in the DSB, which it has refused to do since 2016 for reasons beyond the scope of this chapter.

43 Agreement between the Government of the United Kingdom of Great Britain and Northern Ireland and the Government of the French Republic concerning Fishing in the Bay of Granville, with Exchanges of Notes and Declaration, St. Helier, 4 July 2000, 2269 UNTS 87, including exchanges of notes relating to Guernsey and Sark as well as a French declaration referring to an exchange of correspondence between the French Ministry of Foreign Affairs and the UK Foreign and Commonwealth Office confirming that French nationals would be allowed to continue to fish in certain waters under the terms of the Exchange of Notes concerning the Habitual Rights of French Fishing Vessels within British Fishery Limits (Paris, 24 February 1965), apparently not of treaty status, notwithstanding its termination by the 2000 Agreement, including a defined area off the Isle of Man.

44 C R Symmons, "Recent Developments in Ireland: The Voisinage Doctrine and Irish Waters: Recent Judicial and Legislative Developments" (2018) 49 *Ocean*

that fished in the territorial sea adjacent to the Crown Dependencies of Guernsey, Jersey, the Isle of Man or of a neighbouring EU Member State (i.e. France or Ireland) on more than ten days in any of the three 12-month periods from 1 February to the following 31 January beginning in 2017 and ending in 2020, but excludes from its scope any UK vessels other than those registered in any of the above Crown Dependencies and licensed by a UK fisheries administration. The situation around Jersey led to tensions in May 2021 when the Jersey authorities imposed what were said to be new conditions on the issue of licences to French vessels to fish in the territorial sea around that island, contrary to the implication of this Article read as a whole, that the imposition of any new conditions requires the consent of the other party, which had not been obtained. It transpired, however, that these conditions were in fact not substantive but merely evidential requirements to satisfy the authorities that particular applicant vessels were indeed qualifying vessels.[45]

The Partnership Council formed by Article 7 to administer the Agreement is empowered by paragraph 3 to decide within 90 days of its entry into force, at either party's request, i.e. by the end of July 2021, that this Article, Article 503 on notification periods relating to the importation and direct landing of fisheries products and any other relevant provisions within Heading Five, as well as Article 520(3)–(8) on the Agreement's geographical application, shall cease to apply in respect of one or more of the Crown Dependencies, the decision taking effect 30 days later. Not having been invoked by either party before that date, its force is now spent. This is one of the more peculiar provisions in Heading Five. It is hard to fathom why the UK would have changed its mind so soon in the life of the Agreement; the best this author can suggest is that paragraph 3 allowed time for post-signature consultation with the affected jurisdictions, if none took place prior. A more general power of amendment of the same articles, not temporally restricted, is accorded to the Partnership Council by paragraph 4.

Article 503 provides for the EU to apply notification periods to marine fish, molluscs and crustaceans caught by UK vessels registered in Guernsey or Jersey in the territorial sea adjacent to those territories or to a Member State. Subparagraph 1(a) requires prior notification between three and five hours before fresh product is landed into EU territory, while by subparagraph 1(b) the

Development & International Law 79 at 80, noting at 83 that the UK is disposed to let the arrangement continue despite Brexit; accord S Kopela, "Historic fishing rights in the law of the sea and Brexit" (2019) 32 *Leiden Journal of International Law* 695 at 710. Voisinage arrangements were described by the Supreme Court of Ireland in *Barlow & Ors v. Minister of Agriculture*, [2016] IESC 62, para 11 as the "recognition at official level of practice and tradition whereby fishing boats did not necessarily remain within the national waters but fished neighbouring waters".

45 J Brunsden, S Payne and V Mallet, "Brussels says UK breached trade deal in Jersey fish dispute", *Financial Times*, 6 May 2021, <www.ft.com/content/43297316-6fb1-4caf-abf6-47216f46ec6c> accessed 28 May 2021.

equivalent period for the validated catch certificate[46] for the direct movement by sea of consignments of such products is between one and three hours before the estimated time of arrival at the place of entry into EU territory.

Article 504 deals with a short-term issue, namely advice that by paragraph 1 the parties will have requested from ICES by 1 July 2021 on aligning the management areas and assessment units used by ICES for the stocks identified in Annex 35. Acting jointly, within six months of receiving this advice, they are to review it and consider adjustments to the management areas of the stocks concerned, with a view to agreeing consequential changes to the list of stocks and their shares of them set out in Annex 35. Although this seems to be a purely technical matter, it is not difficult to imagine disagreements emerging around it, perhaps prompted by pressures from the parties' respective fleets for substantive adjustments in their favour, which may in the end most easily be accommodated by doing nothing.

Article 505 governs the parties' respective shares of the TACs for 28 multilaterally managed stocks, which by paragraph 1 are divided between them as set out in Annex 36; paragraph 2 obliges each party to notify the relevant States and regional fisheries management organisations of its shares in accordance with Tables A to D of this Annex. The impression that this is an agreed division of the share of quotas accorded to the EU in those fora while the UK was still a Member State is reinforced by paragraphs 3 and 4, which both make any subsequent changes to those shares a matter for the relevant forum, in the case of Tables A and B once the adjustments of the shares up to 30 June 2026 are complete, although the Partnership Council retains the power to alter Annex 36 under Article 508(3). The assumption that the approval of the other States in these bodies need not be sought, though perhaps practically or politically accurate, nonetheless appears legally questionable, unless all concerned are prepared to treat quotas as a species of property rather than as limitations on the freedom of fishing on the high seas; there is much to be said for the property approach,[47] but only if it is openly adopted and defended rather than occurring *sub rosa*. By paragraph 5 the objectives and principles set out in Article 494 apply without modification as the approach the parties must take in these fora to the management of the stocks concerned.

46 This phrase is not defined, but may refer to the catch certificates required by Council Regulation (EC) No 1005/2008 of 29 September 2008 establishing a community system to prevent, deter and eliminate illegal, unreported and unregulated fishing, amending Regulations (EEC) No 2847/93, (EC) No 1936/2001 and (EC) No 601/2004 and repealing Regulations (EC) No 1093/94 and (EC) No 1447/1999, [2008] OJ L286/1, Art 6 and Chapter III.

47 See by the present author A Serdy, "Property Rights in Areas Beyond National Jurisdiction – Not Too Late for a Proper Debate?" in E J Molenaar and A G Oude Elferink (eds), *The International Legal Regime of Areas Beyond National Jurisdiction* (Leiden: Martinus Nijhoff Publishers, 2010), 143; A Serdy, *The New Entrants Problem in International Fisheries Law* (Cambridge: Cambridge University Press, 2016), 155–157, 174–175 and Chapter 5 *passim*.

Chapter Four (Governance arrangements)

The last Chapter of Heading Five contains a further six articles on governance arrangements, starting with the complex Article 506 covering both remedial measures and dispute settlement.

There is observable influence of WTO law in paragraph 1. After carving out disputes relating to Articles 502, 503 and related provisions, for which there is a separate dispensation, it specifies that if either party alleges non-compliance by the other with any other provision of Heading Five, it may in the first instance, on at least seven days' notice to the other party, suspend wholly or partly access to its waters and the freedom from tariffs normally guaranteed by Article 21, so that the entry into its territory of fishery products becomes subject to whatever customs duty would otherwise be imposable. Should it consider that this "is not commensurate to the economic and societal impact of the alleged failure", it may next suspend the application of Article 21 to other goods, and if it considers this still incommensurate to that impact, may also suspend any or all obligations under Heading One (Trade) of Part Two other than Title XI (the level playing field clauses). If, with the latter exception, Heading One is suspended in its entirety, so too is Heading Three (Road Transport).

If on the other hand the dispute is about alleged breach of Articles 502, 503 or related provisions pertaining to access to waters of Guernsey, Jersey and the Isle of Man, by paragraph 2 the complaining party may, on at least seven days' notice to the other party, suspend, in whole or in part, access to the particular waters defined in Article 502. Should it consider this suspension not commensurate to the economic and societal impact of the alleged failure, it may suspend, in whole or in part, the Article 21 zero tariff treatment for fisheries products, or if that too is not commensurate to the impact, it may go on to suspend the same treatment of any or all other goods under Article 21; neither of these is confined to fisheries products and other goods originating in the Crown Dependencies concerned. In addition, this paragraph protects the arrangements established under Articles 502 and 503 and related provisions of Heading Five from suspension as a remedial measure for the alleged failure by a party to comply with provisions unconnected to those arrangements.

Paragraph 3 requires the remedial measures authorised by paragraphs 1 and 2 to be "proportionate to the alleged failure by the respondent Party and the economic and societal impact thereof". Under paragraph 4, the giving of notice triggers an obligation of the parties to consult within the Specialised Committee on Fisheries with a view to reaching a mutually agreeable solution. The notice itself must identify the way in which the complaining party considers that the other party has failed to comply, the date on which it intends to suspend its own obligations and the level of that suspension. The risk that the complaining party might invoke and impose self-help remedial measures on the basis of its own possibly biased assessment of their proportionality to the alleged harm is addressed by paragraph 5, which ensures that it cannot simply be left at that. Instead, it faces a genuine discipline: within 14 days of the giving of notice it must proceed to refer the other party's alleged non-compliance to an arbitration tribunal under Article 739, without prior recourse to consultations under Article 738.[48] The tribunal is directed to treat the issue as a case of urgency for the purpose of Article 744.[49]

By paragraph 6, the suspension of other obligations must cease when either the complaining party is satisfied that the other party has returned to compliance with its relevant obligations, or the arbitration tribunal decides that the other party has not failed to comply with those obligations. Paragraphs 7 and 8 are parallel to Article 501(5) and (6) above on retaliatory suspension of obligations to the level equivalent to the nullification or impairment of benefits caused by wrongful or significantly excessive application of compensatory measures under paragraphs 1 or 2, and non-recourse to the WTO Agreement or any other international agreement to forestall the suspension of obligations, to which the comments made above in respect of each[50] are equally applicable.

No less significant, however, is what is omitted from Article 506. The parties have made no provision whatever for what may well prove to be the most recurrent of breaches, namely overcatch of quotas. In jumping straight to countermeasures, the text overlooks the longstanding and helpful precedent in the International Commission for the Conservation of Atlantic Tunas, of which both parties are members, for automatic debiting of overages against future quota, possibly with a penalty.[51] Nor does it say anything about what happens to quota left uncaught, implying a use-it-or-lose-it approach, but this is an unwise incentive to try to catch every last tonne of it, with the risk of overshooting, which could have been alleviated by a minor allowance to carry over some or all of the surplus to the following year. Although the omission has since been made good for the short term in the Written Record of the fisheries consultations of 11 June 2021, which provides for 10 per cent flexibility either way for all Annex 35 and 36 stocks,[52] this remains vulnerable to a non-renewal of the decision once it expires. The risk would then revive of overcatches being routinely ignored until their magnitude reaches a political breaking-point that then sees a heavy-handed overreaction collectively punishing not just those

48 The request to establish the tribunal is made by written request to the respondent party in which the complaining party must explicitly identify the measure at issue and explain how it constitutes a breach of the provision(s) concerned "in a manner sufficient to present the legal basis for the complaint clearly": Art 739(2).

49 On the consequences of urgency, see supra text between (nn 32 and 33).

50 Supra, text between (nn 33 and 42).

51 See e.g., ICCAT Recommendation 96–14 (which is how binding decisions of that body are styled), "Recommendation by ICCAT Regarding Compliance in the Bluefin Tuna and North Atlantic Swordfish Fisheries", <https://iccat.int/Documents/Recs/compendiopdf-e/1996-14-e.pdf> accessed 1 June 2021.

52 Written record of fisheries consultations between the United Kingdom and the European Union for 2021, <https://assets.publishing.service.gov.uk/government/uploads/system/uploads/attachment_data/file/993155/written-record-fisheries-consultations-between-uk-eu-2021.pdf> accessed 5 July 2021, at 10 under the heading "14. Inter-annual quota flexibility".

operators responsible for it, but all who export fish across the UK–EU border. The failure to eliminate this risk *ab initio* is poor legal policy.

Article 507 on data sharing is very brief: it merely requires the parties to "share such information as is necessary to support the implementation of this Heading subject to each Party's laws". This may represent an opportunity missed to tailor the availability of data to the requirements of sound modern fisheries management. In particular, the withholding of catch and effort data from scientific advisers because it is deemed commercial-in-confidence is likely to diminish the quality and reliability of the advice they can provide to managers, and shows a questionable sense of policy priorities. Fish stocks are public assets to which licences give privileged access denied to all who are unlicensed, so the commercial interests of individual operators should not be allowed to override and obstruct flows of information that serve the greater good.

The Specialised Committee on Fisheries already mentioned a number of times is created by Article 508. Paragraph 1 is a non-exhaustive list of its functions, to:

a provide a forum for discussion and co-operation in relation to sustainable fisheries management;[53]

b consider the development of multi-year strategies for conservation and management as the basis for the setting of TACs and other management measures;

c develop multi-year strategies to conserve and manage non-quota stocks referred to in Article 500(2);

d consider measures for fisheries management and conservation, including emergency measures and measures to ensure selectivity of fishing;

e consider approaches to the collection of data for science and fisheries management purposes, the sharing of such data (including information relevant to monitoring, controlling and enforcing compliance), and the consultation of scientific bodies;

f consider measures to ensure compliance with the applicable rules, including joint control, monitoring and surveillance programmes and the exchange of data to facilitate monitoring uptake of fishing opportunities and control and enforcement;

g develop the TAC-setting guidelines referred to in Article 499(5);

h prepare for annual consultations;

i consider matters relating to the designation of ports for landings, including facilitation of the timely notification by the parties of such designations and of changes to these;

j establish timelines for the notification of measures, the communication of the lists of vessels and the notice referred to in Articles 496(3), 497(1) and 498(7) respectively;

53 This is an unfortunate turn of phrase, given that it is not the management structures or processes that need to be sustained, but rather the stocks and the fisheries dependent on them.

k provide a forum for consultations on compensatory and remedial measures under Articles 501(2) and 506(4) respectively;
l develop guidelines to support the practical application of Article 500 on access to waters;
m develop a mechanism for voluntary in-year transfers of fishing opportunities between the parties, as referred to in Article 498(8); and
n consider the application and implementation of Articles 502 and 503 on access to waters of Guernsey, Jersey and the Isle of Man and the associated notification periods relating to the importation and direct landing of fisheries products.

Paragraph 2 empowers the Specialised Committee on Fisheries to adopt measures, decisions and recommendations:

a recording matters agreed by the parties following consultations under Article 498 on fishing opportunities;[54]
b in relation to any of the matters referred to in paragraph 1;
c amending the list of pre-existing international obligations referred to in Article 496(2);[55]
d in relation to any other aspect of co-operation on sustainable fisheries management under this Heading; and
e on the modalities of a review under Article 510.[56]

Curiously, by paragraph 3 it is not the Committee, but rather the Partnership Council for the Agreement as a whole, that has the power to amend Annexes 35, 36 and 37.

Article 509 is another special provision enabling termination of the fisheries heading while leaving the rest of the Agreement (mostly) intact. Without prejudice to Articles 521 and 779 on termination of (most of) Part Two and the entire Agreement respectively, paragraph 1 allows either party to terminate Heading Five at any time "by written notification [to the other] through diplomatic channels". In that event, however, not just the fisheries heading but also those on trade, aviation (unless the parties agree otherwise under paragraph 3) and road transport cease to be in force on the first day of the ninth month following the date of notification – severe concomitants doubtless intended to deter invocation of this right.[57] Should that nonetheless occur, through either paragraph 1, Article 521 or Article 779, obligations existing for the parties

54 This is not the same as the written record called for by Art 498(6), although it would have to use the latter as its point of departure.
55 See supra text at (nn 16–19).
56 See infra text at (n 60).
57 See also Art 411(10) and (11) tying the fate of the latter two headings to that of the trade one when the latter is terminated for non-fisheries reasons as part of a broader "rebalancing" of obligations under the Agreement.

under this Heading for the year in which it ceases to be in force would by paragraph 2 continue to apply until the end of that year.

Once more different arrangements apply to the provisions on access to waters of Guernsey, Jersey and the Isle of Man and the associated notification periods for importation and direct landing of fisheries products. Under paragraph 4, again without prejudice to Articles 521 and 779, unless the parties agree otherwise, Articles 502 and 503 together with related provisions of Heading Five[58] shall remain in force until they are terminated by either party giving the other three years' notice of termination; or, if earlier, the date on which paragraphs 3 to 5 of Article 520[59] cease to be in force. This notice may be given singly in respect of one or two of the Crown Dependencies, and if this happens, Articles 502 and 503 together with related provisions of Heading Five remain in force for the other territory or territories. Similarly, if paragraphs 3 to 5 of Article 520 cease to be in force in relation to one or two of the three territories, Articles 502 and 503 plus related provisions of Heading Five continue in force for the other territory or territories in respect of which those paragraphs remain in force.

Article 510 mandates in paragraph 1 a joint review by the parties through the Partnership Council of the implementation of Heading Five, to take place four years after the end of the adjustment period referred to in Article 1 of Annex 38, the Protocol on access to waters, i.e., in 2030, with the aim of considering further codification and strengthening of the arrangements, including in relation to access to waters. Under paragraph 2 reviews may, but need not, be repeated at subsequent intervals of four years. The modalities of the review according to paragraph 3 are to be decided in advance through the Specialised Committee on Fisheries.[60] Paragraph 4 directs that the review should evaluate in particular, in relation to the previous years:

a the provisions for access of parties' vessels to each other's waters under Article 500;
b the TAC shares set out in Annexes 35–37;
c the number and extent of transfers of fishing opportunities under Article 498(8);
d the fluctuations in annual TACs;
e compliance by each party with the provisions of Heading Five and by its vessels with the rules applicable to them in the other Party's waters;
f the nature and extent of co-operation under Heading Five; and
g any other element added in advance by the parties through the Specialised Committee on Fisheries.

58 In this context, the failure to specify precisely which provisions these are may prove more damaging than in other instances where the same formula is used, in the sense that it may create unnecessary and avoidable risks of disagreement and disputes.
59 See supra text following (n 45).
60 See supra text at (n 56).

Finally, Article 511 preserves in paragraph 1 other existing agreements – apparently only those of treaty status, from the contrast in drafting with paragraph 2 below – concerning fishing by vessels of one party within the other party's area of jurisdiction. This no longer includes the London Fisheries Convention permitting access to vessels from Belgium, France, Germany, Ireland, the Netherlands and the UK to fisheries in the outer six miles of each other's territorial seas, which the UK denounced in July 2017,[61] and it is unclear what else it could encompass, as the voisinage arrangement with Ireland[62] is not a treaty, while the 2000 Agreement with France[63] falls under paragraph 2. By the latter, the provisions of Heading Five supersede and replace any existing agreements or arrangements with respect to fishing by EU vessels in the territorial sea adjacent to Guernsey, Jersey or the Isle of Man and by UK fishing vessels registered in any of those territories in the territorial sea adjacent to a Member State, unless the Partnership Council has decided under Article 502(3) that the Agreement will cease to apply in respect of any of the Crown Dependencies, in which event those relevant agreements or arrangements remain on foot in respect of the territory or territories concerned.

Evaluation and Concluding Remarks

Two features of Heading Five stand out. One is just how far short of attaining catch shares commensurate with zonal attachment the UK has fallen, the consequence of manoeuvring itself into a position late in the negotiations where the matter of fisheries was left as the last unsettled sticking point.[64] Thus, instead of serving as a bargaining chip to secure some other aim, it effectively became a matter of either accepting the modest gains offered by the EU or abandoning the negotiations altogether, along with the free-trade deal, on the eve of the expiry of the transitional period. A no-deal outcome would have left the UK with a much larger share of the stocks at issue, thanks to its ability to exclude EU vessels from UK waters, but since the EU is the destination of much of the UK's seafood exports, it would have lost tariff-free access to that market. Far from being willing to separate the catching of fish from their marketing as advocated in the White Paper, and required by the Food and Agriculture Organization of the United Nations (FAO) Code of Conduct for Responsible Fisheries,[65] another of the instruments to be honoured listed in

61 Fisheries Convention, London, 9 March 1964; 581 UNTS 57.

62 Supra, text at (n 44).

63 Supra (n 43).

64 G Parker, S Payne, P Foster and J Brunsden, "EU and UK edge towards Brexit compromise on fisheries", *Financial Times*, 21 December 2020, <www.ft.com/content/90e8e07e-11f7-4a66-881d-a7758676e7b7> accessed 29 May 2021.

65 FAO Code of Conduct for Responsible Fisheries, adopted on 31 October 1995 by the Conference of the FAO; <www.fao.org/3/v9878e/V9878E.pdf> accessed 28 June 2021, Art 11.2.7 ("States should not condition access to markets to access to resources.") The EU, though not itself a State, acts on behalf of its Member States.

Article 404(2)(a),[66] the EU was able to insist on their linkage via a single instrument, not just to each other but also to other goods, and employ this as leverage to drive a hard bargain.

The Government's summary document avers that the Agreement "puts us in a position to rebuild our fishing fleet and increase quotas in the next few years, finally overturning the inequity that British fishermen have faced for over four decades",[67] and highlights that "[t]he UK is now free to create its own laws and fisheries management practices to the benefit of fishers and coastal communities across the whole UK".[68] But it makes no claim to have attained zonal attachment, which it does not even mention, confining itself to the observation that the Agreement "ends the dependence of the UK fleet on the unfair 'relative stability' mechanism enshrined in the EU's Common Fisheries Policy and will mean that the UK vessels are able to take a larger proportion of the total landings from UK and EU waters going forward."[69] Further adjustments of the quota shares in the UK's favour for stocks of particular interest to the UK fleet are not ruled out, but in WTO parlance would have to be "paid for" by other concessions that cannot be predicted (most likely, they would take the form of reduced quotas for other stocks) but may prove too unpalatable to pursue.

The second prominent aspect is that the dispute settlement provisions both fail to deal adequately with overcatch and are back to front and wide open to abuse. Considering that the EU (or more accurately the European Communities, as it then was), with the UK then still a prominent Member State, was instrumental in inserting Article 23(2) into the DSU during the Uruguay Round of multilateral trade negotiations to prohibit what one textbook calls "vigilante justice",[70] it is startling to find them choosing to adopt exactly that tactic against each other in the fisheries field.[71] While it is in line with most observers' views of the disparity in the two sides' bargaining power that the UK

66 Supra, text preceding (n 12).

67 Summary Document, supra (n 24), at 6, para 4.

68 Ibid., at 24, para 123.

69 Ibid., at para 125.

70 P Van den Bossche and W Zdouc, *The Law and Policy of the World Trade Organization: Text, Cases and Materials* (4th edn; Cambridge University Press, 2017), at 188–189. The phrase refers to the pre-WTO era practice whereby Party A would impose GATT-inconsistent trade restrictions against Party B based on a unilateral and not invariably objective determination by A of breach of some provision of GATT by B. DSU Art 23(2)(a) obliges WTO Members seeking the redress of a violation of obligations "not [to] make a determination to the effect that a violation has occurred … except through recourse to dispute settlement in accordance with … this Understanding, and shall make any such determination consistent with the findings contained in the panel or Appellate Body report adopted by the DSB or an arbitration award rendered under this Understanding".

71 See R Churchill, "Fisheries management in European Union and United Kingdom Waters after Brexit – a change for the better?" (forthcoming) *Ocean Yearbook* 36 attributing this to a lack of trust by the EU in the UK engendered by some of its negotiating tactics and statements; on the other hand, a similar provision was in the UK's own draft fisheries agreement, supra (n 6), and see too text at (n 7).

draft ultimately exercised little influence on the content of the 19 articles, it is unfortunate that the two elements of this draft that did survive into the Agreement do not represent best practice. One, annual negotiations, looks decidedly old-fashioned as RFMOs increasingly move to multi-year management cycles and catch share allocations that reduce the transaction costs of frequent renegotiation.[72] The other, authorisation of self-help countermeasures, anticipatory of findings by a dispute settlement forum confirming an alleged breach that may never be made, is more reminiscent of action to counteract dumping (but note that dumping is not itself prohibited by the WTO Agreement and its annexes) and subsidies (only some of which are prohibited), and is ill-suited to fisheries management.

Observers from other goods and services sectors outside the world of fisheries whose interests were subordinated to the fishing sector by the UK in the negotiations for the Agreement may have been expecting to console themselves with the thought that the sacrifices were imposed on them in a good cause if they allowed the UK to redress the real disadvantages borne by the UK fleet in its own waters under the CFP. If so, one must hope for their sake that they have not studied Part Two's Heading Five too closely, lest they come away not merely disabused but chagrined by what they will have found.

72 ICCAT Recommendation 19–04, Recommendation by ICCAT Amending the Recommendation 18–02 Establishing a Multi-Annual Management Plan for Bluefin Tuna in the Eastern Atlantic and the Mediterranean, <https://iccat.int/Documents/Recs/compendiopdf-e/2019-04-e.pdf> accessed 1 June 2021, is a case in point. The UK is not known to have objected at the time to the EU's moves towards multiannual management dating back to the CFP Regulation of 2013, supra (n 22), Arts 9 and 10.

4 Reflections on the Trilateral and Bilateral Fishing Negotiations Between the EU, UK and Norway

Jonatan Echebarria Fernández, Mitchell Lennan and Tafsir Matin Johansson

Introduction

The ocean is a shared open space, and fish stocks do not adhere to or respect international maritime boundaries. International law is clear on the fact that if a resource falls only partly within a State's jurisdiction, that State does not have an unfettered right to exploit that shared resource unilaterally.[1] Some form of cooperative regional management is necessary for fish stocks that move between the exclusive economic zones (EEZs) of States or beyond national jurisdiction to the high seas for both sustainability and legal purposes. Coastal States are obliged under the United Nations Convention on the Law of the Sea (UNCLOS) and the UN Fish Stocks Agreement to take extra steps to manage shared or transboundary stocks, which are defined as "Stocks occurring within the [EEZs] of two or more coastal States or both within the [EEZ] and in an area beyond and adjacent to it".[2] For these stocks, measures in addition to those of the coastal States whose EEZs these stocks inhabit are required for effective conservation and management. UNCLOS obliges coastal States to enter into negotiations to agree on the necessary measures for the conservation and management of such stocks.[3] These consultations "should be meaningful in the sense that substantial effort should be made by all States concerned, with a view to adopting effective measures necessary to coordinate and ensure the conservation and development of shared stocks".[4]

1 Award between the United States and the United Kingdom, Relating to the Rights of Jurisdiction of United States in the Bering's Sea and the Preservation of Fur Seals *(United States v. United Kingdom)* Decision of 15 August 1893 RIAA XXXVIII, at 269.
2 United Nations Convention on the Law of the Sea (UNCLOS), Montego Bay, 10 December 1982, 1833 UNTS 3, Art. 63–64; Agreement for the Implementation of the Provisions of the United Nations Convention on the Law of the Sea of 10 December 1982 relating to the Conservation and Management of Straddling Fish Stocks and Highly Migratory Fish Stocks, New York, 4 August 1995; 2167 UNTS 3, Art. 8.
3 UNCLOS, Art. 63.
4 *Request for an Advisory Opinion Submitted by The Sub-Regional Fisheries Commission (SRFC)*, Advisory Opinion, 2 April 2015, ITLOS Reports 2015 (*Fisheries Advisory Opinion*) at para. 210.

DOI: 10.4324/9781003252481-4

We examine below this obligation in practice. Since the UK shares around 100 stocks with the EU and its other neighbours, cooperation is necessary to ensure sustainable exploitation of shared fish stocks. Brexit has raised concerns about the UK's continued role in relationship-building in the North-East Atlantic. As a new piece in the fisheries cooperation conundrum – will the UK play a disruptive or constructive role? Since the UK has left the EU, both Parties must now proactively engage in negotiations for shared stocks in a trilateral format with Norway for the first time. In addition, Norway and the UK, and the EU and the UK have entered negotiations for bilateral fishing arrangements which raises questions for the future of fisheries cooperation in the North-East Atlantic in a post-Brexit world.

The chapter analyses the outcomes of the annual trilateral (UK–EU–Norway) and bilateral (EU–Norway, UK–Norway and EU–UK) negotiations. Considerations are provided and what the future will be regarding fishing rights for the UK regarding the TCA and the UK–Norway arrangements on fisheries. Norway's long and effective cooperative approach to fisheries management with the EU is especially insightful, so is included here. Prior to these negotiations, the EU had established preliminary fishing opportunities for the first quarter of 2021.[5] Articles 52 and 53 of that Regulation establish fishing opportunities for Norway and the UK, respectively.[6] The UK and Faroe Islands fisheries negotiations on the basis of the bilateral fisheries agreement between the two Parties[7] were also terminated without a fisheries arrangement for 2021, but will remain outside the scope of discussion.

The Trilateral Agreement (UK–EU–Norway)

The trilateral arrangement on jointly managed fisheries stocks in the North Sea for 2021 (TA21) is an example of the EU, Norway and the UK undertaking the above obligations.[8] The three Parties met for the first time in a trilateral fisheries context in January 2021, and "agreed that it was necessary to establish a trilateral framework agreement to underpin their cooperation on the management of North Sea fish stocks".[9] The TA21 has established the total

5 Council Regulation (EU) 2021/92 OJ L 31/31; Regulation (EU) 2017/2403, OJ L 347/81.

6 Ibid.

7 Framework Agreement on Fisheries between the Government of the United Kingdom of Great Britain and Northern Ireland and the Government of the Faroes, Copenhagen, 29 October 2020, <https://assets.publishing.service.gov.uk/government/uploads/system/uploads/attachment_data/file/933792/CS_Faroe_Islands_1.2020_UK_Faroes_Framework_Agreement_on_Fisheries.pdf> accessed 13 July 2021.

8 The EU fisheries agreements with the United Kingdom, Norway, Faroe Islands, Iceland and other coastal states may all be viewed here: <https://ec.europa.eu/oceans-and-fisheries/fisheries/international-agreements/northern-agreements_en> accessed 15 April 2021.

9 Agreed Record of Fisheries Consultations between the European Union, Norway and the United Kingdom for 2021, 16 March 2021, <https://ec.europa.eu/oceans-and-fisheries/fisheries/international-agreements/northern-agreements_en> at para. 8.

allowable catch (TAC) and quota allocation for six fish stocks, totalling over 636,000 tonnes for 2021.[10] Negotiations took two months from January 2021, and a trilateral agreement was signed allowing for the joint management of several stocks (Table 4.1).[11] These were considered by the Parties to be jointly managed stocks in the North Sea (see Figure 4.1),[12] who agreed "to consider and set priorities for joint long-term management strategies for jointly managed stocks".[13] The TAC for five out of six stocks were set at maximum sustainable yield (MSY) in line with advice from the International Council for the Exploration of the Seas (ICES), while the TAC for North Sea/Eastern Channel Skagerrak Cod ("North Sea cod") was set below MSY (see Table 4.1). The state of the North Sea stock has been of concern for quite some time, and a long-term management plan has been in place since the year 2000; however, these have not brought the stock back into recovery.[14] Norway and the EU have jointly adopted a plan of recovery for the North Sea cod stock, including technical measures such as area closures that continue to protect adult and juvenile cod.[15] This considered, the setting of the North Sea cod TAC below MSY does not come as a surprise.

The Parties noted that species such as hake, anglerfish and Norway Pput are shared stocks broadly due to migratory patterns and should be managed jointly.[16] Moving forward, the Parties agreed to preparations for the joint management of these stocks, utilising factual analysis of stock distributions by experts.[17] Parties agreed to share catch information of the jointly managed species by jurisdiction on a monthly basis,[18] and to inform each other of their respective fisheries regulations in the North Sea.[19] In addition, the TA21 also included an agreement on monitoring, control and surveillance (MCS) for joint stocks, and a Working Group on MCS was established.[20] The terms of reference for the working group are annexed to the TA21 with its function and

10 See 'EU, Norway and the United Kingdom conclude key fisheries arrangements on North Sea' European Commission Press release 16 March (2021), <https://ec.europa.eu/commission/presscorner/detail/en/IP_21_1206> accessed 16 April 2021.

11 Agreed Record of Fisheries Consultations between the European Union, Norway and the United Kingdom for 2021 (n 9) para. 8.

12 Ibid., para. 10.

13 Ibid., para. 11.1.

14 OECD, 'Country note on national fisheries management systems – Norway' Online, <www.oecd.org/norway/34430920.pdf> accessed 13 April 2021.

15 Ibid.; Agreed Record of Fisheries Consultations between the European Union, Norway and the United Kingdom for 2021 (n 9) para. 12.7; described in Annex IV; see also (n 10).

16 Agreed Record of Fisheries Consultations between the European Union, Norway and the United Kingdom for 2021 (n 9) para. 18.

17 Ibid.

18 Ibid., para. 19.

19 Ibid., Annex I(II).

20 Ibid., para. 20; Terms of reference for a working group on monitoring, control and surveillance is found in Annex II.I.

Table 4.1 2021 quotas for jointly managed shared stocks in the North Sea between Norway, the EU and UK. Table replicated from TA21 with extra column indicating whether TAC for that species was set at maximum sustainable yield added by authors.

Species	*ICES Area*	*TAC*	*% +/-*	*Set at MSY?*	*Sharing*					
					Norway		*EU*		*UK*	
		Tonnes			*%*	*Tonnes*	*%*	*Tonnes*	*%*	*Tonnes*
Cod	4	13,246	+10%	No	17.0	2,252	39.03	5,170	43.97	5,824
Haddock	4	42,785	+20%	Yes	23.0	9,841	14.21	6,080	62.79	26,865
Saithe	4, 3a	59,512	–25%	Yes	52.0	30,946	37.30	22,198	10.70	6,368
Whiting	4	21,306	+19%	Yes	10.0	2,131	31.30	6,669	58.70	12,507
Plaice	4	143,419	–2.3%	Yes	7.0	1,039	66.53	95,417	26.47	37,963
North Sea Herring	4, 7d	356,357	–7.4%	Yes	29.0	103,344	52.56	187,301	18.44	65,712

Figure 4.1 Detailed boundaries of ICES areas 27.4, 27.5, 27.6, 27.7, 27.8, 27.9.
Source: Figure Reproduced with permission from Food and Agriculture Organization of the United Nations website: www.fao.org/fishery/en/area/27 © FAO 1990–2022.

purpose being "to cooperate, exchange information and best practices related to control of joint stocks, in mutual interest in securing continued responsible fisheries and ensuring the long-term conservation and sustainable exploitation of the marine living resources for which the Parties are responsible".[21] A Working Group on Herring was also established with the objective, *inter alia*, "to recommend how to optimally and sustainably utilise the North Sea Autumn Spawning Herring in the North Sea and explore methods for TAC setting".[22]

Interestingly, the TA21 contains an inter-annual quota flexibility scheme. This allows each Party the option to "transfer to the following year unutilised quantities of up to 10% of the quota allocated to it. The quantity transferred shall be in addition to the quota allocated to the Party concerned in the following year. This quantity cannot be transferred further to the quotas for subsequent years."[23] The scheme is applicable to quotas of herring, haddock,

21 Ibid., Annex III.
22 Ibid., Annex V.
23 Ibid., Annex II.

saithe, plaice and whiting.[24] Parties may authorise vessels to fish up to 10% beyond the allocated quota, and all quantities fished beyond the quota allocated in one year shall be deducted from the following year's annual quota.[25] The scheme relies on complete catch statistics and quotas from previous years being made available to each Party "no later than 1 April", and to ensure transparency, "more detailed information on catch utilisation shall be exchanged".[26] In addition, the scheme is to be terminated if the spawning stock biomass for any of the above stocks falls below precautionary reference points, or is projected to fall below this point in the next two years, or if fishing mortality rises above the precautionary mortality level.[27] The inter-annual quota flexibility scheme is an interesting conclusion in the TA21, since the fisheries provisions of the TCA did not take the same approach and has been criticised for doing so.[28] Based on the quotas allocated in Table 4.1, fishing opportunities within EU Member States were allocated by Council Regulation (EU) 2021/703.[29]

The Bilateral Agreement (UK–Norway)

As has already been mentioned in this chapter, the UK found itself as a new and independent player in the North-East Atlantic fisheries management game, and therefore needed to establish new fishing relationships with the EU and other coastal States, including Norway. The UK and Norway signed a framework agreement on fisheries on 30 September 2020, which entered into force on 1 January 2021.[30] The Agreement contains principles similar to the TCA, including the establishment of cooperation between the two parties to promote the long-term sustainability and optimum utilisation of marine living resources, use of the best scientific evidence available and application of the precautionary approach, etc.[31] The area of application applies to waters "beyond and adjacent to the territorial sea of the Parties and in respect of which they are entitled to exercise sovereign rights or jurisdiction under Part V of UNCLOS".[32] Importantly, the Agreement grants reciprocal access to each Party's vessels for the

24 Ibid.
25 Ibid.
26 Ibid.
27 Ibid.
28 See A Serdy, Chapter 3, text at (n 52).
29 Council Regulation (EU) 2021/703 OJ L 146/1.
30 Framework Agreement on Fisheries between the United Kingdom of Great Britain and Northern Ireland and the Kingdom of Norway, London, 30 September 2020, <https://assets.publishing.service.gov.uk/government/uploads/system/uploads/attachment_data/file/927151/CS_Norway_1.2020_UK_Norway_Framework_Agreement_on_Fisheries.pdf> accessed 20 April 2021.
31 Ibid., Art. 1; for further analysis on this Agreement, see R Barnes 'Framework agreement on fisheries between the United Kingdom of Great Britain and Northern Ireland and the Kingdom of Norway' *The International Journal of Marine and Coastal Law* 36 (2021) 155–164.
32 Framework Agreement (n 30), Art. 2.

purposes of fishing, though the extent and conditions of access is to be the subject of annual consultations between the UK and Norway.[33] The Parties are obliged to produce a written record of the annual consultations and are to determine any access by one Party to the other's waters and vice versa, and any transfer of quota between the Parties.[34] The Agreement also contains provisions on vessel licensing, compliance control and enforcement, consultation relating to questions relating to the interpretation and functioning of the Agreement's application, and in the case of a dispute in the application or interpretation of the agreement, amendments, relationship to other agreements, and relationship with the Law of the Sea.[35]

The UK and Norway, in fulfilment of Article 4 of the Agreement, entered into consultations with the aim of reaching an agreement on fisheries for the year 2021. The consultations were initially projected to conclude by the beginning of 2021; however, the timing of the TCA negotiation delayed this, and Norway prioritised the negotiation of the TA21 ahead of any other bilateral fishing arrangements with the EU or UK.

In April 2021 the talks between Norway and the UK on fishing arrangements for 2021 collapsed. This resulted in loss of reciprocal access by Norwegian and UK vessels. This has consequences for both Parties, particularly with regard to the seasonality of certain fish stocks. Norway, whose vessels catch a majority of blue whiting in UK waters (note in the above Section the EU traded blue whiting to Norway) – however, by April 2021 the season for blue whiting had already passed (an important impacting factor cause by delay in negotiations). The situation is arguably worse for the UK, whose vessels fish throughout the year for cod.[36] UK vessels depend a great deal on access to Norwegian waters for cod stocks, and cod stocks moving further north due to warming seas increases this dependence on access to Norwegian waters.[37] Thus, the failure to achieve a fisheries arrangement was seen as a huge blow to distant water fishing fleets in the UK, particularly in Scotland, as well as Hull and Grimsby.[38] Norwegian vessels also fish for mackerel in UK waters, meaning UK vessels (especially in Scotland – see Chapter 1) may see some benefits in that respect. This followed the unilateral decision by Norway to increase its 2021 share of mackerel by 55% from 191,843 tonnes to 298, 299 tonnes, and was characterised as "irresponsible" by Gerard van Balsfoort, President of the Pelagic Freezer-trawler Association.[39]

33 Ibid., Art. 3.
34 Ibid., Art. 4.
35 Ibid., Arts. 5–10.
36 See Chapter 1.
37 See *ICES Advice on fishing opportunities, catch, and effort Greater North Sea Ecoregion*, 8 November 2019, <www.ices.dk/sites/pub/Publication%20Reports/Advice/2019/2019/cod.27.47d20.pdf> accessed 21 April 2021.
38 C Morris, 'Brexit: Anger over government's failure to get Norway fishing deal' 30 April 2021, <www.bbc.com/news/uk-politics-56940914> accessed 21 April 2021.
39 'EU fishermen strongly rejects Norway's unilateral mackerel quota grab' *The Fishing Daily* 28 May 2021, <https://thefishingdaily.com/featured-news/eu-fishermen-strongly-rejects-norways-unilateral-mackerel-quota-grab/> accessed 21 April 2021; see also G van Balsfoort et al., Chapter 9 in this collection, text between (nn 3 and 4).

The Bilateral Agreements (EU–Norway)

Norway is not an EU Member State, and thus the CFP does not apply to it under EU law. Norway does, however, have access to EU waters as part of a bilateral fisheries agreement, which also allows access of EU and UK vessels to a certain number of fish stocks in Norwegian waters. The EU and Norway have been negotiating bilateral agreements for fisheries with the EU since 1972. When Norway did not join the European Economic Community as it was known at the time through the decision not to ratify the Treaty of Accession.[40] Since its neighbours the UK and Denmark *did* ratify the treaty, meaning fisheries competence was passed to the European Economic Community (EEC), this meant Norway had to undertake negotiations of TACs and quotas with the EEC. The UK's departure from the CFP, and the UK's fisheries agreement with Norway (discussed in the previous section) entering in to force meant that "the EU's fishing operations in Norwegian waters, and vice-versa [...] had been partially discontinued since 31 December 2020".[41] The general political understanding of these specific negotiations is that Norway tends to concede catches to the EU to avoid the Union implementing punitive trade or market measures on fisheries imports from Norway.

As a result, in parallel to the TA21, the EU and Norway entered into consultations and agreed TACs and quota allocations for shared stocks in the North Sea and Skagerrak, as well as quota exchanges and reciprocal access. This resulted in three bilateral agreements signed between the Parties. The EU and Norway renewed their arrangement on reciprocal access for North Sea jointly managed stocks. Importantly, zonal attachment is the basis of quota allocations between the EU and Norway.[42] In the interim or before the conclusion of the negotiations, Article 52 of Council Regulation (EU) 2021/92 provides for access of Norwegian-licensed vessels to fish in EU waters,[43] subject to the conditions of fishing operations by third countries.[44]

The first bilateral arrangement concluded that the EU will have access to catch its allocated quota (29,667 tonnes) of Spring spawning herring in

40 Treaty of Accession of Denmark, Ireland and the United Kingdom [1972] OJ L 73, 27. 3 1972, 5–204; Decision of the Council of the European Communities of 22 January 1972 on the accession of the Kingdom of Denmark, Ireland, the Kingdom of Norway and the United Kingdom of Great Britain and Northern Ireland to the European Economic Community and to the European Atomic Energy Community [1972] OJ L 73, 27.3 (1972) at p. 4; see Churchill, Chapter 2 in this collection, text between (nn 5 and 9).

41 EU, Norway and the United Kingdom conclude key fisheries arrangements on North Sea (n 10); Council Regulation (EU) 2021/92 (n 5) Annex V, Part B.

42 See R Hannesson, 'Zonal attachment of fish stocks and management cooperation' *Fisheries Research* 140 (2013) 149–154; J Hamre, 'A model of estimating biological attachment of fish stocks to exclusive economic zones' *International Council for the Exploration of the Sea* C M 1993/D:43 (Copenhagen, 1993); see Churchill, Chapter 2 in this collection at (n 29).

43 Council Regulation (EU) 2021/92 (n 5), Art. 53.

44 Regulation (EU) 2017/2403 (n 5) Title III.

Norwegian waters.[45] Reciprocal access was also agreed in the case of blue whiting for the two Parties to catch up to 141,648 tonnes each.[46] Another key point of the first bilateral arrangement was quota exchange of stocks of major economic interest to both Parties. Notably, 10,274 tonnes of Arctic cod from the Norwegian fisheries zone were granted to the EU (Table 4.3) in exchange for 37,500 tonnes of blue whiting, and 12,000 tonnes of sprat (to be fished 1 July 2021 to 30 June 2022) for Norway.[47]

Table 4.2 Zonal access for jointly managed stocks in the North Sea. Data from agreed record of conclusions of fisheries consultations between Norway and EU.[48]

Species	*ICES area*	*TAC*	*Norwegian quota*	*EU quota*	*Norwegian access in EU waters*	*EU access in Norwegian waters*
		Tonnes	*Tonnes*	*Tonnes*	*Tonnes*	*Tonnes*
Cod	4	13,246	2,252	5,170	2,252	4,494
Haddock	4	42,785	9,841	6,080	9,841	4,523
Saithe	4, 3a	59,512	30,946	22,198	30,946	22,198
Whiting	4	21,306	2,131	6,669	2,131	4,518
Plaice	4	143,419	1,039	95,417	10,039	39,153
North Sea herring	4, 7d	356,357	103,344	187,301	3,000	3,000

Table 4.3 Quotas to the EU of Norwegian Exclusive Stocks. Data from agreed record of conclusions of fisheries consultations between Norway and EU.[49] For ICES areas, refer to Figure 4.2.

Species	*ICES area*	*Quantity (Tonnes)*
Arcto-Norwegian cod	1;2	10,274
Arcto-Norwegian haddock	1;2	500
Saithe	1;2	770
Greenland halibut (by-catches)	1;2	50
Others (by-catches)	1;2	100

45 Agreed Record of Fisheries Consultations between Norway and EU, 18 June 2021, <https://ec.europa.eu/oceans-and-fisheries/fisheries/international-agreements/northern-agreements_en> accessed 19 April 2021, Table 5.

46 Ibid.

47 Ibid., Table 2.

48 Ibid.

49 Ibid.

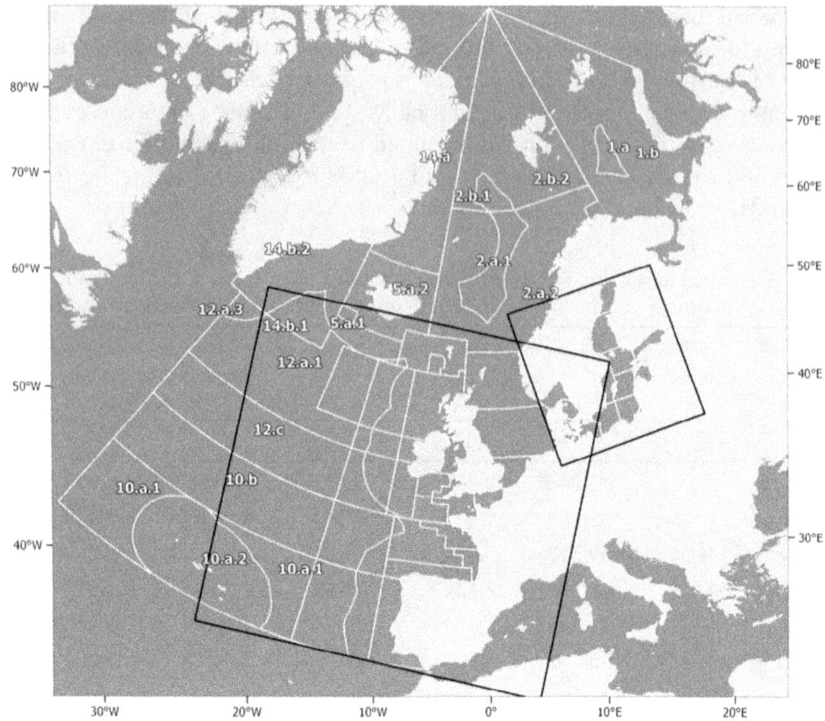

Figure 4.2 Boundaries of the Atlantic, North-East major fishing area and corresponding ICES fishing areas for statistical purposes.
Source: Figure reproduced with permission from Food and Agriculture Organization of the United Nations website: www.fao.org/fishery/en/area/27 © FAO 1990–2021.

The second bilateral arrangement relates to TACs set and quotas shared for Skagerrak and Kattegat straits.[50] TACs were set and quotas allocated for stocks of cod, haddock, whiting, plaice, pandalus, herring and sprat.[51] The Parties "agreed that the negotiated quota arrangements constitute an ad-hoc solution and shall be without prejudice to future fisheries arrangements between the Parties".[52] Norway stipulated that this arrangement was "greatly imbalanced in Norway's disfavour" and will invite the EU for consultations in 2021 with the aim of "establishing a sharing arrangement closer to zonal attachment of the main species".[53]

50 Agreed record of conclusion of fisheries consultations between Norway and the European Union on the regulation of fisheries in Skagerrak and Kattegat for 2021, 16 March 2021, <https://ec.europa.eu/oceans-and-fisheries/fisheries/international-agreements/northern-agreements_en> accessed 20 April 2021.

51 Ibid., Annex I.

52 Ibid., para. 20.1.

53 Ibid., para. 20.2.

The third bilateral arrangement was negotiated by the EU on behalf of Sweden for fishing activity in the Norwegian EEZ south of 62° North for 2021 (within the framework of the fisheries agreement between Norway and Sweden of 9 December 1976).[54] Quotas were allocated to Sweden in the Norwegian EEZ and included cod, saithe, pollack, herring and mackerel.[55]

The Bilateral Agreement (UK–EU)

Article 498 of the TCA indicates that Parties are to enter into annual consolations for setting TACs for the 76 stocks listed in Annex 35.[56] Due to delays, however the UK and EU were not able to achieve an arrangement until June 2021. In the interim, before the conclusion of the negotiations, Article 53 of Council Regulation (EU) 2021/92 provides for access of UK-licensed vessels to fish in EU waters,[57] subject to the conditions of fishing operations by third countries.[58] Further, since the TCA came into force prior to a fisheries arrangement being agreed between the UK and EU, the provisional TACs for shared stocks under Article 499 applied. Article 499(2) aims to ensure that the provisional TACs ensure continued sustainable EU fishing activities until the EU–UK consultations pursuant to Article 498 are concluded and implemented.[59]

The negotiations continued in this collection between January and May 2021, with five rounds of negotiations taking place, concluding with a settlement at the beginning of June 2021. Prior to this, EU Regulations (EU) 2021/91 and (EU) 2021/92 were amended "in order to extend provisional unilateral Union TACs in order to create legal certainty for the Union operators and to ensure the continuation of sustainable fishing activities until those consultations are concluded in compliance with the Union legal framework and the Trade and Cooperation Agreement".[60] This approach, based on Article 499(2) of the TCA, which indicates that if a stocks listed in Annex 35 of the TCA or in Tables A and B of Annex 36 of the TCA remains without a TAC, each party

54 Agreement on fisheries between the Kingdom of Sweden and the Kingdom of Norway, 9 December 1976, <https://ec.europa.eu/oceans-and-fisheries/fisheries/international-agreements/northern-agreements_en> accessed 20 April 2021.

55 Protocol of fisheries consultations between Norway and the European Union, on behalf of Sweden for 2021, 16 March 2021, <https://ec.europa.eu/oceans-and-fisheries/fisheries/international-agreements/northern-agreements_en> accessed 20 April 2021.

56 Trade and Cooperation Agreement Between the European Union and the European Atomic Energy Community, of the One Part and the United Kingdom of Great Britain and Northern Ireland, of the Other Part (TCA), OJ L 444, 31 December 2020, pp.14–1462, Art. 498, Annex 35. See A Serdy, Chapter 3 in this collection.

57 Council Regulation (EU) 2021/92, OJ L 3131–192, Art. 53.

58 Regulation (EU) 2017/2403 (n 5), Title III.

59 TCA (n 56), Art. 499(2); Council Regulation (EU) 2021/703 (n 29).

60 Council Regulation (EU) 2021/703 ibid.

shall set a provisional TAC that corresponds to ICES advice.[61] Provisional TACs were extended until 31 July 2021.[62]

TACs were agreed for 75/76 of the stocks listed in TCA Annex 35, and are listed in Annex I of the arrangement, and so will not be reproduced here.[63] Similar to the arrangements discussed above, the TACs are based on scientific advice from ICES and apply until the end of 2021; while some deep-sea fish stocks apply until 2022. Indeed, the outcome of these negotiations is unique, considering they will apply for less than 6 months of the year in most cases. Similar also to the arrangements analysed above, the arrangement covers quota transfers and inter-annual quota flexibility, technical measures and non-quota stocks. Several factors were important according to the National Federation of Fishermen's Organisations.[64] These were the terms of the TCA: the UK's political position on the "right to regulatory autonomy" as an independent coastal state; the EU's political position to maintain and limit divergence from the CFP; as well as the challenges and limitations presented by the Covid-19 pandemic. The UK had already set TACs for 2021 at the beginning of May and set provisional quotas for the UK fleets. These were formally adopted into the agreement without any significant changes. However, changes in area flexibility (an EU fisheries management practice that aims to guarantee full use of coastal fishing opportunities) between Area 6a (West of Scotland) and Area 4 (North Sea) were made. EU Member States are obliged, by way of Article 7 of amended Regulation (EU) 2021/92, to make use of area flexibilities "in a way which ensures that the overall level of Union catches in 2021 does not exceed the Union share of the maximum provisional TAC level which the Union may set under the [TCA]".[65] The Specialised Committee on Fisheries was charged with discussion of a number of issues, including prohibited species, management of discards, and multi-year strategies on non-quota stocks.[66] Moving forward, the parties agreed that in line with TCA Article 498(2), they should exchange their views early on priorities for 2022 as soon as ICES advice on the level of TACs for the Annex 35 species is available.[67] Negotiations will convene for 2022 on 10 December 2021.[68]

61 TCA (n 56), Art. 499(2).
62 Council Regulation (EU) 2021/703 (n 29).
63 Written record of fisheries consultations between the United Kingdom and the European Union for 2021, <https://ec.europa.eu/oceans-and-fisheries/news/sustainable-fisheries-commission-signs-first-ever-annual-agreement-fishing-united-kingdom-2021_en> accessed 1 July 2021.
64 The National Federation of Fishermen's Organisations, 'UK-EU Fisheries Agreement for 2021', <www.nffo.org.uk/> accessed 22 April 2021.
65 Council Regulation (EU) 2021/703 (n 29), Art. 2, amending Regulation (EU) 2021/92, Article 7.
66 Written record (n 63) at 11.
67 Ibid.
68 Ibid.

Conclusions

The unpredictability of the fisheries management regime in the North-East Atlantic presents a significant challenge in a post-Brexit world. The UK has found itself having to negotiate fishing arrangements in trilateral and bilateral format, and as we have seen, there has been mixed success. The UK–EU–Norway fishing arrangement, while a success, came too late for some species. The failure of the UK and Norway to reach a timely fishing arrangement in 2021 has caused economic harm to the fishing industry, particularly in Scotland, Hull and Grimsby. Thus, it is important to remember that political failures have huge knock-on effects to livelihoods. While the EU–UK finally reached an arrangement by mid-2021, with TACs set that by and large will only apply to most stocks until the end of 2021, there is hope that in this peculiar year, negotiations from 2022 onwards may be smoother sailing.

5 The Fisheries Act 2020 and Devolution

Mitchell Lennan, Jonatan Echebarria Fernández and Tafsir Matin Johansson

Introduction

In leaving the European Union (EU), the UK is now free to regulate its fisheries outside of the constraints of the common fisheries policy (CFP), provided there is still cooperation in shared fish stocks in line with international law.[1] One concern with the UK's departure from the EU was the fact that the majority of the structure and content of fisheries legislation in the UK came from the CFP. Through the European Union (Withdrawal) Act 2018,[2] the UK repealed the European Communities Act 1972,[3] and transposed the provisions of the CFP into its domestic legislation to provide legal continuity until the Withdrawal Agreement and the Trade and Cooperation Agreement (TCA) were reached.[4] The objective of the UK Government in a post-Brexit world is to "reclaim full control" of its waters.[5] With that aim in mind, Parliament approved the Fisheries Act, which received Royal Assent becoming an Act of the Parliament on 23 November 2020. This chapter will first be introducing the Fisheries Act 2020 – a key piece of UK fisheries legislation to replace the EU's CFP; then outline *devolution* of regulatory authority from the central government (UK or state) level to the Scottish, Welsh and Northern Irish legislatures as nations within the UK; and then outline and evaluate the competency of those devolved fishery policies across the nations in the UK. Also considered will be whether this, in combination with the diversity of the fishing industry (Chapter 1) and maritime space (Table 5.1), might cause issues with the sustainable management and conservation of UK fisheries.

The Fisheries Act 2020

The Fisheries Bill 2020 was approved by the UK Parliament and received Royal Assent becoming an Act of UK Parliament on 23 November

1 See Chapters 2, 3, 6, and 7.
2 European Union (Withdrawal) Act 2018, in force 31 January 2020; see also European Union (Withdrawal Agreement) Act 2020.
3 European Communities Act 1972 (repealed), <https://www.legislation.gov.uk/ukpga/1972/68/contents> accessed 21 April 2021.
4 European Union (Withdrawal) Act 2018 (n 2); see Chapters 2 and 3.
5 See Chapter 2.

DOI: 10.4324/9781003252481-5

Table 5.1 National breakdown of UK maritime zones by area in km^2.

Maritime area	*Area (km^2)*	*Approx. % of total UK EEZ*
Scottish Zone	462,315	63%
English Zone	230,190	32%
Welsh Zone	30,778	4%
Northern Irish Zone	6,819	1%
UK Exclusive Economic Zone (Total)	**730,102**	**100%**

Source: Data from the UK Hydrographic Office.[6] This table should be read in reference with Figure 5.1. See Chapter 1 for a breakdown of fisheries industries across the nations in the UK.

2020.[8] Schedule 11 of the Act "contains minor and consequential amendments of retained direct EU legislation"[9] through Article 3(1) of the European Union (Withdrawal) Act 2018 by which directly applicable EU Regulations adopted under the CFP became part of the UK internal legal regime as "retained EU law" with amendments in order to operate and function effectively in a post-Brexit UK.[10] The Fisheries Act established the legislative framework to enable the UK to exercise fisheries management powers as an "independent coastal State".[11]

Fisheries Objectives, Statements and Management Plans

Sections 1–11 contain provisions on fisheries objectives, fisheries statement and fisheries management plans. The fisheries objectives are the: (a) sustainability objective; (b) precautionary objective (exploitation of marine stocks restores and maintains populations of harvest species above biomass levels capable of producing maximum sustainable yield "MSY"); (c) ecosystem objective; (d) scientific evidence objective; (e) bycatch objective; (f) equal access objective; (g) national benefit objective; (h) climate change objective. These objectives are

6 Admiralty Maritime Data Solutions, https://datahub.admiralty.co.uk/portal/apps/sites/#/marine-data-portal/pages/hmnao accessed 22 April 2021.

7 Original figure, metadata and licence details can be viewed here: <https://datahub.admiralty.co.uk/portal/home/item.html?id=05bd4394d25d4b0fb4a1ab0b552ec620> accessed 22 April 2021.

8 Fisheries Act 2020, <https://www.legislation.gov.uk/ukpga/2020/22/contents/enacted> accessed 22 April 2021

9 Ibid., s. 49; Sch 11.

10 These changes include the removal of references to the European Commission and other EU institutions and their replacement with references to the relevant UK regulatory authority and the replacement of the references to EU vessels for British fishing boats, where appropriate, as well as the revocation of provisions which are no longer relevant outside the context of EU membership.

11 E Ares, *Fisheries Act 2020*, House of Commons Library Briefing Paper No. 8994 (2020), <https://researchbriefings.files.parliament.uk/documents/CBP-8994/CBP-8994.pdf> accessed 2 July 2021.

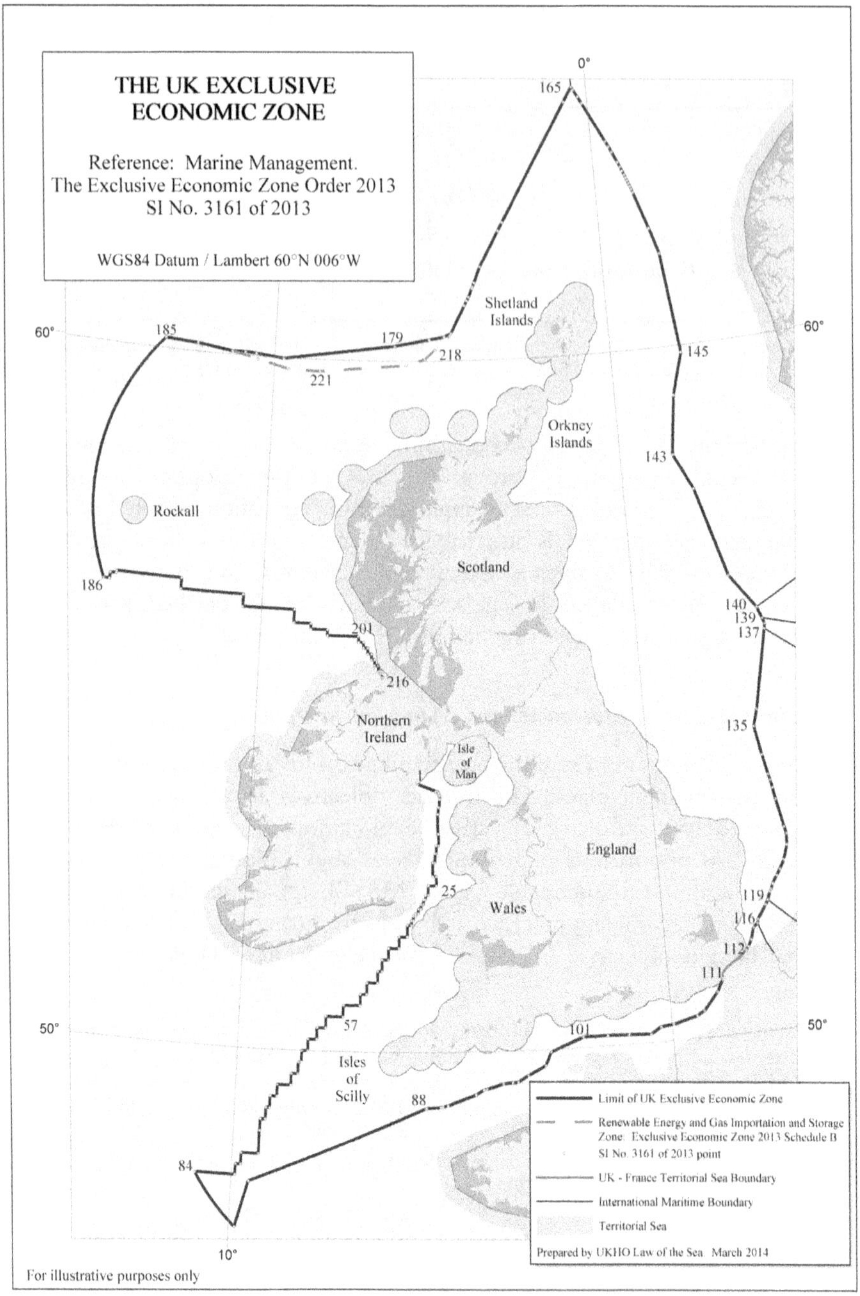

Figure 5.1 The Exclusive Economic Zone of the United Kingdom.
Source: Contains public sector information, licensed under the Open Government Licence v3.0, from The United Kingdom Hydrographic Office.[7]

defined in section 1,[12] and replace the objectives of the CFP found in Article 2 of the Basic Regulation.[13]

Section 2 obliges the fisheries policy authorities (Marine Management Organisation (MMO), Scottish Ministers, Welsh Ministers and the Northern Ireland Department) to prepare and publish a joint fisheries statement (JFS) containing key information including the policies and proposals in use of fisheries management plans for achieving (or contributing to the achievement of) the fisheries objectives outlined above.[14] In terms of content, the JFS must have a statement that explains the fisheries policy authorities' interpretation and applied proportionately in formulating these policies and proposals. Further, these policies set out in the JFS should include "the policies of the fisheries policy authorities relating to the distribution, in accordance with section 25, of catch quotas and effort quotas for use by fishing boats".[15] The JFS should also contain a list of fisheries management plans already in force, plans that authorities plan to prepare and publish, and set out the authorities' reasons "for deciding which stocks of sea fish, types of fishing and geographical areas should be subject to fisheries management plans and which should not".[16] The fisheries policy authorities are to comply with the JFS provisions of the Act by 23 November 2022.[17] Section 3 outlines that the fisheries policy authorities may prepare and publish a replacement or amendment JFS, and review a JFS whenever they consider it appropriate to do so, or within six years of publication.[18] Fisheries policy authorities may also prepare and publish a JFS that omits relevant Secretary of State policy, in which case the Secretary of State must prepare and publish a Secretary of State fisheries statement (SSFS), which sets out any policies omitted from the JFS.[19] Sections 6–11 cover reporting and regulating procedures of SSFS, and provisions and procedures for the preparation and publication of fisheries management plans.[20]

Access, Licences and Offences

Section 12 concerns access to British fisheries by foreign fishing vessels and relates to the removal of Article 5 of Annex 1 to the Basic Regulation of the CFP concerning the right to equal access by vessels from EU Members States. A foreign fishing vessel is prohibited from entering British fishery areas unless it

12 Fisheries Act 2020 (n 8), s. 1.
13 Regulation (EU) 1380/2013 of the European Parliament and of the Council, 11/12/2013, <https://eur-lex.europa.eu/legal-content/EN/TXT/PDF/?uri=CELEX:32013R1380&from=SV> accessed 23 April 2021, Art. 2.
14 Fisheries Act 2020 (n 8), s. 2(1).
15 Ibid., s. 2(2).
16 Ibid., s. 2(3)(d).
17 Ibid., s. 2(4)
18 Ibid., s. 3.
19 Ibid., s. 4.
20 Ibid., s. 6–11.

has a sea fishing licence or "for a purpose recognised by international law or by any international agreement or arrangement to which the United Kingdom is a party." It also must return outside the British fishery zone once this purpose is fulfilled.[21] Failure to comply with this provision constitutes an offence under sections 19–21 of the Fisheries Act and section 12 of the Sea Fisheries Act 1968, and section 13 of that Act by damage caused by offences occurring in Scotland or the Scottish Zone.[22] Schedule 2 of the Fisheries Act contains the amendments of legislation relating to regulation of foreign fishing vessels.[23] Schedule 2 also contains the secondary English and Welsh, Scottish, and Northern Irish legislation applicable to UK vessels and EU vessels in British waters.[24]

Licensing of Fishing Vessels

Sections 14–18 and Schedule 3 outline fishing licensing for British and foreign vessels within the British fisheries zone. Importantly for this chapter, they establish that the Secretary of State cannot amend, remove or vary exceptions to the provision that "fishing anywhere by a British fishing vessel is prohibited unless authorised by a licence"[25] without the consent of the Scottish or Welsh Ministers or the Northern Ireland department.[26] In addition, it is delineated that the power to grant fishing licences to British fishing vessels is by the Scottish Ministers in respect to Scottish fishing vessels, by the Welsh Ministers in respect to Welsh fishing vessels, and by the Northern Ireland Department in respect to Northern Irish fishing vessels. The MMO is responsible for granting licences to any other British fishing vessels.[27] The same power is granted for licences in respect of foreign fishing vessel,[28] i.e., the Scottish Ministers may grant a licence to a foreign vessel provided it does not authorise fishing outside Scotland and the Scottish Zone (Table 5.1). However, how this works in practice is that the United Kingdom Single Issuing Authority (UKSIA), a body of the MMO, acts on behalf of the UK sea fish licensing authorities of England, Scotland, Wales and Northern Ireland and is responsible for granting access of non-UK fishing vessels to UK waters to fish within the UK EEZ.[29] EU

21 Ibid., s. 12.
22 Ibid., s. 12 (3–4); Sea Fisheries Act 1968, <www.legislation.gov.uk/ukpga/1968/77> accessed 23 April 2021, ss. 12 and 13.
23 Fisheries Act 2020 (n 8), s. 2.
24 Ibid., s. 2.
25 Ibid., s. 14(1); Sch 3.
26 Ibid., s. 14(4).
27 Ibid., s. 15.
28 Ibid., s. 17.
29 See <www.gov.uk/guidance/united-kingdom-single-issuing-authority-uksia#foreign-vessels> accessed 23 April 2021; note that the responsibility for the administration and management of UK vessel licensing with the UK EEZ rests with the UK fisheries authorities (Marine Scotland, Department of Agriculture and Rural Affairs in Northern Ireland, the Welsh Government and the MMO).

Member States submit vessel applications to the European Commission who then submit them to UKSIA on their behalf.[30] These authorities also have powers to attach conditions to fishing licences or to suspend, vary or revoke licences.[31] Sections 19–22 and Schedule 4 indicate offences and penalties for breach of the licensing and access provisions.[32]

Fishing Opportunities

Fishing opportunities under the Fisheries Act 2020 is covered by sections 23–27, and Schedule 5. This confers powers on the to the Secretary of State to determine: i) the maximum quantity of sea fish that can be caught by British fishing vessels (i.e., the catch quota);[33] and ii) the maximum number of days at sea British fishing vessels can spend (i.e., the effort quota).[34] Importantly, the Secretary of State is obliged to consult the Scottish and Welsh Ministers, the Northern Ireland Department and the MMO prior to making a decision on catch or effort quotas, and publish as soon as reasonably possible their determination, and send a copy to the Scottish and Welsh Ministers and the Northern Ireland Department.[35] In terms of distribution of fishing opportunities, the responsibility relies on the national fishing authorities (Secretary of State, MMO, Scottish and Welsh Ministers and Northern Ireland Department). The national fisheries authorities are, in distributing catch and effort quotas, obliged to use criteria that are transparent and objective, and include criteria relating to the environment, social and economic factors (so-called "sustainable development"). Interestingly, the criteria considered by the national fishing authorities can be related to: "(a) the impact of fishing on the environment; (b) the history of compliance with regulatory requirements relating to fishing; (c) the contribution of fishing to the local economy; (d) historic catch levels" and the use of selective fishing gear that avoids bycatch (catching of non-target species).[36] National fisheries authorities are also obliged to ensure as far as possible that catch and effort quotas are not exceeded.[37] The Secretary of State is empowered to sell English fishing opportunities, as are the Welsh Ministers with regard to Welsh fishing opportunities.[38]

Charging Scheme and Financial Assistance

Sections 28–32 grant the Secretary of State powers to establish a charging scheme "under which chargeable persons are required to pay a charge in

30 See <www.gov.uk/guidance/united-kingdom-single-issuing-authority-uksia#foreign-vessels> accessed 23 April 2021.
31 Fisheries Act 2020 (n 8), s. 17.
32 Ibid., ss. 19–22; Sch 4.
33 Ibid., s. 23.
34 Ibid., s. 23.
35 Ibid., s. 24.
36 Ibid., s. 25.
37 Ibid., s. 26.
38 Ibid., s. 27.

respect of unauthorised catches of sea fish".[39] How a charge is calculated and when charge payments are due are included here.[40]

Section 33 empowers the Secretary of State to provide or arrange for financial assistance for any person for a list of identified purposes, including: "(a) the conservation, enhancement or restoration of the marine and aquatic environment; (b) the promotion the promotion or development of commercial fish or aquaculture activities; (c) the reorganisation of businesses involved in commercial fish or aquaculture activities; (d) contributing to the expenses of persons involved in commercial fish or aquaculture activities; (e) maintaining or improving the health and safety of individuals who are involved in commercial fish or aquaculture activities; (f) the training of individuals who are, were or intend to become involved in commercial fish or aquaculture activities, or are family members of such individuals; (g) the economic development or social improvement of areas in which commercial fish or aquaculture activities are carried out; (h) improving the arrangements for the use of catch quotas or effort quotas; (i) the promotion or development of recreational fishing". With regard to the other nations in the UK, Schedule 6 of the Act confers powers to the Scottish and Welsh Ministers and the Northern Ireland Department the above powers.[41] Section 34 confers the power to the MMO to impose charges on fishing quotas; ensure that commercial fish activities are carried out lawfully; the registration of buyers and sellers of fish-sale fish; and catch certificates for the import of fish.[42] Schedule 7 confers the same power on the other national fishing authorities.[43]

Power to Make Further Provisions

By way of sections 36–42, the Secretary of State (and Schedule 8 to the national fishing authorities)[44] are conferred the power to make provisions for the purpose of implementing international obligations relating to fisheries, fishing or aquaculture (i.e., regulating to implement outcomes of fishing arrangements outlined in Chapter 4, or environmental obligations outlined in Chapter 7), as well as for conservation or fishing industry purposes,[45] or provisions about aquatic animal diseases.[46] Importantly, regulations made by the Secretary of State under these sections must be made in consultation with the national fishing authorities,[47] and may not include provisions that would be within the legislative competence of the Scottish Parliament if it were included

39 Ibid., s. 28.
40 Ibid., s. 29–32.
41 Ibid., s. 26.
42 Ibid., s. 34.
43 Ibid., Sch 7.
44 Ibid., s. 42, Sch 8.
45 Ibid., s. 36.
46 Ibid., s. 38.
47 Ibid., s. 41.

in an Act of Parliament and identical provisions for the Senedd Cymru (Welsh Parliament) or the Northern Ireland Assembly,[48] unless those legislatures consent to this.[49] However, this provision does not apply should the regulation by the Secretary of State concerning vessels fishing outside their respective national zone, for example, Welsh fishing boats outside the Welsh Zone.[50] Sections 44–55 and Schedules 9–11 are miscellaneous and final provisions concerning, for example, the legislative competence of Senedd Cymru,[51] the conservation of seals,[52] regulations,[53] and interpretation.[54]

Amendments of Retained EU Legislation

As a consequence of the entering into force of the Fisheries Act, the retained EU law gets adapted to the new regime by Schedule 11: 1) Article 5 of and Annex 1 to the Basic Regulation on right of equal access are revoked to give entry to the aforementioned system of licences;[55] 2) Articles 9 and 10 of the Basic Regulation on multiannual plans are revoked, as the UK will start developing its own Fisheries Management Plans (see above), notwithstanding the regulation of jointly managed stocks introduced by the TCA; 3) the landing obligation by which all catches of regulated commercial species onboard are to be landed and counted against quota continues to apply in the UK under retained EU law.[56] Not all discard exemptions that applied under the common EU regime will apply automatically to UK waters;[57] 4) Article 16 of the Basic Regulation on the distribution of fishing opportunities will be revoked and replaced by the TAC determinations approved by the Parliament; 5) Article 17 of the Basic Regulation on the allocation of fishing opportunities by Member States is revoked and replaced by section 25 of the Fisheries Act (see above); 6) Regulation (EU) 2017/2403 on the sustainable management of external fishing fleets is revoked and replaced by a licensing system; and 6) Article 14 (2) to (5) of Council Regulation (EU) 2020/123 determining the 2020 TACs for certain fish stocks and groups of fish stocks, applicable in Union waters and, for Union fishing vessels, in certain non-Union waters has been revoked.

48 Ibid., s. 39(3).
49 Ibid., s. 40.
50 Ibid., s. 39(4)
51 Ibid., ss. 45–47.
52 Ibid., s. 47; Sch 9
53 Ibid., s. 51.
54 Ibid., s. 52.
55 See Chapter 2.
56 'Discarding and the Landing Obligation – Fisheries – European Commission' (*Fisheries – European Commission*, 2021), <https://ec.europa.eu/fisheries/cfp/fishing_rules/discards_en> accessed 16 February 2021.
57 For example, most of the discard exemptions in the North Sea and North Western Waters are kept as retained EU law.

Further critique (both from academic and industry perspectives) of the Fisheries Act can be found in Chapter 9. The next section outlines devolution in the United Kingdom and how this relates to the Fisheries Act.

Devolution in the UK

As outlined above, there are four legislative bodies across the UK. In addition to the UK Parliament in Westminster, London – the main legislature of the UK – there are three other legislatures in the other nations that presently make up the UK. These are the Scottish Parliament, the Welsh Parliament and the Northern Ireland Assembly. These national legislatures exist as a result of a process called "devolution". This means these legislatures can make decisions on certain issues, known as "devolved competences" (or transferred powers in Northern Ireland) without the express permission of the UK Parliament or Government. This means there are four governments in the UK, which allows decisions on devolved matters to be made at a more local level and was introduced in its current form by the UK Government in 1998. The UK parliament still retains legislative competence on several issues; these are known as "reserved" matters.[58] The Scottish and Welsh devolutions specify which matters are reserved to the UK Parliament; in other words, everything else not reserved is devolved.

As indicated from the above section on the Fisheries Act, fisheries policy is a devolved competence in the Scottish, Welsh and Northern Irish legislatures. This means each legislature has the option to decide fisheries policies and how they should be enforced. This is why the eight fisheries objectives are not "nailed down" in the Fisheries Act, and it is down to the devolved legislatures to implement these objectives.

It is apparent from previous chapters in this collection that the UK fishing industry is diverse, and catch, crews and effort are unevenly distributed across the four nations; each faces different social, economic and legal challenges and opportunities due to Brexit in the context of fisheries.[59] The rest of this chapter is dedicated to outlining each nation's issues, to get a more nuanced picture of the legal challenges faced by fishing communities across the UK.

Scotland

Legislative competence in several devolved matters has been devolved to the Scottish Parliament since 1998. This includes the "regulation of sea fishing" within the Scottish Zone (Table 5.1), and to Scottish vessels registered at a Scottish port fishing outside of the Scottish Zone.[60] Scottish Parliament and

58 See UK Civil Service, *What is devolved?* <https://assets.publishing.service.gov.uk/government/uploads/system/uploads/attachment_data/file/769117/Devolution-Postcard.pdf> accessed 23 April 2021.

59 See Chapter 1.

60 Scotland Act 1998, <www.legislation.gov.uk/ukpga/1998/46/contents> accessed 24 April 2021, Sch 5, S C6; a Scottish fishing vessel is defined as "a fishing vessel

Scottish Ministers hold the competence to regulate on this.[61] This competence has been limited somewhat due to the CFP. Prior to the implementation of the Fisheries Act, this left "no proper legal framework on which to construct a system for the sustainable management of Scottish fisheries after Brexit".[62] However, the administration and enforcement of EU fisheries law in the Scottish Zone was the responsibility of Marine Scotland, a directorate of the Scottish Government. Significantly, fisheries policy is very important in Scottish politics, arguably more so than the rest of the UK, and Brexit and fisheries was a key issue for the Scottish electorate at the time of the Brexit referendum.[63] The fishing industry in Scotland is unique to the UK, vocal politically, and is made up of small vessels operating in communities in relatively remote islands fishing for shellfish, as well as larger long-distance fishing vessels. Taking this into account, it was argued the Scottish component, especially in the north east where the larger fishing vessels catch higher-value pelagic species, is likely to benefit the most from extra share of quota.[64]

As outlined in Chapter 1, most of the UK's fishing activity is undertaken in Scotland, and Table 5.1 indicates Scotland possesses the largest maritime space within the UK. It is also important to note the geographic significance of Scotland. For example, it is estimated that Scotland's seas cover an area of 462,315 km^2 (Table 5.1) by definition of the "Scottish Zone" in the 1998 Scotland Act. This means the Scottish Zone comprises 63% of the UK EEZ (Table 5.1).[65]

The UK Government has claimed that the Fisheries Act equips the devolved administrations with greater powers to regulate sea fishing, arguing that the administrations can take a more localised approach, rather than the previous "inflexible" CFP. *Contra*, Scottish Fisheries Secretary Fergus Ewing argued at the time the Fisheries Act was passed that "nothing in this legislation can compensate for the loss of our biggest seafood market in the EU and the wider damage that it will cause to our coastal communities."[66] The Scottish Government does, however, argue that the Act provides a necessary framework to manage fisheries from 1 January 2021, although the trade barriers faced by the Scottish and UK fishing industries are still present. The Scottish Government

which is registered in the register maintained under section 8 of the Merchant Shipping act 1995 and whose entry in the register specifies a port in Scotland as the port to which the vessel is to be treated as belonging".

61 Scotland Act 1998 ibid., ss. 29, 56 and 126(1) and Sch 5, para. C6.

62 R Churchill, 'They're Scotland's Fish! Implications of Brexit for Scots Fisheries Law' *The Edinburgh Law Review* 22 (2018) 110–114, at 111.

63 See Chapter 9; UK in a Changing Europe, 'Fisheries and Brexit' (2020) <https://ukandeu.ac.uk/research-papers/fisheries-and-brexit-3/> accessed 29 April 2021, at 24.

64 UK in a Changing Europe ibid., at 6.

65 See Marine Scotland, <https://marine.gov.scot/data/facts-and-figures-about-scotlands-sea-area-coastline-length-sea-area-sq-kms> accessed 25 April 2021; Chapter 1.

66 See Marine Scotland, UK Fisheries Act, <https://blogs.gov.scot/marine-scotland/2020/11/24/uk-fisheries-act/> accessed 26 April 2021.

has published their "Fisheries Plan 2020–2030", in which it indicates that its JFS will set out the policies of achieving the objectives of the Fisheries Act.[67] It will publish its first JFS at the end of 2021. At the time of writing, it is too early to say the extent to which there will be internal divergences; however, the Scottish Government has indicated it will work together with the other UK fisheries administrations for regulating fisheries in a post-Brexit Scotland.

Wales

The Senedd Cymru has the legislative competence to pass legislation related to fisheries and fishing,[68] with some limitations,[69] in the Welsh Zone (Table 5.1). Prior to devolution of power, much of the fisheries legislation applicable to Wales and the Welsh Zone was made by the Secretary of State, and some of it is still in force, though power was transferred from the Secretary of State to the Senedd Cymru in 1999.[70] The Marine and Coastal Access Act 2009 introduced the "Welsh Zone" (Table 5.1, Figure 5.1) by amendment of the Government of Wales Act 2006.[71] The Boundaries of the Welsh Zone are delineated by the Welsh Zone (Boundaries and Transfer of Functions) Order 2010.[72] Prior to Brexit, the Welsh Ministers were responsible for making subordinate legislation to implement obligations under the CFP in Wales and the Welsh Zone.[73] The Fisheries Act amended the Government of Wales Act 2006 and grants the Welsh authority to administer fisheries in the Welsh Zone.[74] The power to allocate fishing opportunities in Wales and the Welsh Zone has never been used for implementation of reforms for Wales. Post-Brexit, there have been several options outlined extensively by Carpenter.[75] As in Scotland, the fishing

67 Scotland's Fishery Management Strategy (2020–2030), <www.gov.scot/binaries/content/documents/govscot/publications/strategy-plan/2020/12/scotlands-future-fisheries-management-strategy-2020-2030/documents/scotlands-fisheries-management-strategy-2020-2030/scotlands-fisheries-management-strategy-2020-2030/govscot%3Adocument/scotlands-fisheries-management-strategy-2020-2030.pdf> accessed 26 April 2021.

68 Government of Wales Act (2006), <www.legislation.gov.uk/ukpga/2006/32/contents> accessed 26 April 2021, s. 108 and Sch 7(1).

69 Government of Wales Act ibid., Sch 7a.

70 Government of Wales Act 1998; National Assembly for Wales (Transfer of Functions) Order 1999.

71 Marine and Coastal Access Act (2009), <www.legislation.gov.uk/ukpga/2009/23/contents> accessed 27 April 2021, s. 43.

72 Welsh Zone (Boundaries and Transfer of Functions) Order 2010, <www.legislation.gov.uk/uksi/2010/760/contents/made> accessed 27 April 2021.

73 The European Communities Act 1972 (n 3), s. 2(2).

74 Fisheries Act 2020 (n 8), s 45 and 46.

75 See Wales Centre for Public Policy, <www.wcpp.org.uk/wp-content/uploads/2020/09/Policy-options-for-Welsh-fisheries.pdf> and <www.wcpp.org.uk/publication/implications-of-brexit-for-fishing-opportunities-in-wales/> accessed 27 April 2021.

industry in Wales has had non-tariff-related barriers to trade.[76] The Welsh Governments did make several attempts to prepare their fishing industry prior to Brexit,[77] and have announced £1.3m in aid for the Welsh seafood sector to help address Brexit and Covid-19 impacts.[78] At present, the Welsh Government has yet to publish their JFS, so like Scotland and the rest of the UK, the future of the fishing industry in a post-Brexit world remains uncertain.

Northern Ireland

The Northern Ireland Assembly was established by the Northern Ireland Act in 1998;[79] this is the legislature for Northern Ireland, which holds a dual leadership structure between two political parties at opposite ends of the political spectrum. The administrative branch of the Assembly is the Northern Ireland Executive, which is the Devolved Government of Northern Ireland. Similar to Scotland and Wales, the Executive holds competence to regulate fisheries within the Northern Irish Zone (Table 5.1). However, in 2017 the Assembly collapsed when neither party could reconcile issues on social and cultural policies. Northern Ireland remained without a functioning government until 2020. It has been argued that this has led to Northern Ireland's voice remaining unheard in the Brexit discussion, with the situation being "further complicated by the question of the border, or in the case of fisheries the lack of an agreed maritime border between Ireland and Northern Ireland".[80] The Northern Ireland Executive has yet to publish a JFS.

The fishing industry is significant in Northern Ireland relative to its size, with its fleet capacity being 25% of the English equivalent. However, the fishing industry remains unhappy with quota allocations after the promise of a "Brexit dividend",[81] as well as limitations on the number of ports Northern Irish fishing vessels can land their catch on in the Republic of Ireland.[82] Importantly,

76 See, S Dickins, 'Brexit: "My £50,000 shellfish lorry was delayed for 30 hours"', <www.bbc.co.uk/news/uk-wales-politics-55631622> accessed 27 April 2021.

77 Government of Wales, <https://gov.wales/sites/default/files/pdf-versions/2021/1/3/1610564453/preparing-wales-fishing-sector-for-brexit.pdf> accessed 29 April 2021.

78 Government of Wales Policy and Strategy, 'Preparing Wales Fishing Sector for Brexit', <https://gov.wales/sites/default/files/pdf-versions/2021/1/3/1610564453/preparing-wales-fishing-sector-for-brexit.pdf> accessed 28 April 2021.

79 The Northern Ireland Act 1998, <www.legislation.gov.uk/ukpga/1998/47/contents> accessed 29 April 2021.

80 UK in a Changing Europe (n 63) at 24.

81 See BBC, 'Brexit: NI Fishermen "short-changed" in fish quota', <www.bbc.co.uk/news/uk-northern-ireland-56518841> accessed 29 April 2021; see also The Fishing Daily, 'As feared, Westminster has plundered the Northern Ireland Fishing Industry's Brexit Dividend', <https://thefishingdaily.com/featured-news/as-feared-westminster-has-plundered-the-northern-ireland-fishing-industrys-brexit-dividend/> accessed 29 April 2021.

82 BBC, 'Brexit: New NI Fishing Boat Rules "Create Hard Border"', <www.bbc.co.uk/news/uk-northern-ireland-55566214> accessed 29 April 2021.

the fishing industry (catch and processing) relies on migrant labour, which has been significantly affected by Brexit. In addition to the rest of the UK, the Northern Irish fishing industry relies on EU market access. While this has been disrupted elsewhere in the UK, the Northern Ireland Protocol – a key component of the Withdrawal Agreement – ensures fisheries products can enter the EU market without duties or tariffs[83] by maintaining the relevant EU law in Northern Ireland.[84]

Conclusions

This chapter has sought to introduce the UK Fisheries Act 2020 as the key piece of UK fisheries legislation after Brexit. It outlined how fisheries legislation is administrated across the three devolved administrations in the UK: Scotland, Wales and Northern Ireland. Until JFS are made, it is difficult to infer what the future of UK fisheries management holds across the four nations. The key takeaway here is that, arguably, the Fisheries Act facilitates and empowers the devolved administrations with more regulatory authority over their fisheries, with more control, adaptive capacity and flexibility than the CFP. However, the other barriers presented by the UK's departure from the EU, outlined in Chapters 1, 2, 3, and 4, are yet to be worked out and could present further problems in the future. It may be great for the UK fishing industry to catch more fish under control of the UK Governments, *but not if it is difficult or impossible to export.* JFS will, eventually, inform the framework of the Fisheries Act for the sustainable exploitation of fish stocks in UK waters. Prior to this, the UK administrations will publish individual fisheries management plans to be used by industry until the JFS and the SSFS are published.

83 Protocol on Ireland/Northern Ireland, <https://assets.publishing.service.gov.uk/government/uploads/system/uploads/attachment_data/file/840230/Revised_Protocol_to_the_Withdrawal_Agreement.pdf> accessed 19 April 2021, Art. 11.

84 Ibid. para. 46.

6 Fisheries Enforcement in a Post-Brexit World

Mercedes Rosello, Mitchell Lennan, Jonatan Echebarria Fernández and Tafsir Matin Johansson

Introduction

Brexit was heralded as a step towards a status that would allow the United Kingdom (UK) to exist as an "independent coastal state" with "full control" over its fisheries.[1] However, fisheries management often requires substantial international cooperation to be effective in achieving the peaceful and sustainable utilisation of ocean resources.[2] Although advanced forms of international decision-making might be interpreted as a "loss" or "weakening" of sovereignty, the complex realities of marine fisheries management make participation in international law and policy frameworks an unavoidable commitment for any responsible State with an interest in the long-term conservation of fish stocks. As a coastal State, the UK is the custodian of a significant and diverse wealth of marine living resources (MLRs). Managing them sustainably requires participation in shared international frameworks with important implications for enforcement.

As outlined in earlier chapters,[3] prior to Brexit, UK fisheries management was to a great extent carried out through the EU Common Fisheries Policy (CFP). The principle of non-discrimination on grounds of nationality, a fundamental principle of European Union (EU) law, underpins the CFP. As a consequence, EU fisheries are managed on the basis of equal access, save for certain derogations that generally apply to the coastal waters of EU Member States.[4] The legal bases of the CFP are reviewed and updated periodically, and at the time of writing Regulation (EU) No 1380/2013 of the European parliament and the Council on the Common Fisheries Policy is the legal instrument that configures its latest iteration.[5] This regulation modifies and develops

1 *Sustainable Fisheries for Future Generations in July 2018*, Cm. 9660 (2018), <https://assets.publishing.service.gov.uk/government/uploads/system/uploads/attachment_data/file/722074/fisheries-wp-consult-document.pdf> accessed 1 July 2021.
2 See Chapter 4.
3 See Chapters 1, 2 and 3.
4 EU Regulation 1380/2013 permits coastal States to apply restrictions within the 12 nm area, and in some cases beyond it, until 2022.
5 Regulation (EU) 1380/2013 OJ 2013 L354/22.

DOI: 10.4324/9781003252481-6

other EU legal instruments that are important in the context of control and enforcement, such as Regulation (EC) 1224/2009 (the Control Regulation),[6] and Regulation (EC) 1005/2008 (the Illegal, Unreported and Unregulated Fishing [IUU] Fishing Regulation).[7] These regulations are currently under review, but at the time of writing they are in force and directly applicable to EU member States (MS).[8]

These and other instruments integrate a complex legislation framework that directs and conditions MS action in a broad range of activities that are directly relevant to fisheries control and enforcement. In particular, areas such as access to fishery resources, the regulation of fishing effort, technical measures concerning vessel characteristics and gears, the monitoring and verification of fishing activities and documentation of captures are shaped by the CFP. Even though EU MS are responsible for establishing and applying their own sanctioning mechanisms, infractions and sanctions are also influenced by the CFP across the EU, particularly since the introduction of a points sanction system.[9] On the other hand, MS inspections, and control and enforcement efforts, are to a significant extent pooled with and coordinated by EU institutions, such as the European Fisheries Control Agency (EFCA).[10]

Although certain aspects of the UK control and enforcement system have always diverged from EU parameters due to differences in implementation, and in particular in respect of inshore fisheries catch monitoring,[11] much of its control and enforcement framework still largely reflects EU fisheries legislation, much of which has been retained domestically.[12] Beyond this is the case that

6 Council Regulation (EC) No 1224/2009 of 20 November 2009 establishing a Community control system for ensuring compliance with the rules of the common fisheries policy, amending Regulations (EC) No 847/96, (EC) No 2371/2002, (EC) No 811/2004, (EC) No 768/2005, (EC) No 2115/2005, (EC) No 2166/2005, (EC) No 388/2006, (EC) No 509/2007, (EC) No 676/2007, (EC) No 1098/2007, (EC) No 1300/2008, (EC) No 1342/2008 and repealing Regulations (EEC) No 2847/93, (EC) No 1627/94 and (EC) No 1966/2006 OJ L 286 29.10.2008.

7 Council Regulation (EC) No 1005/2008 of 29 September 2008 establishing a Community system to prevent, deter and eliminate illegal, unreported and unregulated fishing, amending Regulations (EEC) No 2847/93, (EC) No 1936/2001 and (EC) No 601/2004 and repealing Regulations (EC) No 1093/94 and (EC) No 1447/1999.

8 For more information on the review of the EU fisheries compliance and control framework, see <https://ec.europa.eu/oceans-and-fisheries/fisheries/rules/enforcing-rules/control-regulation_en> accessed 1 July 2021.

9 See <https://ec.europa.eu/oceans-and-fisheries/fisheries/rules/enforcing-rules/infringements-and-sanctions_en> accessed 21 July 2021.

10 Regulation (EU) 2016/1624 OJ L 251/1, repealed by Regulation (EU) 1052 OJ L 295/1.

11 See <www.gov.uk/guidance/record-your-catch> accessed 22 July 2021.

12 For further information, see <www.gov.uk/government/publications/fishing-regulations-the-blue-book/section-aa-statutory-instruments-amending-retained-eu-legislation> accessed 22 July 2021.

the UK is no longer bound to EU treaties,[13] and it must now operate by reference to a different framework of international obligations. In this chapter, we explore global and regional legal frameworks applicable to the UK as a coastal State,[14] setting out the specific obligations to which it is bound via global and regional agreements to which it is a party.

The analysis commences by outlining the key provisions established by the United Nations Convention on the Law of the Sea (LOSC or Convention)[15] in respect of coastal State obligations relevant to fisheries control and enforcement. The LOSC is a global international agreement subscribed by the majority of the world's coastal and fishing States. The chapter then outlines obligations under the United Nations Fish Stocks Agreement (UNFSA),[16] and the Port State Measures Agreement (PSMA),[17] global international agreements that contain important obligations concerning fisheries enforcement, to which the UK is a party.

Our analysis also includes a brief outline of relevant international guidelines set out in the UN Food and Agriculture Organization (FAO) International Plan of Action to Prevent, Deter and Eliminate Illegal, Unreported and Unregulated Fishing (IPOA-IUU) with regard to the control of illicit activities. A focus is also placed on regional and bilateral instruments, focusing in particular on the legal obligations emanating from the Trade and Cooperation Agreement that the UK and the EU subscribed on 30 December 2020.[18] It then proceeds to discuss key aspects of domestic legislation, and briefly illustrates the application of the previously outlined legal obligations via events which recently occurred in Rockall.

13 In particular, see Articles 3 and 4 of the Treaty on the Functioning of the European Union, in respect of competence distribution, Article 13 regarding respect for animal life, and Articles 38 and 43 on agricultural and fisheries policies.

14 Not including Overseas Territories or Crown Dependencies.

15 United Nations Convention on the Law of the Sea (UNCLOS), Montego Bay, 10 December 1982, 1833 UNTS 3.

16 Agreement for the Implementation of the Provisions of the United Nations Convention on the Law of the Sea of 10 December 1982 relating to the Conservation and Management of Straddling Fish Stocks and Highly Migratory Fish Stocks, New York, 4 August 1995; 2167 UNTS 3.

17 Agreement on Port State Measures to Prevent, Deter and Eliminate Illegal, Unreported and Unregulated Fishing, Adopted 24 November 1993, in force 24 April 2016, 55 ILM 1157.

18 See also, for example, Framework Agreement on Fisheries between the United Kingdom of Great Britain and Northern Ireland and the Kingdom of Norway, London, 30 September 2020, <https://assets.publishing.service.gov.uk/government/uploads/system/uploads/attachment_data/file/927151/CS_Norway_1.2020_UK_Norway_Framework_Agreement_on_Fisheries.pdf> accessed 20 June 2021; Framework Agreement on Fisheries between the Government of the United Kingdom of Great Britain and Northern Ireland and the Government of the Faroes, Copenhagen, 29 October 2020, <https://assets.publishing.service.gov.uk/government/uploads/system/uploads/attachment_data/file/933792/CS_Faroe_Islands_1.2020_UK_Faroes_Framework_Agreement_on_Fisheries.pdf> accessed 5 July 2021.

International Legal Obligations Concerning Fisheries Enforcement

This section outlines the relevant international legal framework applicable to the UK as a coastal State in respect of fisheries enforcement. We commence with the LOSC, which sets out the legal basis for the utilisation of the ocean and its natural resources. The LOSC has been developed and is supported in its implementation by a number of other treaties that deal specifically with, *inter alia*, fisheries enforcement. In particular, the UNFSA and PSMA are significant for the UK, and the key obligations they contained are outlined in this section.

The UN Convention on the Law of the Sea

The LOSC in its Article 192 contains a general obligation to protect and preserve the marine environment. This is an obligation of conduct, one of "due diligence" applying to all maritime areas regardless of jurisdiction.[19] Although this provision is placed in Part XII, which is principally focused on pollution, it has been progressively interpreted by international courts and tribunals to include fisheries.[20] The due diligence nature of this general obligation implies the need for ongoing effort,[21] via the exercise of prescriptive and enforcement jurisdiction.[22] This requires not only the establishment of adequate legal frameworks for the protection of MLRs, but also the effective oversight and control of fishing activities in accordance with domestic legislation. The exercise of due diligence needs appropriate procedures for competent authorities, in order to ensure compliance by fishing actors with applicable legal duties, and to identify and respond to infractions via enforcement action. In Parts II and V, the LOSC outlines the framework of obligations that State parties must incorporate into their domestic law in matters concerning fishing activity control and enforcement, and diligently implement. The responsibility to ensure that fishing activities are consistent with the normative objectives of the Convention

19 *Request for an Advisory Opinion Submitted by The Sub-Regional Fisheries Commission (SRFC)*, Advisory Opinion, 2 April 2015, ITLOS Reports 2015 (*Fisheries Advisory Opinion*), para. 120; *The South China Sea Arbitration* (The Republic of The Philippines v. The People's Republic of China) Award of 12 July [2016], PCA Case No. 2013–19, ICGJ p. 49, para. 940; Chapter 7.

20 *Southern Bluefin Tuna (New Zealand v. Japan; Australia v. Japan)*, Provisional Measures Order of 27 August 1999, ITLOS Reports 1999, p. 280 para. 70; *Chagos Marine Protected Area Arbitration (Mauritius v. United Kingdom)*, Award of 18 March 2015, PCA Case No. 2011–03, paras. 320 and 583; *South China Sea Arbitration* (n 19), para. 945; see also N Bankes 'Legislative and Enforcement Jurisdiction of the Coastal State with Respect to Fisheries in the Exclusive Economic Zone' in Ø Jensen (ed.) *The Development of the Law of the Sea Convention – The Role of International Courts and Tribunals* (Edward Elgar, 2020), at pp. 73–103.

21 See *Fisheries Advisory Opinion* (n 19), para. 129; *Responsibilities and Obligations of States with respect to activities in the Area*, Advisory Opinion 1 February 2011, ITLOS Reports 2011, paras. 108–12; *South China Sea* (n 19), para. 726.

22 N Bankes (n 20).

when the activity occurs *within* the jurisdiction of a coastal State falls primarily on that State.[23] This includes obligations involving the exercise of control and enforcement in both the territorial sea and the Exclusive Economic Zone (EEZ) of that State.[24]

According to the LOSC Article 3, States have "the right to establish the breadth of its territorial sea up to a limit not exceeding 12 nautical miles, measured from baselines determined in accordance with this Convention". Article 4 specifies that the "outer limit of the territorial sea is the line every point of which is at a distance from the nearest point of the baseline equal to the breadth of the territorial sea". The EEZ is, according to Article 55 of the LOSC, "an area beyond and adjacent to the territorial sea", and Article 57 states it "shall not extend beyond 200 nautical miles from the baselines from which the breadth of the territorial sea is measured". The LOSC establishes different regimes in the territorial sea and the EEZ for enforcement purposes.

Although the coastal State must respect the right of innocent passage of vessels flagged to third States in the territorial sea as defined in Article 18 of the Convention, Article 19 specifically excludes from the concept of innocent passage activities of foreign vessels that are "prejudicial to the peace, good order or security of the coastal State". Article 19(2)(i) specifically identifies fishing activity as belonging to the category of prejudicial activities. Hence, other than for the non-discrimination requirements of Articles 24 and 25, in the territorial sea the coastal State can exercise all rights emanating from its sovereignty in matters concerning the control of fishing vessels that are operating within the 12 nautical mile limit.[25] As Article 27 makes clear, coastal States can exercise enforcement jurisdiction, whether of an administrative or criminal nature, in matters involving fishing activity that contravenes the laws established by that coastal State.

In the 200 nautical miles of the EEZ (or other appropriate delimitation in accordance with the LOSC Article 74 with regard to an opposite coast), the LOSC establishes a *sui generis* system based on sovereign rights.[26] In Article 56 (1)(a) the LOSC establishes the coastal State's "sovereign rights for the purpose of exploring and exploiting, conserving and managing" fisheries resources; in subparagraph (b) it establishes their jurisdiction for the purposes of protecting and preserving the marine environment. The exercise of these rights and associated powers must, however, be carried out with due regard to the rights of other States with regard to navigation and the peaceful utilisation of the sea, in accordance with Articles 56(2) and 58. The exercise of enforcement jurisdiction must mirror the legal obligations established to bind persons to the intended conservation and management objectives of the State and ensuring control of fishing activities. The legal bases for the establishment of a domestic legal

23 *Fisheries Advisory Opinion*, (n 19) para. 106.
24 UNCLOS (n 15), Art. 62(4); *Fisheries Advisory Opinion* (n 19), para. 104.
25 Ibid., Art. 27.
26 See N Bankes (n 20), at pp. 73–103.

framework for fisheries conservation and management in the EEZ are set out in LOSC Articles 61 and 62.

Article 61 sets the power of the coastal State to set the total allowable catch (TAC) in the EEZ, which it then conditions with a series of cooperation and conservation obligations, and the requirement to base conservation and management measures on a scientific basis. Under Article 62, any surplus in the TAC is to be made available to other States, albeit without undermining the necessary conservation measures established for the protection of the stocks. This provision is specific to the EEZ, and is not replicated in the context of the territorial sea. The LOSC Article 62(3) establishes the parameters whereby the coastal State should grant access to foreign fishers. Amongst the set criteria, this provision specifically identifies factors for the coastal State to consider, including "the significance of the living resources of the area to the economy of the coastal State concerned" and "the need to minimize economic dislocation in States whose nationals have habitually fished in the zone or which have made substantial efforts in research and identification of stocks". Article 62(4) sets out a non-exhaustive list of measures that the coastal State must take in respect of the management of the resources of the EEZ, which foreign fishermen must comply with. This list includes tools that are essential to the oversight of fishing activity by coastal State authorities, such as licensing, activity and catch reporting, monitoring, landing and enforcement procedures.

The enforcement jurisdiction of the coastal State implies that, where there have been breaches of domestic law, the competent authorities of the coastal State may perform inspections at sea and in port, carry out arrests, and undertake judicial proceedings in accordance with the applicable provisions of their domestic legal framework.[27] Nevertheless, the coastal State must abide by the restrictions established by the Convention in respect of prompt release, prohibition of prison sentences for breaches of fisheries law (except where there is agreement with the flag State) and the prompt notification to the flag State of measures taken in respect of infractions concerning arrests or detention.[28]

The importance of these competences, powers and duties cannot be overestimated, being essential for the successful conservation and management of the living resources in waters under the jurisdiction of the coastal State. The fisheries control and enforcement framework established by the LOSC is mandatory on the coastal State.[29] Nevertheless, foreign flag States are not exonerated from responsibility when it comes to control over the fishing activities of their vessels in the foreign EEZ. As indicated by the LOSC Article 58(3), flag States whose vessels operate in waters under the jurisdiction of the coastal State must observe due regard for the rights and duties of that coastal State. Indeed, flag States have subsidiary obligations to ensure that vessels entitled to fly their flag comply with the laws and regulations of the coastal State in

27 UNCLOS (n 15), Art. 73(1) and 73(3); *Fisheries Advisory Opinion* (n 19), para. 105.
28 UNCLOS (n 15), Art. 73.
29 *Fisheries Advisory Opinion* (n 19), para. 96.

all matters concerning the conservation and management of fisheries located in the EEZ.[30]

Lastly, the LOSC Article 63 establishes a number of obligations in respect of straddling species occurring in the EEZ that are relevant for the exercise of control and enforcement functions. Firstly, there is a duty to seek to agree, "either directly or through appropriate subregional or regional organizations (...) the measures necessary to coordinate and ensure the conservation and development of such stocks", whether the species straddle the EEZs of two or more States, or the EEZ and the high seas. In respect of highly migratory species, Article 64 obligates the "coastal State and other States whose nationals' fish in the region for the highly migratory species listed in Annex I (to) cooperate directly or through appropriate international organizations with a view to ensuring conservation and promoting the objective of optimum utilization of such species throughout the region, both within and beyond the exclusive economic zone". The UK also has specific obligations as a coastal State in respect of anadromous and catadromous fish species under the LOSC Articles 66 and 67. These cooperation obligations are significant in a control and enforcement context: as subsequent sections discuss, they form the legal bedrock for a management and control system that is rooted in international agreement in fundamental ways. As part of this system, the UK must manage stocks and control fishing activities pertaining to these categories by reference to global and regional agreements in which other States with fishing interests and the EU are also participants.

Global Fisheries Instruments

The significance of the LOSC obligations for compliance and enforcement is further brought to light by the UNFSA, a global agreement to which the UK is a party. Particularly important for enforcement are the provisions contained in Article 7, and Articles 20 and 21. Although the UNFSA is principally concerned with the conservation and management of straddling and highly migratory species, it sets out a blueprint for internationally shared fisheries that refines and develops the obligations established by the LOSC. Firstly, it is self-evident that enforcement is carried out by reference to the applicable legal framework. In this respect, UNFSA Article 7(2)(c) clarifies that States need to take into account previously agreed measures established in regional or sub-regional fisheries management organisations. The effect of this provision contributes towards the harmonisation of measures across groups of States whose vessels fish for certain stocks, or in whose waters such stocks occur. Article 20 establishes a cooperation framework for enforcement, seeking the coordination of activities across coastal and flag States. This cooperation framework is refined by Article 21, which in its paragraph 11 also establishes a list of concepts that State parties to the UNFSA must incorporate into their domestic legal

30 Ibid., para. 105.

frameworks as serious infractions. Articles 21, 22 and 23 commit parties to participating and implementing enforcement measures adopted by regional or subregional organisations of which the State is a member.

The UK is also a party to the 2009 FAO Agreement on Port State Measures to Prevent, Deter and Eliminate Illegal, Unreported and Unregulated Fishing (PSMA). The PSMA elaborates on a principle first established in Article 23 of the UNFSA: the right and duty of the port State to take non-discriminatory measures to evaluate the legality of arrivals, and to make sure that they do not undermine regional or subregional cooperation measures. Such measures can include inspections, as well as the prohibition of landings and transhipments. The PSMA elaborates on these provisions. It outlines the minimum standards for the port control of foreign-flagged fishing vessels. Article 6 outlines parties' information exchange obligations. Other obligations include designating ports that vessels may request access to,[31] requesting detailed information, as specified in Annex A of the PSMA,[32] and denying port access to vessel suspected of participating in IUU fishing.[33] Further, parties are required to engage in specific information exchange procedures,[34] as well as deny access to ports when a vessel is suspected of having breached applicable legislation, or regional or subregional conservation and management measures. The PSMA also contains requirement for States to publicise ports in which foreign-flagged vessels may be permitted to enter.[35]

Another fisheries instrument that, despite being non-binding, has been important to the development of enforcement approaches in both the UK and the EU is the International Plan of Action to Prevent, Deter and Eliminate IUU Fishing (IPOA-IUU). The IPOA-IUU contains a definition of IUU fishing in its paragraph 3, which is partially replicated in Article 2 of Regulation 1005/2008. Whilst the designation "IUU fishing" is convenient to assess activities that may contravene the conservation and management and other measures adopted by regional fisheries management organisations, breaches of applicable legal obligations taking place within the EEZ or the territorial sea of the UK are "illegal fishing" events, whether the breach is carried out by a national or foreign vessel.

The influence of the IPOA-IUU has been wide, and also covers a broad range of additional areas that are critical for successful enforcement action. They have been largely reflected in EU legislation, particularly in the Control Regulation and the IUU Fishing Regulation. These regulations have been incorporated into the domestic legislation of the UK, they continue to be relevant to the domestic operation of port and coastal State controls. Of

31 PSMA (n 17), Art. 7.

32 PSMA ibid., Art. 8 and Annex A.

33 Or those on an IUU vessel list of a regional fisheries management organisation; Art. 8 bis (3).

34 PSMA (n 17), Art. 14.

35 FAO IPOA-IUU, <http://www.fao.org/fishery/ipoa-iuu/legal-text/en> accessed 1 July 2021, para. 57.

particular significance for enforcement are measures concerning monitoring, surveillance, inspection, authorisations, regular and special licences and permits, effort regimes and technical measures, transhipment control, electronic and manual catch data recording and reporting, and proportionate and effective sanctions regimes.[36]

Regional and Bilateral Fisheries Agreements

As discussed earlier in this book, the Trade and Cooperation Agreement (TCA) has set out the cooperation parameters between the UK and the EU in respect of the regulation of fisheries in which both parties have an interest.[37] The TCA, which has replaced previous fisheries arrangements with the EU and its MS,[38] reflects the zonal framework of the LOSC whereby the territorial sea is demarcated by a 12-nautical mile limit, etc. The TCA affirms the parties' sovereign rights to explore, exploit, conserve and manage MLRs in their waters through Article 493 and establishes that such activities "should be conducted pursuant to and in accordance with the principles of international law, including [the LOSC]".[39]

The TCA deals with control and enforcement in fisheries matters in several articles. Firstly, in Article 404 on "[t]rade and sustainable management of marine biological resources and aquaculture", the parties highlight their commitment to good fisheries governance within the parameters established in the LOSC and its satellite fisheries treaties, as well as the voluntary instruments of the FAO Code of Conduct for Responsible Fisheries, which incorporates the IPOA-IUU. This provision establishes an obligation on the parties to promote good fisheries governance by participating in regional fisheries bodies, and specifically in the regional fishery management organisations (RFMOs) in respect of which both parties have fishing interests. Article 496 in its paragraph 2 considers the need for both parties to implement and comply with the multilateral obligations to combat IUU fishing emanating from the North-East Atlantic Fisheries Commission (NEAFC), the Northwest Atlantic Fisheries Organization (NAFO) and Recommendation 18–09 of the International Commission for the Conservation of Atlantic Tunas (ICCAT), as well as the

36 Although they are less significant in the context of inshore fisheries and the operation of vessels under 10 metres.

37 Trade and Cooperation Agreement Between the European Union and the European Atomic Energy Community, of the One Part and the United Kingdom of Great Britain and Northern Ireland, of the Other Part, OJ L 444, 31 December 2020, pp.14–1462. A detailed overview and legal analysis of the TCA is given in Chapters 2 and 3.

38 Not just in matters concerning the CFP at large, but also in respect of more specific arrangements. See, for example, Agreement between the Government of the United Kingdom of Great Britain and Northern Ireland and the Government of the French Republic concerning Fishing in the Bay of Granville, with Exchanges of Notes and Declaration (St. Helier, 4 July 2000), 2269 UNTS 87.

39 TCA ibid., Art. 493; see Chapter 3.

PSMA. There is also under paragraph 3 a duty of notification when measures that affect the vessels of the other party are adopted.

The TCA also sets out conditions for reciprocal access, and deals with other related matters. Article 497 of the TCA ("Authorisations, compliance and enforcement") indicates that access by EU and UK vessels to the other's waters is conditional.[40] Firstly, each party must communicate which vessels seek authorisation to fish, and it is for the other party to issue such authorisations or licences.[41] Further, Article 497 stipulates "[e]ach Party shall take all necessary measures to ensure compliance by its vessels with the rules applicable to those vessels in the other Party's waters, including authorisation or license conditions".[42] Article 500 of the TCA, called "Access to waters", in conjunction with Article 497, and Article 502, sets out the parameters for access, which include waters between 6 and 12 nm from the baselines of ICES marine regions IV c and VII d–g (see Figure 5.1) for qualifying vessels.[43] "Qualifying vessels" in this context means a vessel of either party that fished in the aforementioned ICES regions between the years 2012 and 2016.[44]

In Article 508, the TCA establishes a Specialised Committee on Fisheries, which is the forum for discussion and cooperation in respect of a number of areas concerning the management and governance of fisheries shared by the parties. According to paragraph (f), the Committee can consider compliance measures such as joint control, monitoring and surveillance programmes, and other mechanisms of control and enforcement, as appropriate. Another important area for control and enforcement, namely the designation of landing ports, is dealt with in paragraph (i). The Specialised Committee on Fisheries is able to adopt decisions and recommendations in these and other areas relevant to fishery management. Compliance measures can be the subject of joint review.

The UK now participates in the above-mentioned RFMOs, and in the Indian Ocean Tuna Commission (IOTC), and the North Atlantic Salmon Conservation Organization (NASCO).[45] Membership in RFMOs requires the assimilation of monitoring, compliance and enforcement measures in respect of the stocks and areas they manage.[46] This implies participation in and funding of programmes and data collection and sharing, and monitoring control and surveillance tools that are key for enforcement, and that concern vessel activity and catch, as well as access to fishing grounds. For instance, vessels fishing in

40 Ibid., Art. 497; See Chapter 3.
41 Ibid., Art. 497(1).
42 Ibid., Art. 497(2); see Chapter 3, text preceding (n 21).
43 Ibid., Art. 500(4)(c).
44 Ibid., Art. 500(4).
45 See G A Oanta, 'Resolving the United Kingdom and European Union Membership of Regional Fisheries Management Organisations Post Brexit' 1 (2021) *International Journal of Marine and Coastal Law* 1–13; Chapter 8.
46 See in addition Chapter 3 subheading 'Chapter Two (Conservation and sustainable exploitation)'; Chapter 8.

the NEAFC Convention Area and landing NEAFC regulated resources are obliged to complete a Port State Control 1 (PSC1) form if they wish to land their catch in the UK. This is submitted electronically by the vessel Master to the flag State, and then forwarded to the port State (in this case the UK). The implementation of measures adopted by these RFMOs for the conservation and management of regulated stocks must be articulated domestically in accordance with other international obligations, as applicable.[47]

By virtue of Article 511, the TCA supersedes any previously existing agreements or arrangements with respect to "fishing by Union fishing vessels in the territorial sea adjacent to the Bailiwick of Guernsey, the Bailiwick of Jersey or the Isle of Man and with respect to fishing by United Kingdom fishing vessels registered in the Bailiwick of Guernsey, the Bailiwick of Jersey or the Isle of Man in the territorial sea adjacent to a Member State". Nevertheless, this is only the case whilst the TCA remains applicable: it is explicitly stated that such agreements or arrangements can be called upon again by the parties in the event that the relevant provisions of the TCA should cease to apply.

The UK has also made commitments in respect of fisheries compliance in a series of bilateral instruments. In the course of 2020 the UK has entered into a bilateral agreement with the Faroe Islands,[48] and another one with Norway.[49] In the Norway agreement compliance, control and enforcement are dealt with in Article 6. The binding provisions are rather weak, with paragraph 1 establishing that the parties will take "all necessary measures to ensure that, when fishing in the area of jurisdiction of the other Party, vessels flying its flag comply with all conservation and management measures, other terms and conditions, and all rules and regulations governing fishing activities in that area". Paragraph 2 contains a tentative provision whereby parties may agree to further deepen their cooperation in operational compliance matters, such as vessel licensing and data exchange, and vessel monitoring, control and surveillance. Finally, paragraph 3 states that such arrangements may be formulated by way of protocols or guidance documents.[50] These provisions are largely

47 See NEAFC EPSC, Designated Ports and Contracts, <https://psc.neafc.org/designated-contacts#GBR> accessed 2 July 2021.

48 Framework Agreement on Fisheries between the Government of the United Kingdom of Great Britain and Northern Ireland and the Government of the Faroes (Copenhagen, 29 October 2020), <https://www.gov.uk/government/publications/uknorway-framework-agreement-on-fisheries-cs-norway-no12020> accessed 23 July 2021.

49 Framework Agreement on Fisheries between the United Kingdom of Great Britain and Northern Ireland and the Kingdom of Norway (London, 30 September 2020), <https://www.gov.uk/government/publications/ukfaroes-framework-agreement-on-fisheries-cs-faroe-islands-no12020> accessed 23 July 2021; see Chapter 4.

50 For further information on the Norway agreement, see R Barnes, 'Framework Agreement on Fisheries between the United Kingdom of Great Britain and Northern Ireland and the Kingdom of Norway' (2021) 36 *International Journal of Marine and Coastal Law* 155–164.

replicated in Article 5 of the agreement with the Faroe Islands. In addition, the UK has entered into a memorandum of understanding with Iceland,[51] in which the parties set out arrangements to work together on fisheries matters via a mechanism they have called "the Fisheries Dialogue". Compliance, control and enforcement issues are dealt with in paragraph 1 of the memorandum, which refers specifically to monitoring, control and enforcement, but is otherwise open-ended.

Fisheries Enforcement across the UK

As discussed in Chapter 5, fisheries regulation and enforcement are a devolved competence across the four nations of the UK. Prior to Brexit, much of the enforcement activity by the competent authorities within the UK was ensuring compliance with the CFP. Currently, according to the Fisheries Act 2020, fishing within British fishery limits (the UK EEZ) is prohibited by foreign vessels unless authorised by a licence.[52] The power to grant fishing licenses to foreign vessels corresponds to the Scottish and Welsh Ministers, the Northern Ireland Department or the Marine Management Organisation (MMO). Such licences enable fishing within the specified parameters in their respective maritime areas (i.e. licences granted by the MMO do not authorise fishing within the Scottish, Welsh or Northern Irish zones)[53] However, in practice the United Kingdom Single Issuing Authority (UKSIA), a body of the MMO, acts on behalf of the UK sea fish licensing authorities of England, Scotland, Wales and Northern Ireland, and grants access to non-UK fishing vessels to enable them to fish within the UK EEZ.[54] EU MS submit vessel applications to the European Commission, who then submit them to UKSIA on their behalf.[55]

In accordance with the Fisheries Act, foreign fishing vessels are not permitted to enter UK waters with the purpose of fishing unless they have been granted authorisation and are duly licensed. The Act is clear that in this eventuality, or when fishing without a licence occurs, or the fishing activities contravene the

51 Memorandum of Understanding Between the United Kingdom of Great Britain and Northern Ireland and the Government of Iceland on Enhancing Cooperation on Fisheries, <https://www.gov.uk/government/publications/fisheries-memorandum-of-understanding-between-the-uk-and-iceland> accessed 23 July 2021.

52 Fisheries Act 2020, <https://www.legislation.gov.uk/ukpga/2020/22/contents/enacted> accessed 2 July 2021, s 12, s 16.

53 Ibid., s 17.

54 See United Kingdom Single Issuing Authority (UKSIA), <https://www.gov.uk/guidance/united-kingdom-single-issuing-authority-uksia#foreign-vessels> accessed 2 July 2021; note that the responsibility for the administration and management of UK vessel licensing with the UK EEZ rests with the UK fisheries authorities (Marine Scotland, Department of Agriculture and Rural Affairs in Northern Ireland, the Welsh Government and the MMO).

55 Ibid.

parameters established in the licence, the master, owner and where applicable the charterer of the fishing vessel will be committing an offence.[56] If convicted, whether in England, Scotland, Wales, or Northern Ireland, the persons who have committed the offence may be liable for a fine, or may have the catch and/or gear with which the offence was committed forfeited, and in some cases may be disqualified from holding a licence for a specified period.[57] The Fisheries Act also makes clear that offences can be committed by bodies corporate, and in such cases both the body corporate and the person to whom the offence is attributable and who is an officer or member, or a partner,[58] of such body corporate can be guilty of the offence.

In England, fisheries enforcement is divided between the national role of the MMO and ten Inshore Fisheries and Conservation Authorities (IFCAs) who take a regional role. IFCAs are overseen by the Department for Environment, Food and Rural Affairs and hold responsibilities to achieve both conservation objectives and sustainable exploitation of inshore fisheries.[59] Operating within the English territorial sea, IFCAS have the power to both create[60] and enforce[61] byelaws, along with other national legislation within the geographical area of each IFCA district.[62] IFCAs may appoint fishery and conservation officers who engage in monitoring of fishing activities and enforcement of conservation measures.[63] Enforcement activities involve sea patrols and catch inspections to ensure catch is above the legal minimum landing size and not subject to any restrictions at the national or local level.[64] The Sea Fishing (Enforcement) Regulations apply to the whole of the UK and give officers the power to enforce national fisheries conservation measures.[65]

In Scotland, fisheries enforcement is the responsibility of Marine Scotland, a directorate of the Scottish Government and responsible for the monitoring, control and enforcement of fishing within the Scottish zone (see Table 5.1 in Chapter 5). Established in 2009, Marine Scotland is responsible for inspections at sea and in Scottish ports, and reporting infractions of marine and fishing legislation to the relevant prosecuting authorities. Marine Scotland has three marine protection vessels that undertake fisheries patrols, enforcement and inspections, as well as two surveillance aircraft. Relevant legislation includes the

56 Fisheries Act 2020 (n 52), s 12(3), 14(6) and 16(6), and Paragraph 1(4) of Sch 3.
57 Ibid., s 19.
58 If in a Scottish partnership.
59 Marine and Coastal Access Act 2009, c. 23, <https://www.legislation.gov.uk/ukpga/2009/23/contents> accessed 2 July 2021, ss 149–150.
60 Ibid., ss 155–158.
61 Ibid., ss 165–166.
62 See Map of IFCAs in England, <www.association-ifca.org.uk/Content/ifca.map.pdf> accessed 17 July 2021.
63 Ibid., ss 165–166.
64 Ibid., ss 165–166.
65 Sea Fisheries, The Sea Fishing (Enforcement) Regulations 2018, N. 849, <www.legislation.gov.uk/uksi/2018/849/contents> accessed 2 July 2021.

Fisheries Act 2020,[66] the Aquaculture and Fisheries (Scotland) Act 2013,[67] Marine (Scotland) Act 2010[68] and the Marine and Coastal Access Act 2009.[69] Importantly, the Aquaculture and Fisheries (Scotland) Act provides that *any* British sea fishing officer has the power to enforce sea fishing legislation in the Scottish enforcement area (Scotland or the Scottish zone), and in relation to any Scottish fishing vessel "wherever it may be".[70] Officers have the power to detain vessels if there are reasonable grounds to suspect and offence,[71] release vessels,[72] inspect, seize, retain and dispose of fishing gear and other objects.[73] In addition, officers may seize fish, which can then be sold by the Scottish Ministers.[74]

A Brief Illustration: Rockall

Rockall is a small uninhabitable islet,[75] and in accordance with the LOSC generates a 12 nm territorial sea, over which the UK has full jurisdiction.[76] Rockall is in a location, roughly equidistant to the Republic of Ireland and the UK.[77] In the UK, Rockall is familiar to many due to the shipping forecast and weather reports, and in that respect the islet carries some cultural significance.[78] Historically, Rockall has been a cosmopolitan maritime enclave, with fisheries, merchant mariners and explorers from Western Europe utilising its water in various ways.[79]

Rockall was incorporated as part of the County of Inverness in 1972 by the Island of Rockall Act, and "the law of Scotland shall apply accordingly".[80] This

66 Fisheries Act (n 52) offences and penalties for breaches of licences or access provisions are found in ss 19–22; Sch 4.
67 Aquaculture and Fisheries (Scotland) Act 2013, <https://www.legislation.gov.uk/asp/2013/7/pdfs/asp_20130007_en.pdf> Part 3 concerns sea fisheries and enforcement thereof.
68 Marine (Scotland) Act 2010, <https://www.legislation.gov.uk/asp/2010/5/part/7> Part 7 contains specific provisions on enforcement, see ss 151–155 on duties, liabilities of, and offences in relation to, marine enforcement officers.
69 Marine and Coastal Access Act 2009 (n 59).
70 Aquaculture and Fisheries (Scotland) Act 2013 (n 67) s 35.
71 Ibid., s 36.
72 Ibid., s 37.
73 Ibid., ss 39–42.
74 Ibid., ss 43–44.
75 See G S Holland and R A Gardiner, 'The first map of Rockall', *The Geographical Journal* 141 (1975) 94–98.
76 UNCLOS, Art. 121(1).
77 V Lowe, 'The United Kingdom and the Law of the Sea' in Treves and Pineschi (eds.) *The Law of the Sea: The European Union and Its Member States* (Martinus Nijhoff, 1997), at p. 521.
78 See, for example, 'Rockall' in N Compton, *The Shipping Forecast: A Miscellany* (Ebury Publishing, London, 2016), at pp. 171–175.
79 R Derrig, 'An Irish Claim to Rockall' (2021), <https://www.ejiltalk.org/an-irish-claim-to-rockall/> accessed 2 July 2021.
80 Island of Rockall Act 1972, c.2, <https://www.legislation.gov.uk/ukpga/1972/2> accessed 3 July 2021.

Act was amended by the Local Government (Scotland) Act 1973, bringing Rockall in to the Western Isles local government council.[81] As part of Scotland, Rockall fisheries are administered by Scotland,[82] but Ireland also claims a right of access to Rockall for its fishers based on the history of the islet as a site where fishers and sailors of many nationalities have converged over the centuries, as well as the fact the islet is contiguous to the Irish mainland.[83] Nevertheless, according to most academic commentary, UK sovereignty over Rockall appears solid *de jure*, as well as *de facto*,[84] and the UK has included Rockall within its EEZ,[85] without Ireland raising a formal complaint.[86] Rockall was of interest to the UK during the Third UN Conference on the Law of the Sea in Caracas 1974 when States debated the maritime space that could be generated by low-tide elevations, rocks and islands.[87] At that conference, "[t]he promise of jurisdiction over seabed mineral or fisheries could well serve to stimulate or exacerbate disputes over islands. Indeed, it is arguable that this has already begun to happen."[88] This quote is still relevant in the present day.[89]

As mentioned above, prior to Brexit, the UK EEZ was manged under the CFP. Regulation 1380/2013 allows States to restrict fishing by foreign vessels within the 12 nm territorial sea. Under Article 5(2) of that regulation, EU vessels that had traditionally fished in the 12 nm area from ports in coasts adjacent to it were permitted to still have access. Irish vessels that had traditionally operated in Rockall had thus continued to fish there undisturbed whilst the UK was a Member State of the EU. With the UK's withdrawal from the CFP, the competent authorities (see above) in the UK are entitled to

81 Local Government (Scotland) Act 1973, c. 65, <https://www.legislation.gov.uk/ukpga/1973/65/contents> accessed 2 July 2021, s 241(2), Sch 27 para. 202.

82 Island of Rockall Act 1972 (n 80), 2. 1.

83 See C R Symmons, *Ireland and the Law of the Sea* (Blackrock, 1993) at p. 35.

84 See R Collins, 'Sovereignty has "Rock-all" to Do with It … or Has It? What's at Stake in the Recent Diplomatic Spat between Scotland and Ireland?' (2019), <https://www.ejiltalk.org/sovereignty-has-rock-all-to-do-with-it-or has-it-whats-at-stake-in-the-recent-diplomatic-spat-between-scotland-and-ireland/> accessed 22 April 2021; J Harrison, 'Unpacking the Legal Disputes over Rockall' (2019), <https://spice-spotlight.scot/2019/06/18/guest-blog-unpacking-the-legal-disputes-over-rockall/> accessed 22 April 2021; *contra* R Derrig, 'An Irish Claim to Rockall' (n 79).

85 The Exclusive Economic Zone Order 2013, <https://www.legislation.gov.uk/uksi/2013/3161/contents/made> accessed 3 July 2021.

86 S.I. No 86/2014 – Maritime Jurisdiction (Boundaries of Exclusive Economic Zone) Order 2014.

87 See J R Stevenson and B Oxman, 'The Third United Nations Conference on the Law of the Sea: The 1974 Caracas Session', 69 (1975) *The American Journal of International Law* 1–30.

88 J R Stevenson and B Oxman ibid., at p. 25.

89 See M Shaw, 'The Regime of Islands' in Ø Jensen (ed.) *The Development of the Law of the Sea Convention – The Role of International Courts and Tribunals* (Edward Elgar, 2020), at pp. 14–47.

exercise prescriptive and enforcement jurisdiction in the territorial sea around Rockall under Articles 2 and 3 of the LOSC.[90] In principle, this means that access to fisheries in the territorial sea can only take place via the procedures agreed internationally between the UK as coastal State and third States or the EU. If granted, any fishing activity must be carried out in accordance with the licences assigned to individual vessels, and in accordance with the provisions established in the Fisheries Act 2020.

The waters around Rockall are home to complex fisheries with a transnational dimension,[91] which attract considerable interest,[92] being important not only to vessels from the UK and Ireland, but also to fleets from other EU MS and beyond, to the Icelandic and Russian fleets, for example. Cases where enforcement responses have been prompted are recent: just a few hours into Brexit, the Scottish marine protection vessel *Jura* had stopped Irish fishing vessel *Northern Celt* from entering Rockall waters beyond the 12 nm of the UK territorial waters.[93] This action resulted in a diplomatic incident between Ireland and the UK, and even prompted calls for Ireland to step up claims over Rockall.[94] Unfortunately, this incident has not been the only one in the short history of Brexit fisheries so far.[95]

Conclusions

The above illustration brings to light the relevance that the international legal framework in matters of control and enforcement possesses, furnishing the coastal State with a balanced framework of competences, rights and obligations, and fostering international cooperation with neighbouring coastal States and flag States alike. The content of this chapter shows how the transition undertaken by the UK from EU MS and CFP participant to independent coastal State does not extricate it from a complex framework of international commitments, which specify what may be considered illegal fishing, and shape and condition control and enforcement responses.

90 R Collins (n 84).

91 See ME Certification Ltd, 'Marine Stewardship Council (MSC) Public Comment Draft Report SFSAG Rockall haddock on behalf of Scottish Fisheries Sustainable Accreditation Group (SFSAG)' (2018), <https://cert.msc.org/FileLoader/FileLinkDownload.asmx/GetFile?encryptedKey=CeswdM1Ypz5E+5Ds/wS7etIJq119rb7OA/2C/Tl8ByCY9J4r+/4BmSShcOMmEM/6> accessed 22 May 2021.

92 See Chapter 4.

93 See V Kearney, 'Donegal Vessel Blocked from Fishing around Rockall by Scottish Patrol Boat' RTE (2021) <https://www.rte.ie/news/brexit/2021/0105/1187865-rockall-fishing/> accessed 22 April 2021.

94 See *Irish Examiner* 'Irish Examiner View: Time for Ireland to Claim Rockall' 7 January 2021 <https://www.irishexaminer.com/opinion/ourview/arid-40202453.html>.

95 See, for example: <https://www.bloomberg.com/news/articles/2021-06-28/fresh-brexit-fish-spat-averted-as-jersey-extends-french-amnesty> and <https://www.ft.com/content/f58eb8b0-c5fd-4ba5-b387-189f2f194f4b>.

Whilst this framework permits and obliges independent coastal States such as the UK to ensure that there is a domestic legal system that ensures sustainable management of fishing resources in the waters under the jurisdiction of the coastal State, it also fosters a deeper level of cooperation, especially at the regional level. The UNFSA requires cooperation with RFMO measures, including for compliance purposes, and the PSMA sets out procedures to combat IUU fishing. The control and enforcement provisions contained in these agreements, and in the IPOA-IUU, are largely replicated in CFP legislation, much of which has been retained by the UK. Yet, as a new relationship is being forged with the EU and MS with fishing interests neighbouring the UK, new agreements have emerged. The TCA and the bilateral agreements that the UK has entered since 2020 provide additional framework upon which to base this new relationship.

The confrontation at Rockall and other examples of discontent that have followed since Brexit suggest that these agreements and the legal foundations that they contain for control and enforcement should not be underestimated.[96] Control and enforcement are needed to ensure and maintain sustainability, but they can also both foster and defuse conflict. Further, the cooperative framework of the LOSC and its satellite treaties strongly shows that no State exists in isolation, and that the international context always involves a balancing of interests. Indeed, this is the case with the UK, which although no longer a part of the CFP, nevertheless remains a trading partner of the EU.[97] Consequently, the UK is unlikely to remain impermeable to legal evolution in the EU in all matters involving fisheries governance, including compliance, control and enforcement.[98] Whether the TCA and the new agreements entered into by the UK and the control and enforcement policies developed on the legal bases they provide are sufficient to ensure sustainability and conflict-free oceans in the UK and its neighbouring waters is yet to be seen.

96 See R Barnes and M Rosello, 'Fisheries and Maritime Security: Understanding and Enhancing the Connection' in Evans and Galani (eds.) *Maritime Security and the Law of the Sea* (Edward Elgar, 2020), at pp. 48–82, 80.

97 For more information on trade data, see <https://www.seafish.org/insight-and-research/market-supply-data-and-insight/seafood-trade-and-brexit/> accessed 22 July 2021.

98 This is likely to be the case in particular with regard to the review of Council Regulation 1005/2008, the EU IUU Regulation, which specifically aims to foster minimum IUU fishing control standards and mechanisms vis-à-vis third countries that export fish products to the EU.

7 Conservation of Fisheries Resources and Protection of the Marine Environment Post-Brexit

International Obligations

Mitchell Lennan, Jonatan Echebarria Fernández and Tafsir Matin Johansson

Introduction

As discussed throughout this book, despite leaving the EU and the CFP and becoming a so-called "independent coastal State," the UK is still bound by various international environmental legal obligations. Post-Brexit UK remains party to over 40 international environmental treaties (or over 100 agreements when one considers protocols and amendments).[1] The UK Government has gone on record stating that it intends to remain bound by its international environmental obligations laid out in Multilateral Environmental Agreements (MEAs)[2] and that, "we will of course continue to honour our international commitments and follow international law".[3] The MEAs to which the UK is party concern an array of subjects including climate change, nuclear safety and access to information.[4] To ensure regulatory stability, the UK Government has maintained a policy of retaining EU environmental law until the opportunity for regulatory evaluation presents itself.[5] However, this regulatory evaluation and potential reshaping is limited by the UK's obligations to treaties which it is

1 UK Environmental Law Association (UKLEA), *Brexit and Environmental Law: The UK and International Environmental Law* (London, UK, UKELA, 2017) at 5; R Macrory and J Newbigin, *Brexit and International Environmental Law* (London, UK, Centre for International Governance Innovation, 2017), <https://www.cigionline.org/static/documents/documents/Brexit%20Paper%20no.8.pdf> accessed 1 May 2021.

2 Written statement to the House of Commons by Thérèse Coffey, Parliamentary Under Secretary of State for the Department for Environment, Food and Rural Affairs, in response to written questions from Caroline Lucas, MP, "Environment: Treaties: Written question – 9691" (asked on 8 September 2017, answered on 18 September 2017) ["Environment: Treaties"], <https://members.parliament.uk/member/3930/writtenquestions?page=41> accessed 1 May 2021.

3 Brexit White Paper, <https://www.gov.uk/government/publications/the-united-kingdoms-exit-from-and-new-partnership-with-the-european-union-white-paper> accessed 1 May 2021.

4 UKLEA (n 1), Annex.

5 Brexit White Paper (n 3), at para. 2.7.

DOI: 10.4324/9781003252481-7

party. Therefore "international environmental law could be seen to provide an important underpinning of future national environmental obligations, rights and minimum standards",[6] as a "backstop beyond which we cannot fall in terms of environmental standards".[7]

Because the EU has legal personality,[8] and has the power to conclude international treaties if those treaties allow, or where concluding an agreement is necessary to achieve one of the EU's policies, or the objective of the treaty.[9] The exercise of the EU's power in this regard depends on the legal competence the EU possesses on the subject of the treaty.[10] Generally, there are three categories of international agreements relevant for our purposes:

1 International agreements exclusively within the EU's competence and that only the EU can ratify;
2 International agreements where MS retain exclusive competence and may negotiate and ratify alone and without the EU's involvement; and
3 International agreements where the subject "straddles" the competence of the EU and MS, and where the EU and MS will both be parties.

The first and third categories of agreement are of key interest for this chapter. As mentioned throughout this book, regional fisheries agreements and agreements on the conservation of marine biological resources fall under exclusive EU competence under the CFP, and so fall into category 1.[11] Prior to Brexit, the UK was party to any agreement in category 1 by way of Article 216(1) of the Treaty on the Functioning of the European Union, which binds MS to international agreements entered into by the EU. Obligations of those agreements are to be implemented through directly applicable EU regulations or by implementation of EU directives. However, *international* agreements relating to fisheries, such as UNCLOS or the UNFSA, were signed and ratified by the UK prior to the EU, and the external dimension of fisheries was only adopted

6 R Macrory and J Newbigin (n 1), at 1.
7 See also evidence of M Lee, House of Lords Select Committee on the European Union, Energy and Environment Sub-Committee, Brexit: environment and climate change (London, UK: 2016) at 156 [House of Lords], <https://www.parliament.uk/globalassets/documents/lords-committees/eu-energy-environment-subcommittee/Brexit-environment-climate-change/Brexit-Environment-Climate-Change-Written-Oral-Evidence-Volume.pdf> accessed 1 May 2021.
8 Treaty on European Union, 7 February 1992, OJ, C 325/5, Art. 47.
9 Treaty on the Functioning of the European Union (TFEU), 13 December 2007 OJ, C 115/47, Art. 216.
10 G De Baer, *Constitutional Principles of EU External Relations* (Oxford, UK: Oxford University Press, 2008) at 10; see R Macrory and J Newbigin (n. 1); See also TFEU (n 9) Art. 216; *Commission of the European Communities v Council of the European Communities: European Agreement on Road Transport*, C-22/70, [1971] ECR, at 263.
11 TFEU (n 9), Art. 3(1).

by the EU as a pillar of fisheries policy in 2013.[12] After Brexit, the UK was still bound by these treaties.

Category 3 is the most common form of MEA; they are known as mixed agreements. These contain elements that fall within both the UK and EU's competence and as such both are party to said agreement. Mixed agreements "are frequently used to ensure member state support even in areas where the EU strictly appears to have exclusive legal competence"[13] (45 agreements to which the UK is party fall under this category).[14] On leaving the EU, the UK assumed the competences previously held by the EU and as such are bound automatically by these mixed agreements that the UK has signed and ratified.[15]

For reasons of space, and in keeping with the theme of this book, the UK's international obligations for the conservation and management of fisheries and the protection and preservation of the marine environment will be examined here.

The environmental component of fisheries resources management and regulation are interlinked and indivisible. Of special focus are the marine environmental protection obligations under international law applicable to fisheries, which the UK remains bound by despite Brexit. In particular, it outlines the obligations under the UN Convention on the Law of the Sea (UNCLOS),[16] the UN Fish Stocks Agreement (UNFSA),[17] the Convention on Migratory Species (CMS),[18] the Convention on Biological Diversity (CBD),[19] as well instruments adopted under the UN Food and Agriculture Organization (FAO). This is important as despite Brexit, there is still a layer of international obligations applicable to the UK and EU to ensure the conservation and sustainable exploitation of fish stocks. It should also be noted that generally, international fisheries instruments apply to recreational fisheries as well as commercial fisheries.[20]

12 Regulation (EU) No 1380/2013 OJ L 354/22.

13 R Macrory and J Newbigin (n 1), at 3; J Weiler, *The Constitution of Europe* (Cambridge, UK: Cambridge University Press, 1999) at 177; P Koutrakos and C Hillion (eds.) *Mixed Agreements Revisited: The EU and its Member States in the World* (Oxford, UK: Hart Publishing, 2010).

14 UKLEA (n 1), Annex.

15 R Macrory and J Newbigin (n 1), at 4.

16 United Nations Convention on the Law of the Sea (UNCLOS), Montego Bay, 10 December 1982, 1833 UNTS 3. The UK acceded to UNCLOS on 24 July 1993.

17 Agreement for the Implementation of the Provisions of the United Nations Convention on the Law of the Sea of 10 December 1982 relating to the Conservation and Management of Straddling Fish Stocks and Highly Migratory Fish Stocks, New York, 4 August 1995, 2167 UNTS 3. The UK acceded to UNFSA on 10 December 2001.

18 Convention on the Conservation of Migratory Species of Wild Animals (CMS), Bonn, 23 June 1979, 1651 UNTS 333. The UK became a party to the CMS on 1 October 1985.

19 United Nations Convention on Biological Diversity (CBD), Rio de Janeiro, 22 May 1992, 1760 UNTS 79. The UK became a party to the CBD on 1 September 1994.

20 D Diz, M Lennan and K Hyder, 'Assessment of governance structures and legal instruments for recreational sea fishing and its inclusion in broader fisheries

International Environmental Obligations in Fisheries Management and Conservation

UNCLOS

UNCLOS sets out the legal framework for ocean governance, establishing the rights and duties of States relating to all activities that occur at sea. The scope of the Convention is vast, and it was negotiated by consensus and in a holistic manner. UNCLOS is referred to either explicitly or implicitly by the other instruments covered in this chapter. These instruments should be interpreted and applied through UNCLOS, which lays out the rights and duties of States whose nationals engage in fishing activities in waters both within and beyond national jurisdiction. The UK has been a party to UNCLOS since 25 July 1997.[21]

Coastal State obligations have been laid out previously in Chapter 6. However, as a key reminder, UNCLOS in its Part XII explicitly requires all States to protect and preserve the marine environment. This is an obligation of conduct, one of "due diligence" applying to all maritime areas regardless of jurisdiction.[22] Such obligations are *erga omnes* – meaning they are owed to, and enforceable by, any member of the international community.[23] The provisions covering marine living resources (MLRs), such as, for example, Conservation and Management Measures (CMMs) of both coastal States, "constitute an integral element in the protection and preservation of the marine environment",[24] and failure to ensure respect of CMMs constitutes a violation of UNCLOS Part XII. Article 194(5) of UNCLOS establishes the obligation to protect and preserve rare or fragile ecosystems and habitats of depleted, threatened or endangered species as well as other forms of marine life. UNCLOS, however, does not provide criteria for identifying and managing such areas, and relies on other instruments to do so. These instruments, such as the CBD, complement UNCLOS by providing further guidance, including on minimum standards.

UNFSA

The rather vague provisions found in UNCLOS pertaining to straddling fish stocks and highly migratory (HM) fish stocks are further elaborated by

governance' Report for Centre for Environment, Fisheries and Aquaculture Science (forthcoming – on file with authors).

21 See United Nations Treaty Collection, <https://treaties.un.org/Pages/ViewDetailsIII.aspx?src=TREATY&mtdsg_no=XXI-6&chapter=21&Temp=mtdsg3&clang=_en#10> accessed 2 May 2021.

22 *The South China Sea Arbitration* (The Republic of The Philippines v. The People's Republic of China) Award of 12 July [2016], PCA Case No 2013–19, ICGJ p. 49.

23 See generally: *Case Concerning the Barcelona Traction, Light and Power Co., Ltd.* (Belgium v. Spain), Judgment of 5 February [1970] ICJ Reports 1970, p. 3.

24 *Request for an Advisory Opinion Submitted by The Sub-Regional Fisheries Commission (SRFC)*, Advisory Opinion, 2 April [2015], ITLOS Reports 2015, p. 4 (*Fisheries Advisory Opinion*) at para. 120.

UNFSA.[25] In terms of geographic scope, Articles 5 (principles), 6 (precautionary approach) and 7 (compatible measures) are applicable both within and beyond national jurisdiction, while the rest apply to areas beyond national jurisdiction.[26] UNFSA should be interpreted and applied consistently with UNCLOS,[27] and it requires the application of the precautionary approach to fisheries,[28] an ecosystem approach;[29] and the protection of marine biodiversity.[30] Parties to UNFSA must comply with CMMs established by an RFMO or fisheries arrangement, or refrain from fishing altogether.

Convention on Migratory Species of Wild Animals (CMS)

The CMS is a global multilateral conservation treaty which aims to protect migratory species, and especially those species that are threatened, vulnerable or have unfavourable conservation status. Applying to areas within and beyond national jurisdiction, the Convention defines migratory species as: "the entire population or any geographically separate part of the population of any species or lower taxon of wild animals, a significant proportion of whose members cyclically and predictably cross one or more national jurisdictional boundaries".[31] The UK has been a party to the CMS since 1985.[32] The CMS lists species that are considered threatened or endangered in its Appendix I,[33] lesser threatened species in Appendix II.[34] With regard to fisheries, parties are expected to take measures to protect Appendix I species against bycatch.[35]

Memoranda of Understanding (MoU) under the CMS

Like agreements for Appendix II species, parties to the CMS may outline specific measures necessary for the protection of migratory species through the adoption of memoranda of understanding (MoU). MoU are not legally binding; instead they guide States on how to implement the general obligations of

25 "Highly Migratory Fish Stocks" are listed in Annex I of UNCLOS.
26 Agreement for the Implementation of the Provisions of the United Nations Convention on the Law of the Sea of 10 December 1982 relating to the Conservation and Management of Straddling Fish Stocks and Highly Migratory Fish Stocks, New York, 4 August 1995; 2167 UNTS 3.
27 Ibid., Art. 4.
28 Ibid., Art. 5(c); Application of the precautionary approach is laid out in UNFSA Art. 6 and Annex II; See Rio Declaration on Environment and Development, 31 ILM 874. Concluded 13 June 1992, Principle 15.
29 UNFSA (n 17), Arts. 5(d–e).
30 Ibid., Art. 5 (g).
31 Ibid., Art. I(a).
32 See Convention on the Conservation of Migratory Species of Wild Animals, <https://www.cms.int/en/country/united-kingdom> accessed 4 May 2021.
33 Ibid., Art. III (1).
34 Ibid., Art. IV (3).
35 CMS COP Resolution 6.2 (1999).

the CMS in the context of specific species. For example, the Memorandum of Understanding on the Conservation of Migratory Sharks[36] has 48 parties, including the UK and EU, and lists 29 species of shark and ray in its Annex.[37] The MoU aims to achieve a favourable conservation status for migratory sharks based on the best available scientific information, accounting for the socio-economic value of species. The MoU outlines a Conservation Plan to improve understanding of migratory sharks, ensure fisheries for sharks are sustainable, protect critical shark habitat and migratory corridors, and enhance national, regional and international cooperation.[38]

Agreement on the Conservation of Small Cetaceans of the Baltic, North East Atlantic, Irish and North Seas (ASCOBANS)

ASCOBANS is an agreement to conserve all small cetaceans found in the Baltic, North-East Atlantic, Irish, and North Seas, which was adopted under the auspices of CMS.[39] The agreement applies to toothed whales (Odonotoceti) apart from the sperm whale. The UK has been party to ASCOBANS since 1993, and "appl[ies] in all UK waters in accordance with existing statutory protection for cetacean species".[40] Parties are obliged to adopt CMMs listed in an Annex to the Agreement[41] and also obliged to work towards the development of modifications of fishing gear and practices to reduce bycatches as well as preventing marine litter from fishing gear being discarded at sea.[42] Through their own national legislation, parties must prevent the intentional taking and killing of small cetaceans and abide by the requirement to release at once any animal covered by the agreement that is caught alive and in good health.[43] ASCOBANS also requires the introduction of measures to reduce and minimise bycatch of listed migratory species[44] covered by ASCOBANS, such as the harbour porpoise, which is vulnerable to bycatch and vessel collision.

36 CMS Memorandum of Understanding on the Conservation of Migratory Sharks (MoU-Sharks), Bonn, 1 March 2010. The UK became a signatory on 18 June 2012.
37 Annex I of MoU Sharks listing species is available online here: <https://www.cms.int/en/document/amendments-annex-1-sharks-mou-species-covered-mou-and-their-ranges> accessed 7 September 2020.
38 MoU-Sharks ibid., Art. 12.
39 Agreement on the Conservation of Small Cetaceans of the Baltic, North East Atlantic, Irish and North Seas (ASCOBANS), Bonn, 13 September 19911772 UNTS 217. The UK became a party to ASCOBANS on 13 July 1993.
40 Joint Nature Conservation Committee, <https://jncc.gov.uk/about-jncc/careers/technical-support-analyst-202149/?gclid=CjwKCAjwz_WGBhA1EiwAUAxIcTyPv-Hmx0jyid72qT5hwu5hzx0Ehqcu7PFtK0YuwWVysut_16b45xoCfFgQAvD_BwE> accessed 5 May 2021; see ASCOBANS ibid.
41 ASCOBANS ibid., Annex.
42 Ibid., Annex (1)(b).
43 Ibid., para. 4.
44 Ibid., Art. 2.2.

The Convention on Biological Diversity (CBD)

The UK ratified the CBD in June 1994. Two key objectives of the CBD are the conservation and sustainable use of biological diversity.[45] The CBD's provisions apply to terrestrial and marine biodiversity within a party's national jurisdiction; and to activities or processes regardless of where their effects occur under a State's jurisdiction or control, which must not harm the environment whether within or beyond national jurisdiction.[46] States are obliged to implement CBD provisions into their national law; cooperate on matters of mutual interest directly or through a competent international organisation;[47] and to adopt measures to minimise or avoid significant adverse impacts on biodiversity.[48] Importantly, CBD parties must read the obligations under the Convention consistently with UNCLOS,[49] which informs and strengthens its provisions relating to the marine environment.[50] This can be understood as an interpretative tool for the marine environmental provisions of UNCLOS Part XII.[51]

The CBD promotes *in situ* [52] conservation, Article 8 provides an exhaustive "toolkit" of measures to be applied, case by case, to achieve conservation *in situ*, [53] including establishing protected areas or areas requiring special measures,[54] rehabilitating degraded ecosystems[55] and adopting legislation for protection of threatened species.[56] Articles 6–20 elaborate the general principles of the CBD[57] into binding commitments.[58] Building on those, parties had adopted commitments to establish and adequately manage ecologically representative systems of MPAs and other effective area-based conservation measures (OECMs) by 2020.[59] The UK has declared 372 MPAs or OECMs with varying levels of protection.[60] Moving forward beyond 2020, at the time of writing, the first draft of the Post-2020 Global Biodiversity Framework proposes to

45 CBD (n 19), Art. 1.
46 Ibid., Arts. 3 and 4.
47 Ibid., Art. 5.
48 Ibid., Art. 10(b).
49 Ibid., Art. 22.
50 *South China Sea Arbitration* (n 22), para. 908.
51 A Boyle and C Chinkin, *The Making of International Law* (Oxford: OUP, 2007), at 256–257.
52 CBD (n 19), Art. 2.
53 Ibid., Art. 8.
54 Ibid., Art. 8(a).
55 Ibid., Art. 8(f).
56 Ibid., Art. 8(k).
57 Ibid., Art. 1.
58 P Birnie, A Boyle and C Redgwell, *International Law and the Environment* 3rd Ed. (Oxford: OUP, 2009), at 639 at 616.
59 CBD Decision X/2, *Strategic Plan for Biodiversity 2011–2020 and the Aichi Biodiversity Targets* (2010) Aichi Biodiversity Target 11.
60 Joint Nature Conservation Committee, 'UK Marine Protected Area Network', <https://jncc.gov.uk/our-work/uk-marine-protected-area-network-statistics/> accessed 7 May 2021.

increase protection to 30% with at least 10% of protected areas under strict protection.[61] Obligations relating to conservation and sustainable use of biological diversity apply to fisheries. For example, CBD parties are encouraged to review their national environmental laws and relevant legislation and consider appropriate institutional mechanisms relevant to integrated marine and coastal management.[62] CBD parties have also indicated the necessity for further implementation and improvement of Ecosystem Approach to Fisheries.[63] In addition, CBD parties (including the UK) have committed to achieving Aichi Target 6, which outlines that by 2020 all fish and invertebrate stocks and aquatic plans are managed and harvested sustainably and legally, applying ecosystem-based approaches, avoiding overfishing, with recovery plans for species which need them, and that fisheries have no significant adverse impacts on stocks, species and ecosystems are.[64] Clearly, the target for this has passed, and replacement targets have not yet been agreed at the time of writing. However, the UK reported despite the fact it had made insufficient progress overall, it had "made significant progress in introducing sustainable fisheries measures … UK stocks are now showing signs of recovery following their historic overexploitation".[65]

FAO Code of Conduct for Responsible Fisheries

There are several instruments related to fisheries adopted under the auspices of the FAO. For reasons of space, this section will only outline the Code of Conduct for Responsible Fisheries (the Code) and instruments adopted in its implementation. Instruments adopted to promote compliance with CMMs or prevent, deter, and eliminate IUU fishing, are not covered here for reasons of space.[66]

Adopted in 1995 by FAO, the Code provides an international and national framework in the sustainable exploitation of aquatic living resources, while protecting the aquatic environment. The Code promotes sustainable use of fishery resources while protecting the aquatic environment and its biodiversity.

61 CBD, *First Draft of the Post-2020 Global Biodiversity Framework*, 6 January 2002 CBD/WG2020/2/3, <https://www.cbd.int/conferences/post2020/wg2020-03/documents> accessed 20 July 2021.

62 CBD Decision VIII/22, *Marine and Coastal Biological Diversity: Enhancing the Implementation of integrated Marine and Coastal Area Management* (2006).

63 CBD Decision X/2; CBD Decision XI/18, *Marine and Coastal Biological Diversity: Sustainable fisheries and addressing adverse impacts of human activities, voluntary guidelines for environmental assessment, and marine spatial planning* (2012), para. 2; see also: Decision XIII/2, *Progress towards the achievement of Aichi Biodiversity Targets 11 and 12* (2016).

64 CBD Decision X/2 ibid.

65 JNCC, *Sixth National Report to the United Nations Convention on Biological Diversity: United Kingdom of Great Britain and Northern Ireland. Overview of the UK Assessments of Progress for the Aichi Targets* (JNCC, Peterborough 2019), at 4.

66 On illegal fisheries and enforcement, see Chapter 6.

The Code is not legally binding, but is in part "based on relevant rules of international law", and as such may be used to interpret other instruments related to fisheries.[67] Three key points on the Code are: i) Its application is not limited to the EEZ and the high seas, but also applies to internal waters, territorial seas and archipelagic waters; ii) Unlike the UNFSA, the guidance offered is not limited to aspects of conservation and management but also covers fisheries development, marketing, trade, energy use, food hygiene and quality, a safe working environment, marine pollution and integrated coastal zone management; iii) The Code is directed at States as well as persons, financial institutions and vessel-owners and charterers. States are also encouraged to prevent excess fishing capacity, adjusting capacity accordingly to avoid overcatch.[68]

Article 2(d) of the Code of Conduct promotes the development of international agreements in furtherance of the Code's objectives. So far, this has led to non-legally binding International Plans of Action (IPOAs) on Sharks, IUU fishing, management of fishing capacity, and seabirds. The FAO Fisheries Department has developed various technical guidelines for responsible fisheries in support of the implementation of the Code of Conduct. These instruments and technical guidelines assist governments, industry and fisheries in taking the necessary steps to implement the various obligations in the Code, for example, the International Guidelines on Bycatch Management and Reduction of Discards (Bycatch Guidelines).[69] While these are not binding on the UK *per se*, they are considered generally agreed international rules and standards that inform obligations under UNCLOS, to which the UK is bound to abide by.

Conclusion

The purpose of this chapter was to outline the international legal obligations and options for the conservation and management of fish stocks, and the protection and preservation of the marine environment after Brexit. Despite leaving the EU and the CFP, the UK is still bound by a framework of international environmental obligations, which will shape any future fisheries legislation or policy relating to the conservation and sustainable use of the marine environment. This is primarily because the UK was a party to the treaties discussed in this chapter as category 2 or 3, and, as mentioned in the introduction, the UK Government's position is to maintain and uphold its international obligations with respect to the environment. With an aim to outline these obligations and examples of best practice, this chapter first outlined obligations under UNCLOS, the UNFSA and the CBD, among others, and then outlined key principles applicable to the UK in its fisheries management post-Brexit. Indeed,

67 FAO Code of Conduct for Responsible Fisheries (The Code), <http://www.fao.org/docrep/005/v9878e/v9878e00.htm> accessed 6 May 2021, Art. 1.1.

68 Ibid., Arts. 6.3 and 7.1.

69 International Guidelines on Bycatch Management and Reduction of Discards (Bycatch Guidelines) (2010), <http://www.fao.org/docrep/015/ba0022t/ba0022t00.pdf> accessed 7 May 2021, paras. 9.1–4

since international law can exert influence over domestic legal systems, in particular the interpretation and development of national law, we see this demonstrated through the inclusion of some, but not all, key fisheries governance elements in the Fisheries Act 2020, as discussed in Chapter 5.

8 Disentanglement from the EU

Consequences for the UK's Role in International Fisheries Organisations

Jonatan Echebarria Fernández, Mitchell Lennan and Tafsir Matin Johansson

Introduction

As has been elaborated throughout this book, the UK is no longer part of the Common Fisheries Policy (CFP) and finds itself a so-called "independent coastal state". The UK must now independently participate in the same organisations and agreements that the EU previously participated in on the UK's behalf. This includes, for example, the specialised agency of the United Nations for international fisheries, the Food and Agriculture Organization (FAO) of the United Nations. Additionally, by way of the CFP, the European Commission represents EU Member States' interests at the intergovernmental bodies for management of fisheries on the high seas. These are known as regional fisheries management organisations (RFMOs), which manage straddling and highly migratory stocks (see Chapter 7) on the high seas in a specific geographical area, or for a specific species.[1] Presently, the Commission participates in five tuna RFMOs[2] and 11 non-tuna RFMOs.

Up until 31 January 2020, the UK was represented on behalf of the EU in RFMOs. Since the UK now finds itself outside of the CFP, the UK Government is faced with the choice of which RFMOs it should choose to become a member of as an "independent coastal state". The UK would need to apply for membership to these organisations as a Contracting Party in its own right, should it wish for vessels flying the UK flag to fish with the RFMOs' regulatory area or for species managed by a particular RFMO. At the time of writing, the UK has already done so for several RFMOs.[3] This chapter will explore the legal consequences of the UK's departure from the EU within international fisheries management structures. Based on its fishing interests (see Chapter 1), there are five RFMOs of interest. These are: the North-East

1 See FAO Regional Fisheries Bodies Map Viewer, <www.fao.org/figis/geoserver/factsheets/rfbs.html> accessed 1 July 2021.

2 The Commission for the Conservation of Southern Bluefin Tuna (CCSBT) is geographically non-specific.

3 See A Serdy, 'The 2018 Fisheries White Paper, the Fisheries Act 2020 and their legal dimensions' 10 *Cambridge International Law Journal*, 73–95.

DOI: 10.4324/9781003252481-8

Atlantic Fisheries Commission (NEAFC),[4] the Northwest Atlantic Fisheries Organization (NAFO),[5] the International Commission for the Conservation of Atlantic Tunas (ICCAT),[6] the Indian Ocean Tuna Commission (IOTC)[7] and the North Atlantic Salmon Conservation Organization (NASCO).[8] After first outlining the legal developments concerning these issues post-Brexit, this chapter specifically looks at these RFMOs, and then makes some inferences for the UK moving forward in international fisheries. It is important to note that the UK is party to several other RFMOs,[9] and could join other RFMOs if it so wished, by virtue of its territories outside of the EU[10] (but these will not be considered here).

Regional Fisheries Management Organisations: Consequences for the UK

The key international fisheries instruments, United Nations Convention on the Law of the Sea (UNCLOS) and the UN Fish Stocks Agreement (UNFSA) provide for regional coordination to manage fish stocks on the high seas for conservation and cooperation.[11] As previously discussed, this coordination is

4 Originally established by the North-East Atlantic Fisheries Convention (signed 24 January 1959, entered into force 27 June 1963) 486 UNTS 157, replaced by the Convention on Future Multilateral Cooperation in the North-East Atlantic Fisheries, 1982 (adopted 18 November 1980, in force 17 March 1982) 1285 UNTS 129.

5 Established by the Convention on Future Multilateral Cooperation in the Northwest Atlantic Fisheries (adopted 24 October 1978, entered into force 1 January 1979) 1135 UNTS 369.

6 International Convention for the Conservation of Atlantic Tunas (Rio Convention) (adopted 14 May 1966, entered into force 21 March 1969) 673 UNTS 63.

7 Established by the Agreement for the Establishment of the Indian Ocean Tuna Commission (adopted 25 November 1993, entered into force 27 March 1996) 1927 UNTS 329.

8 Established by the Convention for the Conservation of Salmon in the North Atlantic Ocean (opened for signature 2 March 1982, entered into force 1 October 1983) 1338 UNTS 33.

9 For example, the Commission for the Conservation of Antarctic Marine Living Resources (CCAMLR), created by the Convention on the Conservation of Antarctic Marine Living Resources (adopted 20 May 1980, entered into force 7 April 1982) 1329 UNTS 47.

10 For example, the Western and Central Pacific Fisheries Commission (WCPFC), created by the Convention on the Conservation and Management of Highly Migratory Fish Stocks in the Western and Central Pacific Ocean (adopted 5 September 2000, entered into force 19 June 2004) 2275 UNTS 43.

11 United Nations Convention on the Law of the Sea, adopted 10 December 1982, UNTS 1833, ILM 1261 (entered into force 16 November 1994), Arts. 117–118; Agreement for the Implementation of the Provisions of the United Nations Convention on the Law of the Sea 10 December 1982 relating to the Conservation and Management of Straddling Fish Stocks and Highly Migratory Fish Stocks (UNFSA), 2167 UNTS 3 (concluded 4 August 1995, entered into force 11 November 2001), Art. 8.

achieved primarily through RFMOs, which are the intergovernmental bodies though which straddling and highly migratory fish stocks are managed within a specific geographical area, or for a specific species. RFMOs are considered to be "at the forefront of international efforts to achieve the conservation and sustainable utilisation of fish stocks".[12] One of their key functions is to facilitate inter-State coordination through conservation and management measures (CMMs), for example through setting of total allowable catches (TACs) and quota allocation in their convention area or for species they manage. As discussed in Chapters 6, 7 and 8, the UK and the EU have an obligation to protect and preserve the marine environment, and to cooperate in doing so.[13] As Oanta notes, "[t]his duty includes, among others, the promotion of sustainable fisheries and international fisheries governance in the framework of relevant RFMOs of which they are members." This is enshrined in Article 8.8 of Title XI of the TCA,[14] which "further reinforces the commitments of both parties to conserve and sustainably manage marine biological resources and aquaculture".[15]

In leaving the CFP, the UK was at risk of finding itself outside the RFMOs it held fishing interests in, and so had to consider which RFMOs it should rejoin. Indeed, "to avoid legal hiatus [the UK] needed to do so by the end of the transition period on 31 December 2020, until this date the UK remained under the CFP, including the relative stability principle for quotas".[16] The Withdrawal Agreement, in its Article 130 titled "Specific arrangements relating to fishing opportunities," provided that during the transition period, the UK "shall be consulted in respect of the fishing opportunities related to the [UK], including the context of the preparation of relevant international consultations and negotiations".[17] The UK was also permitted to "provide comments on the Annual Communication on fishing opportunities, the scientific advice form the relevant scientific bodies and the proposals from the European Commission for fishing opportunities for any period falling within the transition period".[18]

12 J Harrison, *Making the Law of the Sea* (Cambridge University Press, Cambridge: 2011), at 226.; see also J Harrison, 'Key challenges relating to the governance of regional fisheries' in R Caddell and E Molenaar (eds.) *Strengthening International Fisheries Law in an Era of Changing Oceans* (Hart Publishing, Oxford: 2011), at pp. 79–102.

13 See also G Oanta, 'Resolving the United Kingdom and European Union membership of regional fisheries management organisations post Brexit' 36 (2021) *The International Journal of Marine and Coastal Law* 1–13.

14 Trade and Cooperation Agreement between the European Union and the European Atomic Energy Community, of the one part, and the United Kingdom of Great Britain and Northern Ireland, of the other part, Brussels and London, December 30, 2020 (entered into force provisionally on 1 January 2021 and definitively on 1 May 2021) UKTS 2021 No. 8; OJ 2021 L149/10 (TCA).

15 G Oanta (n 13), at 3.

16 A Serdy (n 3).

17 The EU–UK Withdrawal Agreement (2019), <https://ec.europa.eu/info/relations-united-kingdom/eu-uk-withdrawal-agreement_en> accessed 1 July 2021, Art. 130(1).

18 Ibid., Art. 130(2).

Importantly, the Withdrawal Agreement aims to allow the UK to "prepare its future membership in relevant international fora"; this would be operationalised through the EU, in exceptional circumstances, inviting the UK "to attend, as part of the Union's delegation, international consultations and negotiations referred to in paragraph 1 of this Article, to the extent allowed for Member States and permitted by the specific forum".[19]

Further, the Withdrawal Agreement aimed to help buy the UK some time in order to apply to the necessary organisations without being outside the RFMOs it had an interest in.[20] As discussed in Chapter 6, after the end of the transition period, the EU's international agreements are no longer applicable to the UK.[21] Article 129(1) of the Withdrawal Agreement states that "during the transition period, the [UK] shall be bound by the obligations stemming from the international agreements concluded by the Union, by [Member States – MS] acting on its behalf, or by the Union and its [MS] acting jointly".[22] As also discussed in Chapter 6, since 1973 and before February 2020 the UK and EU had "mixed" membership status in some international organisations. There were three scenarios here. First, the UK and EU had joint or cumulative membership in certain international organisations. Second, in some organisations, the EU was the sole member and so the UK's fishing interests were represented by the EU. Third, "both the UK and the Union were members, but the former acted only in respect of the fishing interests of its overseas territories".[23] The UK Government explained its intention to become a member of the several RFMOs in the explanatory notes of the Fisheries Bill but did not clarify which ones.[24] Further guidance published in February 2019 highlighted four of the five RFMOs mentioned above (NEAFC omitted).[25] However, the UK was "already a member in its own right of two of these RFMOs [IOTC and ICCAT] by virtue of territories outside the EU".[26]

The Withdrawal Agreement permitted the UK to "negotiate, sign and ratify international agreements entered into in its own capacity in the areas of exclusive competence of the Union, provided those agreements do not enter into force or apply during the transition period unless so authorised by the Union".[27] On 3 April 2020 the UK requested permission from the EU to become a party to the constitutive treaties of the five RFMOs mentioned

19 Ibid., Art. 130(3).
20 Ibid., Art. 130(4).
21 Ibid., Art. 129(1).
22 Ibid., Art. 129(1).
23 G Oanta (n 13), at 3.
24 UK Government, *Fisheries Bill [HL] Explanatory Notes*, <https://publications.parliament.uk/pa/bills/lbill/58-01/071/5801071en.pdf> accessed 1 July 2021.
25 Department for Exiting the European Union, 'Guidance: Fisheries' (5 November 2019), <https://www.gov.uk/government/publications/international-agreements-if-the-uk-leaves-theeu-without-a-deal/fisheries> accessed 1 July 2021.
26 A Serdy (n 3), at 79; Department for Exiting the European Union ibid.
27 Withdrawal Agreement (n 17), Art. 129(4).

above during the transition period.[28] The EU authorised this request on 18 September 2020, granting the UK authorisation to express its consent in its own capacity to be bound by certain international agreements to be applied during the transition period of the CFP. This allowed the UK "to take part in decision-making within these bodies on all matters taking effect in or after 2021, such as quotas".[29] Serdy notes that this decision can be understood for ICCAT "since the UK could not otherwise represent the British Isles and Gibraltar as a coastal State before the transition period's end, but not for the IOTC, as other territories are the basis of its eligibility for membership of the latter".[30] Indeed, whether the UK needed to request authorisation in the first place is questionable, as Article 129(4) could be interpreted as only applying to the negotiation, signature and ratification of new treaties, rather than existing treaties.[31] However, since RFMOs negotiate quotas a year in advance, i.e. quotas for 2021 would be negotiated and set by the end of 2020, the EU would be in a "conflicted position if it were still negotiating these on the UK's behalf. Hence it was vital for the UK to take the requisite treaty action to achieve membership of [aforementioned RFMOs] in time to negotiate quotas its own interest, and not obvious what reason the EU could have for seeking to prevent this without risking accusations of bad faith."[32]

To summarise, as a consequence of Brexit, the UK has found itself in the position where it has had to apply for membership of three of the five RFMOs it holds fishing interests in where it was previously represented as part of the EU. Through the Withdrawal Agreement, the UK was given time during the transition period to apply to the necessary organisations without being outside the regulatory framework of the RFMOs it had an interest in. The next section will go through these five RFMOs in turn.

North-East Atlantic Fisheries Commission (NEAFC)

NEAFC is the intergovernmental organisation responsible for the management of fisheries in the high seas in the North-East Atlantic.[33] As discussed in Chapter 1, several species managed by NEAFC are of interest to the UK.

28 COM (2020) 489 final, Proposal for a Council Implementing Decision on the authorisation of the United Kingdom to express its consent to be bound, in its own capacity, by certain international agreements to be applied during the transition period in the area of the Union's common fisheries policy, Brussels, 7 September 2020, at 1–2.

29 A Serdy (n 3), at 80; Council Implementing Decision (EU) 2020/1305 of 18 September 2020 authorising the United Kingdom to express its consent, in its own capacity, to be bound by certain international agreements to be applied during the transition period in the area of the Union's common fisheries policy (2020) OJ L305/27, recital 6 and Art. 1.

30 A Serdy (n 3), at 80.

31 Ibid., at 80.

32 Ibid., at 81.

33 Supra (n 4).

NEAFC adopts CMMs based on the latest scientific advice provided by ICES. NEAFC CMMs take "due account" of fishery impacts on marine ecosystems, as well as the conservation of marine biodiversity (see Chapter 7). NEAFC exercises an environmental protection component through the protection of vulnerable marine ecosystems, such as deep-sea sponges and corals from bottom fishing. Contracting parties are the EU, Iceland, Norway, the Russian Federation and Denmark (Faroe Islands and Greenland).

As pointed out by Serdy, it is interesting that NEAFC was the only RFMO mentioned in the UK Government's White Paper (the policy document that sets out the UK Government's aims for its future relationship with the EU after Brexit).[34] The UK applied to become a party to NEAFC's constitutional treaty, and became a Contracting Party on 7 October 2020, the same day as it submitted its application.[35] This not only demonstrates Article 1(1) of the Implementing Decision (EU) 2002/1305 in action, but "suggests that the approval must have been pre-negotiated".[36] There is no evidence publicly available to confirm this, but Oanta was also surprised at the fact the UK was able to negotiate accession to NEAFC in such a short space of time.[37] Since the UK has had fishery disputes with Iceland over mackerel since 2009, and Norway several years ago, this could in theory have jeopardised the UK's accession.[38] However, the UK clearly has a "real interest" in the fisheries of the North-East Atlantic, considering it is a coastal State within that area.[39] NEAFC's headquarters are found in London, and the UK is the depository of its convention.[40]

As a new member, the UK may have issues with quota allocation in NEAFC (and the other RFMOs discussed in this chapter, for that matter). For example, NEAFC adopted in 2003 "Guidelines for the Expectation of Future New and Contracting Parties with Regard to Fishing Opportunities in the NEAFC Regulatory Area".[41] These guidelines state that "Non-Contracting Parties of NEAFC should be aware that presently and for the foreseeable future, stocks regulated by NEAFC are fully allocated, and fishing opportunities for new

34 UK Government Department for Exiting the European Union, *The future relationship between the United Kingdom and the European Union* 12 July 2018, <https://www.gov.uk/government/publications/the-future-relationship-between-the-united-kingdom-and-the-european-union> accessed 2 July 2021; A Serdy (n 3).

35 NEAFC, *The United Kingdom Becomes 6th Contracting Party to NEAFC* 7 October 2020, <https://www.neafc.org/news/34327> accessed 2 July 2021.

36 A Serdy (n 3), at 81.

37 G Oanta (n 13), at 5–6.

38 Ibid., at 6.

39 UNFSA (n 11), Art. 8(3).

40 Convention on Future Multilateral Cooperation in the North-East Atlantic Fisheries (n 4), Art. 22.

41 NEAFC, 'Guidelines for the expectation for future new and contracting parties with regard to fishing opportunities in the NEAFC regulatory area' (2003) <https://www.neafc.org/becomingacp> accessed 10 May 2021.

members are likely to be limited to new fisheries (stocks not currently allocated)".[42]

Northwest Atlantic Fisheries Organization (NAFO)

The EU is a founding member of NAFO and has represented its MS in this forum from the beginning.[43] The UK joined NAFO as the 13th Contracting Party in September 2020,[44] through Article XXIII (4) of NAFO's Convention. According to Oanta, it was necessary for the UK to join NAFO so as to not lose access to fisheries resources within NAFO's management jurisdiction; though it is not yet apparent whether the UK's fishing interests will conflict with the EU or Canada.[45] NAFO quotas were allocated to EU MS as fishing opportunities fixed by the EU for 2020,[46] including UK vessels to catch, for example, cod and herring.[47] This is in line with the Withdrawal Agreement, outlined above (with the UK remaining a part of the CFP during the transition period).

In terms of quota allocation for 2021, the UK and EU have agreed to divide the EU quota for Atlantic cod in the NAFO regulatory area for 2021 found in Table D Annex 36 of the Trade and Cooperation Agreement (TCA) (see Chapter 2), with the UK being allocated a 16.34% share, and the EU allocated the remaining lion's share.[48] The TCA requires both parties to notify NAFO of their divided quota shares (any changes are to be discussed multilaterally at the meeting of the Contracting Parties to NAFO).[49]

International Commission for the Conservation of Atlantic Tunas (ICCAT)

ICCAT is the intergovernmental organization responsible for the collective management of tuna species in the North and South Atlantic, the Mediterranean, and the Black Sea,[50] with 52 contracting parties and five "cooperating non-parties". The UK was already a member of ICCAT prior to Brexit on account of having several island territories in the Convention area that exist

42 Ibid.

43 Council Regulation (EEC) No 3172/78, OJ L 378/1 30.12.1978.

44 NAFO, 'NAFO Hosts 42nd Annual Meeting Virtually and Welcomes United Kingdom as a NAFO Contracting Party' Press Release of 25 September 2020, <https://www.nafo.int/Portals/0/PDFs/press/PressRelease_AM2020.pdf> accessed 2 July 2021.

45 G Oanta, 'Resolving the United Kingdom and European Union membership of regional fisheries management organisations post Brexit' *The International Journal of Marine and Coastal Law* 36 (2021) 1–13 at 4.

46 Council Regulation (EU) 2020/123, OJ L 25/1 30.1.2020.

47 Ibid., Annex 1B.

48 TCA (n 14), Annex 36, Table D.

49 TCA ibid., Art. 505(2)–(3).

50 See ICCAT, Convention Area, <https://www.iccat.int/en/> accessed 7 September 2020.

outside the EU[51] (Ascension Island, Bermuda, the British Virgin Islands, Saint Helena and Tristan da Cunha, and the Turks and Caicos Islands). In spite of already being a member, the UK alerted the United Nations Food and Agriculture Organization (FAO) – the depository of the Rio Convention – on 21 October 2020, stating that it would be party to ICCAT on the basis of the British Isles and Gibraltar.[52] Serdy notes the fact that the return of Atlantic bluefin tuna to UK waters, likely due to climate change,[53] would allow the UK to argue for a quota allocation for the stocks under the ICCAT allocation guidelines[54] (although, when a member of the EU the UK was not allocated bluefin quota).[55] At present, the UK prohibits fishing for Atlantic bluefin in its EEZ.[56]

As a member of ICCAT, the EU allocates quotas between its MS and sets minimum conservation reference sizes,[57] and prior to Brexit it did not allocate a quota for bluefin to the UK.[58] On the basis of the TCA, for 2021, the UK has been allocated a slither of four ICCAT quotas; with regard to bluefin tuna, the UK has been allocated 0.25% of the quota, with the EU taking the remaining 99.75%.[59] Indeed, considering the ban on fishing for this stock in UK waters, this comes as no surprise, but if this stock becomes of interest to the UK, any changes must be discussed as "a matter for the relevant multilateral fora".

Bluefin Tuna: Emerging Challenges

Despite the potential issue above, the UK's approach appears to be aiding the recovery of the Atlantic bluefin tuna stock. For example, the International

51 See ICCAT, *ICCAT geographical definitions* 2016.02.EN, <www.iccat.int/Data/ICCAT_maps.pdf> accessed 2 July 2021.
52 See ICCAT, *Adherence by the United Kingdom of Great Britain and Northern Ireland* 28/X/2020 <http://extwprlegs1.fao.org/treaty/docs/CSL000252.pdf> accessed 2 July 2021.
53 T W Horton et al., 'Evidence of increased occurrence of Atlantic bluefin tuna in territorial waters of the United Kingdom and Ireland' *ICES Journal of Marine Science* (2021), <10.1093/icesjms/fsab039> accessed 2 July 2021.
54 ICCAT, 'Compendium: Management Recommendations and Resolutions Adopted by ICCAT for the Conservation of Atlantic Tunas and Tuna-Like Species' (2020), <https://www.iccat.int/Documents/Recs/COMPENDIUM_ACTIVE_ENG.pdf> accessed 2 July 2021; A Serdy (n 3), at 84.
55 See, for example, ICCAT, Recommendation 17–07, *Amending the Recommendation 14–04 on Bluefin Tuna in the Easter Atlantic and Mediterranean* (2017), para. 5.
56 See Marine Management Organisation, *Bluefin tuna in the UK* 12 June 2020, <https://www.gov.uk/government/news/bluefin-tuna-in-the-uk> accessed 2 July 2021.
57 See, for example, Commission Regulation (EU) 2016/1627, OJ L 252/1, Arts. 14 and 15.
58 See, for example, Council Regulation (EU) 2018/120, OJ L 27/1, Annex ID.
59 TCA (n 14), Annex 36, Table C; UK allocations for the three other ICCAT stocks in question are albacore tuna (North Atlantic): 1.52%, blue shark (North Atlantic): 0.10%, and swordfish (North Atlantic): 0.10%.

Union for Conservation of Nature revised their listing of the Atlantic bluefin tuna from "endangered" to "near threatened" in 2015, and the Marine Stewardship Council has certified some bluefin tuna fisheries in the North Atlantic as sustainable.[60] The latest report from ICCAT indicates that there has been an increase in abundance in the Atlantic bluefin tuna stock.[61] This has prompted ICCAT to replace the management plans for the stock from conservation to exploitation – by moving from a "recovery management plan" for eastern Atlantic bluefin to a "multi-annual management plan" in 2020.[62]

It may be unlikely that other ICCAT members would be willing to pass up a share of their quota to the UK should the UK not intend to make use of it.[63] Indeed, "[t]o overcome this, it may be necessary for the UK to affirm that, once given a stock recovery threshold is reached, it will use the quota for fishing".[64] However, one small point is that ICCAT does grant contracting parties the right to allocate quota for the "purpose of sport and recreational fishing" and permits recreational and sport fishing of bluefin tuna in the Eastern Atlantic and Mediterranean from 16 June to 14 October annually.[65] Marketing of bluefin tuna in recreational and sport fishing is prohibited, recreational fisheries can operate for the purposes of "tag and release".[66] This is problematic for some EU MS not allocated a tuna quota; however, with the UK outside the EU, it could be a benefit for the recreational sea fishers who are interested in catching bluefin tuna.[67]

Indian Ocean Tuna Commission (IOTC)

The IOTC is a tuna RFMO in the Indian Ocean. Operating under the auspices of the FAO, membership is open to any State that is a member of FAO, or non-members of FAO but members of the United Nations, on the condition they are "situated wholly or partly within the [management] Area" or

60 International Union for the Conservation of Nature (IUCN) *Atlantic Bluefin Tuna*, <https://www.iucnredlist.org/species/21860/97778482> accessed 2 July 2021; Marine Stewardship Council, *Recent History of Atlantic Bluefin Tuna*, <https://www.msc.org/species/tuna/recent-history-of-bluefin-tuna> accessed 2 July 2021.

61 ICCAT, *2019 SCRS Report*, <https://www.iccat.int/Documents/SCRS/ExecSum/BFT_ENG.pdf> accessed 2 July 2021.

62 ICCAT, *Recommendation by ICCAT Amending the Recommendation 18–02 Establishing a Multi-Annual Management Plan for Bluefin Tuna in the Eastern Atlantic and the Mediterranean* 19–04, <www.iccat.int/Documents/Recs/compendiopdf-e/2019-04-e.pdf> accessed 2 July 2021.

63 A Serdy (n 3), at 84.

64 Ibid.

65 ICCAT (n 62), paras. 39–47.

66 Ibid.

67 D Diz, M Lennan and K Hyder, 'Assessment of governance structures and legal instruments for recreational sea fishing and its inclusion in broader fisheries governance' Report for Centre for Environment, Fisheries and Aquaculture Science (forthcoming – on file with authors).

whose vessels fish for stocks managed by IOTC in the management area.[68] The UK maintains its membership of the IOTC on the basis of its claim to sovereignty over the Chagos Archipelago, or so-called British Indian Ocean Territory (BIOT), and has been a member of the IOTC on behalf of the BIOT since 31 March 1995. The EU has been a member since 27 October 1995,[69] and France since 3 December 1996 on account of its overseas territories in the region. Since the UK's fishing interests are only represented on behalf of the BIOT with this set up, in order to have its fishing interests represented, the UK expressed interest in acceding to the IOTC and being represented not just on behalf of BIOT on 3 April 2021.[70] The EU granted permission for the UK to apply for "full" membership of the IOTC during the transition period.[71]

The UK deposited an instrument of accession to the Agreement for the Establishment of the IOTC in 2020, the Agreement entering into force (for the UK) on 22 December 2020.[72] This was not without controversy. The republic of Mauritius maintains a sovereignty claim over the Chagos Archipelago, and the consequences of its separation from Mauritius as the UK's "bargaining chip" for Mauritian independence and in February 2019 was the subject of an Advisory Opinion of the International Court of Justice.[73] That Advisory Opinion determined that the UK's continued occupation of the Archipelago constitutes and internationally wrongful act. Furthermore, "the process of decolonisation of Mauritius was not lawfully completed when that country acceded to independence in 1968, following the separation of the Chagos Archipelago"[74] and that the UK has the obligation to "bring to an end its administration of the Chagos Archipelago as rapidly as possible".[75] On that basis, Mauritius formally requested that this issue be formally discussed at the 24th IOTC session, stating Mauritius "is the sole State lawfully entitled to exercise sovereignty rights over the Chagos Archipelago and its maritime zone".[76] Mauritius argued its position based on this Advisory Opinion, as well as United Nations General Assembly Resolution 73/295 of May 2019 which:

68 Constitution of the Food and Agricultural Organization of the United Nations, Art. XIV in *Basic Texts of the Food and Agriculture Organization of the United Nations* Vols. I and II (2015) at 3–16, <http://www.fao.org/3/mp046e/mp046e.pdf> accessed 2 July 2021.

69 Council Decision 95/399/EEC OJ L 236/24.

70 COM (2020) (n 28), at pp. 1–2.

71 Implementing Decision (EU) 2020/1305, OJ L 25/1, Art. (1)(d).

72 IOTC Circular 7 January 2021, 'The United Kingdom of Great Britain and Northern Ireland Joins IOTC', <https://iotc.org/documents/united-kingdom-great-britain-and-northern-ireland-joins-iotc> 2 July 2021.

73 *Legal Consequences of the Separation of the Chagos Archipelago from Mauritius in 1965 (Advisory Opinion)* 2019 ICJ Rep 95.

74 Ibid., para. 183(3).

75 Ibid., para. 183(4).

76 Sixth Meeting of IOTC Technical Committee on Allocation Criteria, Statement by the Republic of Mauritius, 15–16 September 2020, <https://iotc.org/sites/default/files/documents/2020/09/Statement_by_Mauritius_under_Item_2_6th_IOTC_TCAC_fv.pdf> accessed 2 July 2021, para 4; see also The Chairperson's Report of the 6th

> [c]alls upon the United Nations and all its specialized agencies to recognize that the Chagos Archipelago forms an integral part of the territory of Mauritius, to support the decolonization of Mauritius as rapidly as possible, and to refrain from impeding that process by recognizing, or giving effect to any measure taken by or on behalf of the "British Indian Territory".

The UK, in response to the Mauritian request, argued that it had sovereignty over the Chagos Archipelago and was unequivocally entitled to be a member of IOTC on that basis.[77]

The IOTC decided that discussion of the Mauritian issue would take place at the 25th session (June 2021) due to the Covid-19 pandemic.[78] In the meantime, a case was brought to a Special Chamber of the International Tribunal for the Law of the Sea (ITLOS) by Mauritius concerning the maritime boundary between Mauritius and the Maldives on the basis of Mauritius's sovereignty over the Chagos Archipelago. The substantive part of this case concerns Mauritius's claim for delimitation of the maritime boundary between the Chagos Archipelago and the Maldives. The Maldives raised preliminary objections to this case, including the question of whether the Special Chamber had jurisdiction to delimit a maritime boundary in the circumstances where a third State, the UK, maintained a sovereignty claim over the Archipelago. The objections were heard in October 2020 and the Special Chamber delivered its judgment on 28 January 2021.[79] The Special Chamber held that, on the basis of the ICJ's Advisory Opinion:

> Mauritius can be regarded as the coastal State in respect of the Chagos Archipelago for the purpose of the delimitation of a maritime boundary even before the process of the decolonization of Mauritius is completed. In the Special Chamber's view, to treat Mauritius as such State is consistent with the determinations made … in the *Chagos* advisory opinion which were acted upon by UNGA resolution 73/295.[80]

The Chamber found it had jurisdiction on this basis, and the case will now proceed to the merits phase, and the Chamber may delimit a maritime

Technical Committee on Allocation Criteria, 15–16 September 2020, IOTC-2020-TCAC06-R, Appendix 2, pp. 15–17, <https://www.iotc.org/sites/default/files/documents/2020/10/IOTC-2020-TCAC06-RE_0.pdf> accessed 2 July 2021.

77 Chairperson's Report ibid.

78 Sixth Meeting of IOTC Technical Committee on Allocation Criteria (n 76), para 5.

79 *Dispute Concerning the Delimitation of the Maritime Boundary Between Mauritius and Maldives in the Indian Ocean (Mauritius/Maldives) Preliminary Objections* Judgment of 28 January 2021 ITLOS Reports 2021; Mitchell Lennan acted as assistant to Counsel for the Republic of Maldives in this case and may do so as it proceeds to the merits. His views, and the views expressed in this chapter, do not necessarily reflect the views of the Republic of Maldives.

80 Ibid., at para. 250.

boundary between the two States.[81] Indeed, several compelling legal developments are happening in this area that may affect, *inter alia*, the UK's membership of the IOTC. The latest development in the implementation of the UNGA Resolution 73/295 outside of the IOTC framework at the time of writing is the UN Universal Postal Union council recommendation, by reference to the above judicial decisions, that stamps issued by BIOT should no longer be recognised by UN Member States.[82]

The IOTC met to discuss Mauritius's request, as well as the FAO's plan to implement paragraph 6 of UNGA Resolution 73/295,[83] in their 25th session in the second week of June 2021.[84] At time of writing, a decision has not been made on this issue.

North Atlantic Salmon Conservation Organization (NASCO)

NASCO was established by the Salmon Convention in 1984. The main aim of NASCO is the conservation and enhancement of salmon stocks based on the best scientific evidence available to it. NASCO prohibits fishing for salmon on the high seas, and beyond the 12 nm territorial sea of contracting parties, but cannot adopt decisions regulating the management of salmon within parties' 2 nm territorial seas. NASCO does, however, have the power to adopt decisions regulating fishing of salmon within the jurisdiction of one State party where it affects salmon that originate in the rivers of another party.

Prior to Brexit, NASCO had six contracting parties: the EU, Canada, USA, Russian Federation, Denmark (Faroe Islands and Greenland) and Norway. NASCO's headquarters are located in Edinburgh; however, up until 2020 the UK was not a party as it was not an eligible signatory of the Convention of Salmon in the North Atlantic Ocean listed in Article 17(1). However, Brexit presented "the UK this opportunity, for the first time, as paragraph 3 of the same Article opens the Convention to accession 'subject to the approval of the Council, by any other State that exercises fisheries jurisdiction in the North Atlantic Ocean or is a State of origin for salmon stocks subject to this Convention'".[85] Similar to NEAFC, the UK was clearly eligible based on it exercising fisheries jurisdiction in the North Atlantic. The UK had engaged with NASCO in early 2019, indicating it wished approval from NASCO's Council to accede to the Convention only on the condition that the UK left the EU

81 Ibid., at para. 354(6).

82 See *The Guardian*, 'UN favours Mauritian control over the Chagos Islands by rejecting UK stamps' 16 May 2021, <https://www.theguardian.com/world/2021/may/16/un-favours-mauritian-control-over-chagos-islands-by-rejecting-uk-stamps> accessed 2 July 2021.

83 IOTC, 'Implementation of paragraph 6 of the UNGA Resolution 73/295' IOTC-2021-S25–07(E).

84 IOTC, '25th Session of the Indian Ocean Tuna Commission', <https://www.iotc.org/meetings/25th-session-indian-ocean-tuna-commission> accessed 2 July 2021.

85 Serdy (n 3), at 81–82.

without a Withdrawal Agreement. The request was made again without that condition on 6 July 2020. The Council of NASCO, "agreed that the decision on whether to approve the UK's accession to the Convention would be taken, by email, in accordance with Article 6 of the Convention, once the European Council publishes its Decision authorising the UK to join during the transition period".[86] As discussed above, the EU authorised the UK to do so in September 2020, and as permitted by Article 1(1) of that EU Decision, the UK deposited its instrument of accession on 27 November 2020 and became the seventh contracting party to NASCO.[87]

Finally, while the NASCO Council could have vetoed the entry of the UK as a seventh contracting party, it was not in the best interests of the other parties. This is because, as described above, NASCO does not have the power to regulate the fishing of salmon within the jurisdiction of one State party (or non-party) where it affects salmon that originate in the rivers of another party (or non-party). This means that for the contracting parties the UK being outside of the obligations of NASCO's Convention "would expose salmon spawned in their own rivers, and passing through the UK's EEZ on their migratory path to and from the Atlantic Ocean, to being caught there by UK-licensed vessels".[88] Serdy also argues that in the process of the UK joining the organisation, the Secretariat of NASCO did not consult the existing contracting parties on the conditions of Articles 129 and 130 of the Withdrawal Agreement. Indeed, this may "simply be because the other members were relieved at the prospect of a seamless transition in the UK's status to shield them from exposure to the turmoil engulfing many other aspects of the Brexit negotiations, and cared little for the attendant legal niceties".[89] The authors, based on the issues laid out throughout this book, are inclined to agree, and it is not surprising that a "seamless transition" was the most attractive option.

Moving Forward

International fisheries participation within RFMOs for the UK in a post-Brexit may see delegations in negotiations in RFMOs with considerably more freedom as a member in its own right, and will not have to maintain an EU

86 NASCO, 'Report of the September 2020 Inter-Sessional Meeting of the Council of the North Atlantic Salmon conservation Organization', <https://nasco.int/wp-content/uploads/2020/10/CNL_IS2018_Report-of-the-September-2020-Inter-Sessional-Meeting-of-the-Council-of-the-North-Atlantic-Salmon-Conservation-Organization.docx.pdf> accessed 2 July 2021, para. 4.8.

87 NASCO, 'Decision of the Council of the North Atlantic Salmon Conservation Organization on the Accession of the United Kingdom of Great Britain and Northern Ireland on the Convention for the Conservation of Salmon in the North Atlantic Ocean', <https://nasco.int/wp-content/uploads/2020/11/CNL2057_Decision-of-the-Council-of-NASCO-on-the-Accession-of-the-UK-to-the-NASCO-Convention.pdf> accessed 1 July 2021.

88 Serdy (n 3), at 82.

89 Ibid., at 82.

position. However, the UK may have issues in negotiating allocation of catch or effort quotas within the RFMOs where it is a new or "returning" member outside of the EU, since RFMOs are not always eager to allocate new participants a share of quota. It is not yet apparent on what basis the UK will approach negotiating quotas for the abovementioned RFMOs, which could be either "(a) the continuity with any existing or previous UK membership of the RFMO and the catch history before and during its EU Membership, or (b) the fact that a given stock resides in or migrates through UK waters".[90] Further, it is expected that the EU would argue that quotas awarded to it by any of the above five RFMOs discussed are solely theirs and should not change simply because the UK has departed. To avoid this and end up in an unfortunate situation, the UK may need to make a consistent claim across these five RFMOs that it is entitled to a portion of the EU quota, based on the level at which the UK participates in that fishery. Future multilateral negotiations within these RFMOs will prove interesting to follow, especially to see which approach each party takes and the extent to which they cooperate in these fora. Finally, perhaps the most interesting outcome will be the decision of the IOTC on the outcome of Mauritius's request to discuss the legitimacy of the UK's membership of that organisation.

90 Ibid., at 85.

9 A Synoptic Overview of Expert Opinion on Fisheries in a Post-Brexit World[1]

Gerard van Balsfoort, Catherine Barnard, Mercedes Rosello, Miguel Núñez Sánchez, Richard Barnes, Elizabeth Bourke, Seán Marriott, Rod Cappell, Ciarán O'Driscoll, Jimmy Buchan, Tafsir Matin Johansson, Jonatan Echebarria Fernández and Mitchell Lennan

Why is (Almost) Everybody Complaining?[2]

Complaints emanate from two sides. On the UK side, the small-scale fleets are complaining as the Brexit bonus has not arrived and their main market, i.e., the EU, has become difficult to export to. The UK white fish fleets (cod, haddock, etc.) are complaining as their quota situation has deteriorated significantly when compared to the pre-Brexit period. Markedly, the UK fleet lost the extra quota that came with The Hague Preferences (part of the relative stability linked to the CFP) and with the quota swaps with the fishing industry with respect to the continent. Until now these quota exchanges have not been possible. In addition, the processing and export industry all over the UK are struggling with the fact that the UK Government chose to leave the Single Market and the Customs Union, which makes it difficult to comply with the rather complicated red tape that comes with being a third country that wants to export to the EU single market. It is worth giving particular mention to the British bivalve sector (mussels), which because of the sudden impossibility to export to the EU, is currently imploding. On top of these issues there are strong signals that the UK's independent new fisheries policy might be greener than many fishermen had anticipated.

Complaints have been raised throughout the EU fisheries and seafood industry; the pelagic sector because of the loss of mackerel and herring, the Irish fleets because of the loss of access in the Irish Sea and in the waters off

1 Based on the outcome of the Workshop titled 'Legal Challenges Faced by Coastal and Fishing Communities, Brexit and the New British Fisheries Policy" jointly organised by the City Law School, the International Law and Affairs Group, the Institute for the Study of European Law, the London Universities Maritime Law and Policy Research Group and the World Maritime University.

2 This section takes from the keynote address delivered by Gerard van Balsfoort (European Union Fisheries Alliance/EUFA, Europêche) during the workshop under the same title.

DOI: 10.4324/9781003252481-9

West Scotland, and the Danish industrial fleet for the loss of Norway pout and sand-eel. The UK has indicated that they would like to phase out the sand-eel fishery, conducted almost entirely by Danish vessels in UK waters.

At this point, it is difficult to project whether the situation will improve. This realisation of interdependency on all these levels has been translated in the position that the EU has taken during the Brexit negotiations. From the Political Declaration that gave guidance to the negotiations on the future relationship and in all subsequent negotiation mandates for Michel Barnier formulated by the Council, the linkage of the wider trade agreement to the fisheries dossier has always been a central element. And this linkage has also found its way into the Fish Chapter of the Trade and Cooperation Agreement (TCA).[3] And this linkage will also emerge in 2025 or 2026 when discussions revolving around reciprocal, bilateral access arrangements for the years after 2026, as agreed in the TCA, will take place.

The EU fishing industry is aware that the EU Single Market is the largest seafood importing market in the world. To this end, the EU has been able to connect this huge EU market to the bilateral fisheries negotiations with the UK in the Brexit deal. The EU plans on utilising the "market attractiveness" negotiating fisheries agreements with the coastal States in the Northeast Atlantic to remind us that mutual interdependency continues to exist and that constructive attitude by all coastal States is very much needed.

At this stage, it is too early to determine how the post-Brexit era will develop. The UK as the new coastal State could be struggling to find its place. That being said, it is necessary to become a constructive coastal State and support collaborative approaches in the pursuit of effective management of our many shared fish stocks. It is opined that it may take time before the UK will be a stable force in the Northeast Atlantic part of the seas. From the EU standpoint, it is important to maintain the positive force as it was observed during pre-Brexit times. It is therefore important to remind all neighbouring coastal States that access to the EU single market comes at a price. And that price is being collaborative and constructive – also for the needs of the EU fishermen.

Jersey and Fisheries[4]

On the day of local elections in part of the UK on 6 May 2021, the UK sent gunboats to the waters around Jersey. Why this show of force, and is it compatible with the trade remedies' provisions in the TCA?

Article 502 TCA contains "specific access arrangements: relating to Jersey, Guernsey and the Isle of Man". Post-Brexit, it is possible for the French

3 Trade and Cooperation Agreement Between the European Union and the European Atomic Energy Community, of the One Part, and the United Kingdom of Great Britain and Northern Ireland, of the Other Part, OJ L 444, 31 December 2020 (TCA), pp. 14–1462.

4 This section takes from the speech delivered by Catherine Barnard (University of Cambridge) in session 1 of the workshop.

fishermen to fish in the waters of the Channel Islands. The dispute in May concerned licences granted by the Jersey authorities. Based on historic fishing patterns, Jersey granted licences to 41 larger vessels but not to 17 smaller vessels that did not have the necessary satellite tracking equipment.

Faced with an escalating situation in these contested waters, the European Commission held a video conference and said that the (general) dispute resolution mechanism under Part Six of the TCA should be applied. This has a three-stage process: (1) political consultation, which, if unsuccessful, is followed by (2) an arbitration tribunal. If the tribunal finds in favour of the claimant, the losing party is obliged to pay compensation. Refusal to pay compensation means that the losing party may be subject to tariffs.

In addition to the general dispute resolution mechanism (DRMs) there are separate and specific DRMs for fisheries:

- Article 501 TCA concerns disputes over "access to waters". Unlike the general DRM, if the political consultations fail the complaining party can go straight for remedies (compensatory measures and suspension of access and preferential tariffs for fish) and only then can the matter be considered by the Arbitration Tribunal.
- Article 506(1) TCA deals with any breach of the heading on fisheries. Here again the model, more or less, follows the model under Article 501 where the remedy is applied before the matter is considered by the Arbitration Tribunal. The remedies range from suspension of access to waters and suspension of preferential tariffs on fish to suspension of preferential tariffs in respect of other goods, to suspension of all obligations under Heading One of the TCA (trade) which automatically triggers suspension under Heading Three (road transport).

Finally, there is an express remedial provision in respect of a breach of Article 502 on the Channel Islands and the Isle of Man. Article 506(2) broadly maps the dispute resolution under Article 506(1), but in terms of what can be done the first mechanism is suspending access to the relevant waters around the Channel Islands and Isle of Man.

It is unclear how the general DRM relates to the specific DRMs. Generally, the law favours specific remedies over general mechanisms but it is early days and none of this has been tested.

Rockall: Northwest Moderate Becoming Rough[5]

Perhaps due to the United Kingdom's history as a maritime power, its fishing industry has a political importance that significantly transcends its economic weight. Something similar occurs with Rockall, a small and remote sea rock

5 This section takes from the speech delivered by Mercedes Rosello (Leeds Beckett University) in session 1 of the workshop.

that has emblematic significance as a site of UK sovereignty, as well as being valued for its fish. Indeed, although friction over Rockall involves a variety of interests, at least one international dispute gravitates around access to fisheries: the Republic of Ireland disputes UK sovereignty over Rockall, and claims freedom of access for its fishermen.

The UK exercises *de facto* sovereignty over Rockall, and its position also appears valid *de jure*.[6] Sovereignty over an islet has consequences at sea: according to the United Nations Convention on the Law of the Sea (UNCLOS),[7] islets like Rockall attract a 12 nautical mile (nm) territorial sea, in which the coastal States with corresponding sovereignty can exercise full prescriptive and enforcement jurisdiction.

When UK fish stocks were managed under the Common Fisheries Policy (CFP) of the European Union (EU), they were subject to the equal access and relative stability principles, and pooled with those of other Member States. EU Regulation 1380/2013 permits coastal States to apply restrictions within the 12 nm area, and in some cases beyond it, until 2022. Yet, under Article 5(2) of the Regulation, EU vessels that had traditionally fished in the 12 nm area from ports in adjacent coasts could continue to have access. Irish vessels that had traditionally operated in Rockall had thus continued to fish there undisturbed whilst the UK was a Member State of the EU.

Following Brexit the CFP has been replaced by the UNCLOS framework and the 2020 EU–UK Trade and Cooperation Agreement. Under the UNCLOS, coastal State sovereignty in the territorial sea has very few caveats, and unlike in the EEZ the coastal State has here no obligation to share surplus stock.[8] The TCA permits some EU vessels that meet certain criteria to continue to have access in some areas. Specifically, Article 500(c) of the TCA sets out parameters for access to waters between 6 and 12 nm in the areas comprised by ICES regions IVc and VIId–g, none of which concern Rockall. Accordingly, access to fisheries in the Rockall 12 nm area can now only take place with agreement from the UK, as coastal State with sovereignty over the islet.

Rockall is home to valuable fish stocks, which are not only of interest to UK fishing vessels, but also to others, including Russian, Icelandic, Irish and wider EU fleets. In any context in which economically attractive stock may be vulnerable to being captured in furtive or otherwise illicit ways, the risk of illegal, unreported and unregulated (IUU) fishing needs to be considered. In fully

6 See R Collins, 'Sovereignty has "Rock-all" to do with it … or has it? What's at stake in the recent diplomatic spat between Scotland and Ireland?' 2019, <https://www.ejiltalk.org/sovereignty-has-rock-all-to-do-with-it-or-has-it-whats-at-stake-in-the-recent-diplomatic-spat-between-scotland-and-ireland/> accessed 1 June 2021; J Harrison, 'Unpacking the Legal Disputes over Rockall', 2019, <https://spice-spotlight.scot/2019/06/18/guest-blog-unpacking-the- legal-disputes-over-rockall/> accessed 2 June 2021.

7 United Nations Convention on the Law of the Sea (UNCLOS), Montego Bay, 10 December 1982, 1833 UNTS 3.

8 UNCLOS ibid., Article 62(1).

regulated areas such as the territorial sea of the UK, however, only a potential designation of *illegal fishing* is relevant.

In summary,[9] fishing within the UK's territorial sea around Rockall can only be carried out upon authorisation granted by the competent fisheries authorities in the UK. Any fishing activity carried out without a valid licence would constitute illegal fishing. If access is granted, all licence conditions must be observed, otherwise illegal fishing will also occur. Should any non-UK vessels be granted access, their flag States will need to cooperate with the UK in ensuring compliance with licence conditions and the applicable legal framework. They should also undertake timely investigation and appropriate information sharing in the event of a suspected infraction.

Brexit as an Opportunity to Assist in Sustainability in the Fisheries Sector: Engaging Coastal Communities on a Bottom-Up Approach[10]

Commercial fisheries, either as industrial or artisanal, are activities that provide welfare to the society, but these activities would not be carried out if they were not profitable. In the UK, the regional structures for fisheries have allowed its development as economic and social motors at local level. However, the impact of fisheries in the UK's Gross Domestic Product (GDP) is limited. This means that in any negotiation process dealing with larger economic drivers to reach a satisfactory trade agreement, fishing would run the risk of being used as a bargaining chip or left to the end of the process, as it happened during the Agreement between the EU and the UK.

However, the possibility of real control of the Exclusive Economic Zones (EEZs) and the waters under jurisdiction as an extension of the country combined with historic "fish wars" provide a different impression. The events of May 2021 in the waters under the jurisdiction of Jersey are examples of how fishermen will grapple for resources. This has the potential of occurring again at local levels, until there are clear mechanisms to understand how quotas are going to be established and sea fishing licences granted to foreign fishing vessels. In addition, the exploration and exploitation of renewable energy resources in British waters, i.e., in the already harmed Dogger Bank, may have an impact in catches and local communities. Finally, the negotiations between the UK and the EU after the five-year period may lead to some unknown consequences that will allow the UK to choose between adding more quota to British fishing vessels or protecting the stocks, providing an excellent

9 Save for exceptional cases involving possible traditional fishing rights. However, the academic literature is pessimistic about the viability of such rights. See, in particular, V Schatz, 'Access to Fisheries in the United Kingdom's Territorial Sea after Its Withdrawal from the European Union: A European and International Law Perspective' (2019) 9(3) *Goettingen Journal of International Law* 457–500.

10 This section takes from the speech delivered by Miguel Núñez Sánchez (Spanish Ministry of Transport, Mobility and Urban Agenda) in session 1 of the workshop.

opportunity to restore the maximum sustainable yields. Notwithstanding the mere fact that this also provides the UK with the possibility to fully rule their waters, it offers an excellent opportunity to consider how these developments may affect the sustainability of the affected communities and the country.

Since the promulgation of the White Paper entitled "Sustainable fisheries for future generations" in 2018 up to the adoption of the "Fisheries Act" in 2020, there has been continuous advocacy for the use of the term sustainability. Upon examination of the Fisheries Act it is then interpreted that fisheries activities need to be conducted sustainably. The wording used in the Fisheries Act gives a higher weighting to the environmental and ecologic pillar of sustainability, referring to the fact that fisheries is a key activity providing nutrition to humankind, bearing in mind that sustainability needs to be provided in different dimensions.[11] The Fisheries Management Plans in their power to depart from proposals in the Joint Fisheries Statement need to consider circumstances that are capable of being relevant and include changes relating to available evidence concerning social, economic or environmental elements of sustainable development. The question would then be how to measure or consider these changes affecting sustainability into the sovereign waters of the UK and in fisheries, and whether this can be extrapolated to enhance the role of the UK at international fora.

Firstly, fishing out of UK waters on board British flagged ships needs to be sustainable, complying with both UK legislation and the requirements by the nation that granted the fishing licences. Since the UK is a developed nation, these fishing vessels should be a paragon, because if these activities are not carried out in a sustainable manner it may result in poverty or imbalance to the coastal states. This is one of the potential consequences of industrial fisheries, carried out in EEZs when the means to control of the activity are not coordinated.[12]

Secondly, fisheries in UK waters need to be sustainable, when carried out by UK-flagged or foreign-flagged fishing vessels. In this regard, the sea fishing licences granted by the UK should also take into consideration how the flag States intend to implement sustainability. At UK level there is a duty to protect local fishermen and their communities, because if fish stocks go down, partly due to the activity of large commercial fishing vessels, local fishermen dedicated to artisanal fisheries will have to consider other alternatives that might result in a lower income and higher risks.

11 M Nunez, L Perez-Rojas, L Sciberras and E Silva, 'Grounds for a safety level approach in the development of long-lasting regulations based on costs to reduce fatalities for sustaining industrial fishing vessel fleets' 113 (2020) *Marine Policy* 10386, <https://doi.org/10.1016/j.marpol.2019.103806>.

12 D J McCauley, C Jablonicky, E H Allison, C D Golden, F H Joyce and D Kroosma, 'Wealthy countries dominate industrial fisheries' 4 (2018) 8 *Science Advances*, eaau2161. DOI: 10.1126/sciadv.aau2161.

All of the above implies the need to provide measurable sustainability in the economic, societal and environmental dimensions and working through cooperative approaches to guarantee the future of the sector. At the national level there will be new opportunities when the devolved quotas may be redistributed in the UK and help boost local economies. At the international level the UK can enhance its role at UN agencies dealing with fisheries activities, such as the Food and Agriculture Organization (FAO), the International Labour Organization (ILO) and the International Maritime Organization (IMO), whose missions are related to food, health and working conditions, safety and marine environmental pollution prevention, respectively, where the European Commission has been claiming exclusive competence, assisting in the development of a framework to contribute towards the Sustainable Development Goals of 2030 (SDGs).

In terms of drawback, the UK Fisheries Governance regime may find it difficult to frame detailed policy at the national level due to the particular emphasis on biological and ecosystems indicators that might not address the essential issue of managing fisheries in all dimensions. The UK Administrations need to strike the right balance with a high coordination effort since the risk of devolving powers to different administrations may lead to different interpretations of sustainability in Scotland, Wales or Northern Ireland.

In the UK, the responsibilities pertaining to the sector are spread across a number of ministries, e.g., safety under the Maritime and Coastguard Agency (MCA), Department for Transport. This helps avoid paternalistic approaches, which may occur when responsibility falls under one Ministry of Fisheries. As an example, the White Paper mentions the need to consider fishermen's safety, and the exemplary tasks carried out by the MCA and the Marine Accident Investigation Branch (MABI) have been outstanding for the last 30 years. Their role will be now equally important; however, it seems that the financial assistance to achieve a good management in all dimensions will be shared among administrations at national or regional level. In this regard, if the focus is mainly on fisheries, the social aspects of the industry have the potential of being overlooked. Once this point is reached, silos are created and the possibility to develop a very much needed capacity becomes more difficult. It would also affect the way to integrate sustainability in the overall picture of ocean governance from the coastal communities to the limit of the EEZs.

In the implementation of a holistic approach, which includes the Fisheries Act of 2020 as a main element, considering the special focus needed on coastal fishing communities, and the administrations' needs, a bottom-up approach using performance indicators would allow measuring the level of sustainability within UK waters. This enables the UK to take into account the above-mentioned challenges in a harmonised manner, avoiding silos as much as possible and being able to measure sustainability at national level. As an example of how this could be achieved, one could turn to the readily available indicators such as the Fish Performance Indicators (FPIs) developed by Anderson et al., which are used by the World Bank in relation to different communities both in developed and developing countries.[13] This approach helps to evaluate how management approaches interact with resource, community and market conditions not only to assure stock health, but also to create economic and community benefits, considering also the environment. This approach could also be used by the UK to assist FAO, ILO and the IMO in measuring sustainability at international fora.

The FPIs stress that data availability is a problem and needs to be substituted with qualitative analysis carried out by suitable experts. To serve its purpose the qualitative analysis could be converted into quantitative indicators by the UK at a later stage. The FPIs are divided into enabling factors, which act as inputs, and assess the country to determine output indicators as a result of the evaluation of the community, with a total of 68 indicators using a scale of 1 to 5. These indicators offer a sound assessment instrument for measuring the fishery-derived benefits created not only in the fish stock in the water, but also in the harvest and post-harvest sectors and fishing communities in accordance with the World Bank's emphasis on the triple bottom line and the importance of an integrated ecosystem management approach that can be used to measure the achievement of the respective goals under the United Nations 2030 Agenda for Sustainable Development Goals (SDG 2030).

Figure 9.1 was developed in relation to the implementation of national requirements and FAO/ILO/IMO conventions, which are also connected with the SDG 2030 after a suitable analysis of all Inter Agency Expert Group on SDGs (IAEG-SDGs) Tier I, II and III indicators. In addition to the above outputs, there was a need to consider the suitable inputs or enablers. In this regard, Figure 9.2 was developed as a simplification of the PFIs for the purpose of this chapter.

The inputs or enablers are primarily related to the countries themselves and also allow for the translation into indicators for a top-bottom approach. The concepts of spatial management, level of chronic pollution and governance quality together with the GDP allow for a better connection to SDGs, such as SDG 17 (partnership for the goals), which could measure the collaboration between the UK and the devolved authorities.

Bearing in mind the above, the sustainability of the UK fisheries sector could be established integrating the local communities around the country. The process would need to be iterative so that the inputs representing the performance of a country in terms of sustainability reflect the status of the individual communities.

13 J L Anderson et al., 'The Fishery Performance Indicators: A Management Tool for Triple Bottom Line Outcomes' (2015A), PLOS, <https://doi.org/10.1371/journal.pone.0122809> accessed 12 December 2019; see also J L Anderson et al., 'Economic, environmental and social evaluation of Africa's small fisheries' (2015B), World Bank, wbGROUP report N 955557-glb.

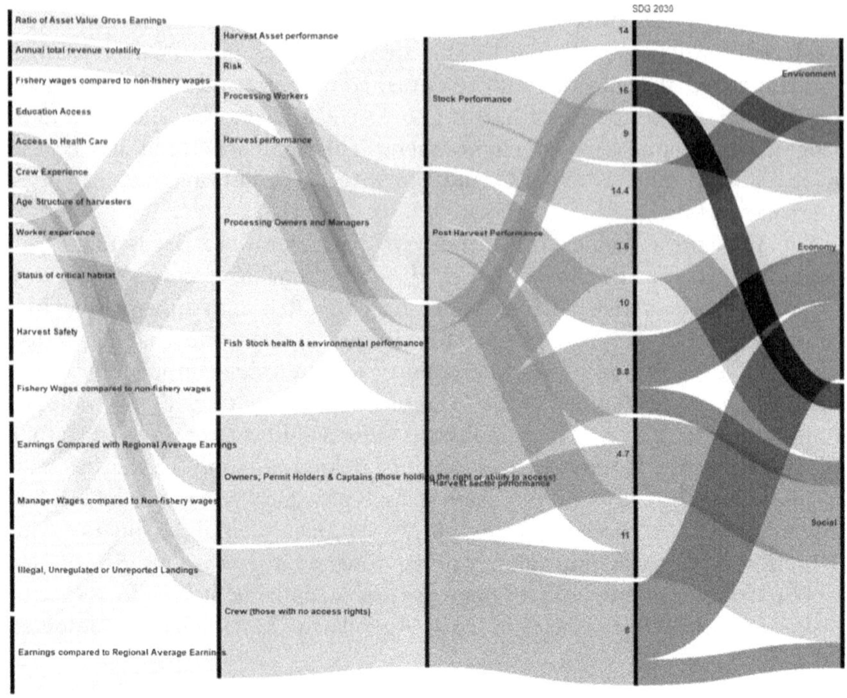

Figure 9.1 Output indicators with alluvial flow towards SDG 2030.
Source: Copyright Miguel Núñez Sánchez

Once these metrics for the high seas sustainability have been selected, there are some inputs for consideration that will catalyse conditions to incentivise socio-ecologically sustainable fisheries. In this regard the effort from the UK should be focused in the achievement of high markings of these indicators, and this needs to be done through careful coordination without creating an unnecessary burden on UK fishermen. Finally, the UK may promote its achieved sustainability in fisheries and be consistent with the Fisheries Act.

Options for Change Post-Brexit: Where Next?[14]

The UK has a number of key objectives for fisheries post-Brexit. However, although change is possible, we need to be realistic and honest about the extent of changes. Much will depend upon goodwill and the ability to compromise in light of the wider fishing and trade interests at stake, as the challenges of negotiating Brexit and the first rounds of annual fisheries negotiations post-Brexit have shown. In the second part of this contribution, the author outlines

14 This section takes from the speech delivered by Richard Barnes (University of Lincoln, University of Tromsø) in session 1 of the workshop.

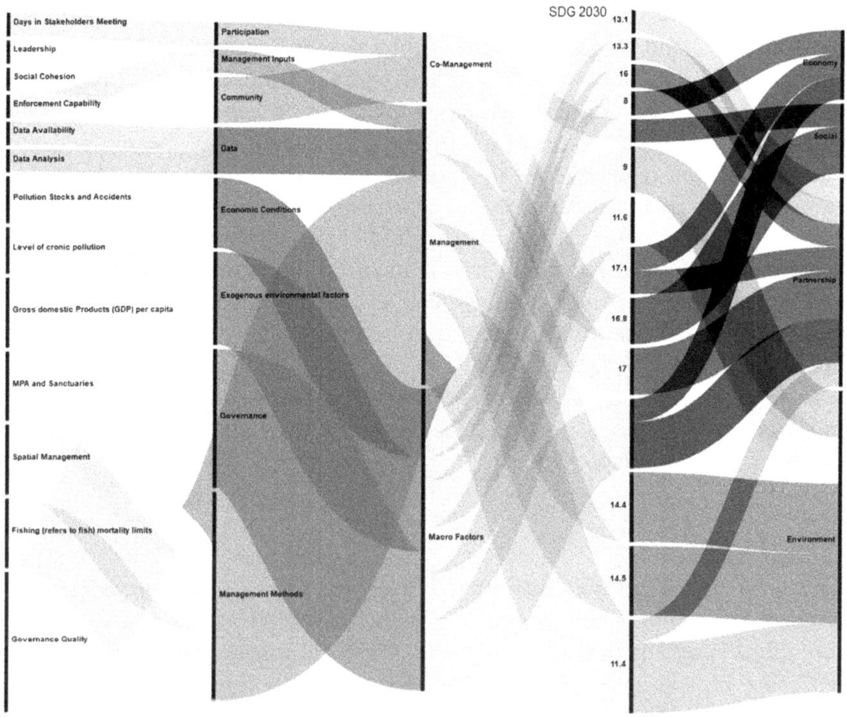

Figure 9.2 Input indicators (enablers) with alluvial flow towards SDG 2030.
Source: Copyright Miguel Núñez Sánchez

some key lessons from Brexit and fisheries negotiations to show how key structural factors continue in fisheries management. In the third part, the author examines the avenues and barriers for change, focusing specifically on key elements of the TCA and the Fisheries Act 2020.

Future Fisheries Goals

There is no single statement of UK fisheries' overarching goals post-Brexit, but key goals can be derived from a range of instruments and commitments revealed in policy and regulatory fora.[15] These include, first and foremost, a fisheries management regime that is both sustainable and responsive to the local needs of UK fishing interests; in other words, improving the quality of the

15 See, for example, Defra, Sustainable fisheries for future generation (July 2018, Cm 9660); House of Lords European Union Committee, Beyond Brexit: Food, environment, energy, and health. 22nd Report of Session 2019–21 (23 March 2021, HL Paper 247); APPG on Fisheries, 'The Brexit Deal: How it affects fisheries', 7 January 2021, <https://www.fisheriesappg.org/blog/2021/1/7/the-brexit-deal-how-it-affects-fisheries> accessed 7 January 2021.

resource base and making better use of it. This also includes reducing the environmental and carbon footprint of the catch and seafood trade sectors, and improving food security across the fisheries sector. If nothing else, Brexit failed to deliver on quota and hamper market access, so addressing these failings will be critical to support the British finishing industry. This means increasing quota, including regular access to quota in third State waters, e.g., Norway.[16] Alongside this is the acute need to alleviate or mitigate barriers to seafood export.[17] Finally, some stability is required. It is only reasonable that a regulatory regime provides a stable environment within which to conduct fishing and trade. Fishermen and exporters need to plan and invest. Without having a reasonably clear sense of what regulatory demands or barriers may be placed upon them, this will be impossible.

In summary, the objectives of regulatory autonomy, a better resource base, more quota, easy access to markets and stability are ongoing goals. These are much the same as before Brexit.

Recent Lessons

The general consensus is that Brexit failed to deliver the expected fisheries windfall that was promised prior to Brexit, and maintained as an objective through the negotiations.[18] The expected windfall gains of taking back control fell short of what the industry expected in terms of increased quotas.[19] In addition to this, the export of fish to the EU is now slower and more difficult. For some seafood, e.g., live bivalve molluscs, this has been seriously curtailed.[20]

I suggest that there are four important lessons to be taken from the deal, and these should be borne in mind when we think about how best to achieve the ambitions that we have for the future management of fisheries in the UK. First, we need to be realistic. This deal seems poor because of the unrealistic expectations generated by politicians and a refusal to acknowledge the wider trade-

16 Notably, the UK and Norway failed to reach agreement on access and quota for 2021: See Defra in the Media, <https://deframedia.blog.gov.uk/2021/04/30/fisheries-negotiations-with-norway-concluded/> accessed 6 June 2021; see Environment, Food and Rural Affairs Committee, Seafood and Meat Exports to the EU, Eighth Report of the Session 2019–21 (29 April 2021, HC 1189).

17 See Environment, Food and Rural Affairs Committee, Seafood and Meat Exports to the EU ibid.

18 R Barnes, G Carpenter, B Stewart, S Walmsley and C Williams, 'The Brexit deal and fisheries – has reality attached the rhetoric?' unpublished manuscript on file with author.

19 See, e.g., SFF, 'Brexit deal falls far short of commitments and promises', 29 December 2020, <https://www.sff.co.uk/brexit-deal-falls-far-short-of-commitments-and-promises/> accessed 6 June 2021; NFFO, 'A letter to the prime Minister, Boris Johnson' 15 January 2021, <https://www.nffo.org.uk/a-letter-to-the-prime-minister-boris-johnson/> accessed 6 June 2021.

20 See Environment, Food and Rural Affairs Committee, Seafood and Meat Exports to the EU (n 17).

offs that would be needed to secure a trade deal. There was much rhetoric about the sea of opportunity, and potential gains of hundreds of thousands of tonnes of fish. However, the reality is quite different. I am currently working on a paper that shows that the overall change in quota is much lower than initially expected when you look at predicted landed weight and value – i.e., fish that are actually caught and not just quota on paper.[21] Whilst the headline figure remains a return of 25% of quota from the EU share enjoyed under the CFP, the reality is around 14% and 10% gain, respectively.

Second, although the UK sought to achieve the status of "independent coastal state", with the theoretical power to management exclusively its fisheries, this ambition was both a political and legal mirage.[22] The UK has always been an independent coastal State – but through political choice decided to manage this by way of cooperation under the CFP as part of the deal to be a member of the EU. It remains the case that most stocks in UK waters are shared, and so there was always going to be some degree of shared management or shared decision-making over access and quotas.[23] This is both a practical reality and a legal requirement – with duties to cooperate under the UNCLOS[24] and the United Nations Fish Stocks Agreement 1995,[25] and reinforced through regional fisheries agreements – including those entrenched in the Trade and Cooperation Agreement 2021.[26]

Third, fisheries cannot be separated from wider trade relationships. The UK sought to detach fisheries from trade, but the asymmetrical nature of the negotiations, and the overarching importance of securing some kind of trade deal meant that fisheries would always form part of a wider package deal. Indeed, it is arguable that fisheries are more firmly wedded to trade measures now than they were under the CFP, since it is explicitly linked to trade measures in the TCA. Here unilateral changes to agree access/quota measures, or a general failure to comply with the TCA provisions on fisheries, may result in a range of retaliatory trade measures.[27]

Finally, it has become all too clear that negotiating change in fisheries is a difficult and time-consuming process. Agreement on the detail of fisheries was only reached at the last minute.[28] And post-Brexit agreements on TAC/quotas

21 R Barnes, G Carpenter, B Stewart, S Walmsley and C Williams (n 18).

22 See The UK in a Changing Europe, Fisheries and Brexit (June 2020), <https://ukandeu.ac.uk/wp-content/uploads/2020/06/Fisheries-and-Brexit.pdf> accessed 6 June 2021.

23 Ibid.

24 UNCLOS (n 7).

25 Agreement for the Implementation of the Provisions of the United Nations Convention on the Law of the Sea of 10 December 1982 Relating to the Conservation and Management of Straddling Fish Stocks and Highly Migratory Fish Stocks, adopted 4 August 1995, in force 11 December 2001, 2167 UNTS 3.

26 TCA (n 3), Heading Five: Fisheries.

27 TCA ibid., Arts. 501 and 506.

28 N Morris, 'Brexit deal was delayed by last minute blunder over fishing quotas', iNews, 25 December 2020, <https://inews.co.uk/news/brexit/trade-deal-delayed-last-minute-blunder-fishing-quotas-808459> accessed 7 June 2021.

between the UK and EU have taken five months to determine.[29] And the UK/Norway failed to agree any TACs and quotas for 2021. Although this may become easier over time and as new compromises are reached, there will be continuing challenges presented in efforts to change the status quo. Framework agreements are easy.[30] However, agreeing the detail on specific catch levels and quota is far more challenging.

In summary, this points towards the importance of the following principles when moving forward: cooperation, a holistic approach and the need for compromise and realism.

Avenues and Barriers to Change

Options for the development of fisheries management exists under the Fisheries Act, the Trade and Cooperation Agreement and other agreements. However, any such change within an individual legal arrangement must be sensitive to constraints that exist within related arrangements. For example, whilst wide powers to manage fisheries exist under the Fisheries Act, these must be consistent with UK's international commitments under the TCA, and measures adopted by the Specialised Committee on Fisheries. In short, we cannot ignore the interconnectedness of issues and legal regimes.

Given the general dissatisfaction with the fisheries settlement, there are four areas where one might expect pressure for change: access, quotas, flagging and new technical regulations.

First, access to waters. Although the Fisheries Act restricts the access of foreign fishing vessels to UK fishery limits, access is permitted when vessels are licensed or access is permitted under an international agreement.[31] Although the power of exclusion exists, this is restricted by the TCA, which establishes rights of access into UK waters for EU vessels.[32] Access to waters is contingent upon the outcome of annual negotiations and generally follows from the agreed distribution of fishing opportunities. However, such negotiations should normally result in access to EEZ to catch fish in accordance with the share of stocks set out in the TCA, which is now locked in. For non-quota species access continues to be in line with the level of catch during a reference period 2012–2016, and for waters between 6–12 m, access is at a level that qualifying vessels enjoyed as of 31 December 2020.[33]

29 NFFO, UK-EU Fisheries Agreement for 2021, 7 June 2021, <https://www.nffo.org.uk/uk-eu-fisheries-agreement-for-2021/> accessed 7 June 2021.

30 See R Barnes, 'Framework Agreement on Fisheries between the United Kingdom of Great Britain and Northern Ireland and the Kingdom of Norway' 36 (2021) *International Journal of Marine and Coastal Law* 1–10.

31 Fisheries Act 2020, <https://www.legislation.gov.uk/ukpga/2020/22/contents/enacted> accessed 8 June 2021, ss. 12, 13 and 17.

32 TCA (n 3), Article 500, Specific access arrangements relating to the Bailiwick of Guernsey, the Bailiwick of Jersey and the Isle of Man under Art. 502.

33 TCA (n 3), Art. 500(4).

Second, if access follows quota, then can quota be changed and so impact access? Under the Fisheries Act, there is the power to determine quota.[34] However, this only concerns domestic distribution of quota and the UK discretion to determine quota exclusively is again circumscribed by the TCA. It is generally understood that the TCA fixed quota shares for a five-year period, which will gradually restore around 15% of quota in UK waters to UK vessels.[35] At the end of this period, it is claimed that the UK can further adjust quota. However, this runs counter to the text of the TCA. The use of the term "onwards" to describe fishing quota at the end of the five-year transition period suggests that the division of quota settled in 2026 will continue as long as the TCA remains in force. It also runs counter to the wider objective of stabilising fishing and trading rights after an adjustment period. There is no provision in the TCA that supports any unilateral changing of quota beyond 2026. This is a matter to be determined in annual negotiations. If one side seeks to unilaterally determine quota at variance to existing levels, then this requires that party to notify the other party of changes to the level and conditions of access. However, this is subject to retaliatory measures.[36]

There is nothing to prevent ad hoc exchanges of quota in the TCA. This was common practice under the CFP, where adjustments of quota were often made to accommodate variations in bycatch. In theory, this could be done in return for payments for reductions in quota or to enable quota swaps. However, there is yet no mechanism to enable this under the TCA. We will have to await the outcome of decisions by the Specialised Committee on Fisheries to see if and how this is possible. The Specialised Committee has a wide mandate to adopt conservation and management measures.[37]

Third, there may be scope to change UK rules on the flagging of fishing vessels. The EU principle of free movement meant that EU citizens and businesses were able to register fishing vessels in the UK and take advantage of opportunities to secure UK fishing quota.[38] Foreign ownership of UK vessels remains permitted under the Merchant Shipping Act and Regulations. In theory, it is open for the UK to change the conditions for the registration of vessels in the UK, to restrict ownership by EU companies and persons, and exclude foreign ownership of quota.[39] Indeed, this has been advocated by some in the industry.[40]

34 Fisheries Act 2020 (n 31), s. 23.

35 This is set out in the TCA (n 5), Annexes 35 and 36.

36 TCA (n 3), 501 and 506, described as compensatory and remedial measures, respectively.

37 TCA (n 3), Art. 508.

38 See R Churchill and D Owen, *The EC Common Fisheries Policy* (Oxford University Press, 2010), pp. 202ff.

39 See European Parliament, *Research for PECH Committee – Common Fisheries Policy and Brexit* (June 2017), <https://www.europarl.europa.eu/RegData/etudes/STUD/2017/601981/IPOL_STU(2017)601981_EN.pdf> accessed 8 June 2021.

40 See UK to toughen economic link requirement, <https://mag.hookandnet.com/2021/04/09/2021-04flagships/content.html> accessed 9 June 2021.

Moreover, under the TCA, the UK reserved the right to introduce new conditions that could restrict flagging of vessels to British companies or nationals, or require that the crew of a UK-flagged vessel be British nationals.[41] Additionally, the UK reserves the right to limit licences granting the right to fish in UK territorial waters to UK-flagged vessels. Although this power exists, it would be surprising if the UK made any radical changes to ship registration for two reasons. First, it would run counter to the idea of global Britain and the idea that the UK wants to seek foreign investment in the UK industry. Second, and perhaps more compellingly, such changes could amount to a de facto and de jure removal of legitimately held quotas. As we have seen in the past, any such changes would likely result in legal challenge.[42]

A final point is to note that under both the Fisheries Act and the TCA, the UK enjoys extensive powers to set management and other technical measures for fisheries in its waters. However, it is unlikely that such powers can be exercised as freely as the UK might desire. First, measures must be consistent with existing bodies of law and given that much of the CFP remains part of domestic law, future domestic fisheries law will develop under the long shadow of a EU law for a time.[43] In order to ensure smooth transition to any new rules, changes will be mostly evolutionary. Second, it would be impractical for the UK and EU to adopt widely divergent regulatory regimes. Indeed, as the EU Scrutiny Committee recently observed, the EU is revising its Control Regulation, and this means UK vessels fishing in EU waters will need to comply with any changes.[44] This may include remote electronic monitoring, CCTV and controls on pre-notification of landings, and it will entail costs. However, it will also give rise to practical problems if different standards apply to vessels depending upon whether they are in UK or EU waters. Third, to maintain access to EU markets, UK catch will still have to comply with EU health and safety standards. The UK is now a third country and it will have to meet the EU's robust conditions for access to its markets.[45] As such, future regulation of fisheries needs to be sensitive to wider developments in EU fisheries regulations.

Brexit represents a significant failure to deliver on over-inflated political promises. It also represents a high watermark in ignorance of the wider legal, economic and political realities that shape fisheries management. This points towards the importance of the following principles or approaches when considering change: *cooperation, holistic approaches, compromise and realism.* Whilst

41 UK reservation No 13 'Fishing and Water' TCA (n 3), at p. 1583.

42 See *United Kingdom Association of Fish Producer Organisations v. Secretary of State for Environment, Food and Rural Affairs* [2013] EWHC 1959 (Admin).

43 This was done under the European Union (Withdrawal) Act 2018, c. 16, <https://www.legislation.gov.uk/ukpga/2018/16/contents/enacted> accessed 9 June 2021.

44 House of Commons European Union Scrutiny Committee, *Second Report of Session 2021–22* (26 May 2021, HC 121-ii), part 4.

45 See House of Lords European Union Committee (n 15).

there is scope to change and improve fisheries post-Brexit, failure to accept these principles or approaches can only compound the problems Brexit delivered for the fishing industry.

Key Difficulties Facing the English Fishing Industry Post-Brexit[46]

The fishing industry is prone to uncertainty and risk. Every year plans are made and investments are planned within a context where the data underlying policy decisions is often out of date or lacking. This gap increases risk and also stresses the need to mitigate those risks. Whilst a framework of stability is important, flexibility is essential.

For most people, the obvious manifestation of all this is the difficulty that is now attached to exporting to the EU. Exports are very important to the UK fishing industry since the UK largely exports what it catches and consumes what it imports. As of 1 January 2021, largely due to the lack of a Sanitary and Phytosanitary Agreement (SPS Agreement), approximately 10% has been added to the cost of exporting, which means that UK fish are less competitive and may take longer to arrive. From an extremely low point, volumes have been rising over the first quarter of the year, both because of a relaxation in Covid-19 restrictions and the gradual reopening of some hospitality operations.

Larger companies have been doing better – both because of their larger resources and because their logistics are simpler. Smaller fishermen have not done as well. They have been particularly badly hit by the Covid-19 closures, although direct sales have increased. Coping with a lot of paperwork is not their forte (and there is a shortage of agents). In addition, finding any hauler who is willing to take on groupage deliveries is problematic at the present time. While the situation may well improve – the UK is talking of digitisation of the whole customs process by October 2022, which would reduce the possibility of errors and therefore delays – the profitability of exports has been reduced, leaving the industry in a less positive position to respond to Covid-19 and other challenges.

One of the major drivers for Brexit in the fishing industry was the belief that it would lead to a greater share of fishing opportunities. The TCA, revealed on 24 December 2020, in fact, provided far less than was expected, meaning that there was less available to mitigate the market effects. In addition, for the first time, non-quota stocks were brought into the agreement. These had traditionally been seen as an escape valve for the fishing industry when fishing opportunities for pressure stocks (quota stocks) were reduced. In fact, England is now responsible for 55% of the value of total landings. The TCA introduces tonnage limits on the non-quota stocks that are fished in each other's waters. Whilst these are to be based on the period 2012–2016, the UK would prefer

46 This section takes from the speech delivered by Elizabeth Bourke (National Federation of Fishermen's Organisations) in session 2 of the workshop.

the period 2016–2019 when prices were increasing, as were volumes of exports. There are also difficulties over the evidence base since there was no obligation to report landings for the small-scale coastal fleet, and under the CFP vessels were not obliged to carry REM under 12 metres. These matters are unlikely to be resolved before 2022–2023.

For quota stocks the problems lie with the provision assigning the exchange of quota to the State level – although it is understandable why the State should wish to have control over any extra quota, but at the same time giving up quota for dubious benefit (political or otherwise) is not universally popular. In the past, as stocks moved northwards – there are calls for the realignment of management areas – fishing patterns changed and generations of fishermen changed their target fisheries and gears and vessels, and as a result, in the UK, the quota held by boats no longer matched their operations. As a result, the producer organisations (POs) organised exchanges of quota among themselves, registering them with the MMO for approval, and at times they undertook exchanges with POs in other Member States. These exchanges could take place at any time of the year, and in the case of Norway were negotiated at the time of the Annual Agreement in December so that they could take effect at once and take advantage of the seasonality of cod in Norwegian waters.

Under the TCA exchanges and transfers will only take place towards the end of the year when it becomes clear that they will not be fished: this ignores the whole problem of seasonality. It has become clear that operating this provision causes problems – both for the UK and for certain Member States. It is likely that, once it has been constituted, the issue will be delegated to the Specialised Committee on Fisheries: but it is unlikely that it will be resolved immediately, so an important flexibility has effectively been lost at least until 2022 (and possibly 2023).

The concentration at State level is an important indication of the UK's insistence on "taking back control" and regulatory autonomy as an independent coastal State – ICS.

The CFP was a major cause of dissatisfaction with the EU among UK fishermen, largely because of its inflexibility and also because it seemed to pay little attention to the feasibility of implementation. Although much of the CFP was passed into retained legislation, the Fisheries Act 2020 was supposed to provide a semi-blueprint for future fisheries management. In fact, it provides more of a menu than a blueprint and was based on the assumption that the UK would be receiving many more fishing opportunities and would therefore be faced with the luxury of choice as to what it would do.

Of particular interest to the fishing industry is the provision relating to over-quota landings and the possibility of adopting something more similar to the Norwegian system, taking away any profit but allowing mixed fisheries to continue. The elaborate list of the possibilities as to how additional quota may be apportioned appears somewhat hollow now – especially to the inshore fleet. In addition, the possible introduction of UK landing requirements of 70% as outlined in the Economic Link consultation are likely to have an impact on profitability, whilst it is unclear how far they could aid in the regeneration of coastal communities.

The reality is that 2026 seems a long way away and that the fishing industry has been downgraded in importance: the fishing industry does not fit the technical/digital/green image that the Government now seeks to project. The policy announcements concerning Highly Protected Marine Areas and whole site closures, 40 GW of offshore wind farms, floating wind farms, and the proliferation of cables (which are not always sufficiently buried) mean that displacement is likely, and, whether or not fishing opportunities are available, they may well not be accessible – particularly to the small-scale coastal fleet.

In addition, the absence of a clear dispute mechanism means that relations with the Devolved Administrations over the Joint Fisheries Statement and the Fisheries Management Plans are likely to be difficult. It is possible, however, that the Government will use affirmative resolutions should the Devolved Administrations seek to change any primary legislation.

The elaboration of a new Fisheries Management Plan will need to try and satisfy a number of very different interests with very little slack to accommodate them. At the same time, the paradigm has shifted and politics has become more important in the UK at the same time trust has diminished among the fishing community. This begs the question: what happens in 2026?

Always assuming that things do not fall apart over the Northern Ireland Protocol, the provisions of the TCA relating to fishing opportunities are set to expire in 2026 and the question inevitably arises as to what, if anything, will take its place. It is clear that the EU does not envisage any change – that in fact any alteration could lead to countervailing measures. On the other hand, the UK fishing industry cannot wait for more change. By then, however, there may have been other changes in relation to the following:

- A more cooperative ambience may prevail and the schism over convergence and divergence may have had time to cool;
- Climate change and the green agenda may have led to improved cooperation;
- The small-scale coastal fleet may have declined due to problems over markets and access;
- Coastal communities will need to have started to find alternative types of jobs – although offshore windfarms and turbines will not require the same level of maintenance, employment and skills as the oil industry in the past; and
- The final question is what all these changes will have done to prices for fisheries products and what sort of profitability can be expected for the remaining vessels in the future, because, essentially, we want our fleet to have a future.

A Critique of the Fisheries Act 2020 as a "Gold Standard Model" for Sustainability[47]

As part of the preparation for the post-Brexit future, the Department for Environment, Food and Rural Affairs (Defra) published in 2018 a White Paper,[48] which laid out the proposed changes to fisheries policy and introduced for consultation a draft Fisheries Bill that would be the means for delivering these. In the foreword, Michael Gove made the point that, as an independent coastal State, the UK would be free to: "promote a more competitive, profitable and sustainable fishing industry … setting a gold standard for sustainable fishing around the world".[49]

The Bill, described as being a "significant change to the way fisheries are managed in the UK", had a number of specific provisions that would achieve this change by, *inter alia*, enabling the UK to: take back control of access to its waters, with equal access for UK vessels throughout; improve environmental protection, making use of scientific advice; introduce quota schemes, reducing discards; and develop policy statements … *applying sustainability principles and objectives.*[50]

The Fisheries Act 2020 received Royal Assent on 23 November 2020. It is the sustainability principles that should be at the heart of the legislation, but closer examination shows that these are, in reality, paid only lip service as opposed to the political objectives of resource access and allocation, which are the main concern of the legislation. The critical issues of sustainable resource use that this paper identifies are: the sustainability objective; the relevance of precautionary principle; and the use of the concept of maximum sustainable yield (MSY) as the guarantor of sustainable management.

The Sustainability Objective

Section 1 (1) of the Bill lists the "Fisheries Objectives", which are intended to be the focus of the "Fisheries Statements", which will lay out how these objectives are to achieved. Each of these is seen as equal with the other. The objectives are:

a the sustainability objective;
b the precautionary objective;
c the ecosystem objective;
d the scientific evidence objective;
e the bycatch objective;
f the equal access objective;

47 This section takes from the speech delivered by Seán Marriott (University of Lincoln) in session 2 of the workshop.
48 Defra (n 15).
49 Defra (n 15), at 6.
50 Defra (n 15), at 16.

g the national benefit objective; and
h the climate change objective.

During its passage through Parliament, a number of amendments were proposed. Amongst these was Lord Kreb's amendment, proposing that: "The sustainability objective is the prime fisheries objective" (passed by 310–251 votes).[51] In proposing his amendment, he said: "the Bill as drafted allows for the possibility of short-term economic and social factors overruling environmental sustainability in making trade-offs".

In challenging the amendment, Lord Gardiner of Kimble, for the Government, stressed that the wording of the Objectives Section: "gives equal weight to environmental, social and economic considerations. That follows the concept of the three pillars of sustainable development, a concept that is well established in international law and practice."[52]

The "Three Pillars" argument was repeated later, in the Commons, by Victoria Prentice, for Defra, and the amendment was rejected.

The theoretical equivalence assigned to the eight Fisheries Objectives of the Act become a critical issue in relation to Section 7, which grants power to the "policy authorities" to depart from proposals in a Joint Fisheries Statement when making a fisheries management plan (under Section 6). Subsection 7 (4) allows for a change to a plan where there is a "relevant change of circumstances"; subsection 7 (7) lists these "relevant changes"; of particular significance is subsection 7 (7) (d): "available evidence relating to the social, economic or environmental elements of sustainable development."

This provides for the possibility of the sustainability objective being overturned by short-term political considerations relating to economic and social pressures.

The original criticism of the basis of sustainability remains: the policy objectives do not sit on three equal pillars; they sit on eight. It is clear that the Government has chosen to present these objectives as part of the sustainable development discourse, where the subject of sustainability is development. But the subject of natural resource sustainability is the resource, not its development. The analogy is not three equal pillars holding up sustainability but rather a triangle of forces, at the apex of which rests sustainable development. But the base of the triangle is the sustainable resource upon which the others rest. If the resource fails, then so do the economic and social objectives.

There is a clear contrast between the UK Act and the Australian *Fisheries Management Act* 1991 (as amended at 2017) where, under Section 3A, titled *Principles of ecologically sustainable development*, subsections (c) and (d), it states:

51 E Ares, *Fisheries Act 2020*, House of Commons Library Briefing Paper No 8994 1 December 2020, <https://researchbriefings.files.parliament.uk/documents/CBP-8994/CBP-8994.pdf> accessed 8 June 2021, at. 12.

52 E Ares ibid., at pp. 12–13.

a the principle of inter-generational equity … the environment is maintained or enhanced for the benefit of future generations
b the conservation of biological diversity and ecological integrity should be a fundamental consideration in decision-making;

It is these principles that are missing from the Fisheries Act.

The Precautionary Principle

Under Section 1 (3), the Act defines the precautionary principle as:

a the precautionary approach to fisheries management is applied; and
b exploitation of marine stocks restores and maintains populations of harvested species above biomass levels capable of producing maximum sustainable yield.

This wording is a curious choice because it fails to make explicit the key point of the principle that the "absence of adequate scientific information should not justify postponing or failing to take management measures";[53] the wording here is taken from the 2013 Common Fisheries Policy Regulation, which bases its definition on Art. 6 of the 1995 *United Nations Fish Stocks Agreement* (FSA).[54] The reference to the FSA is crucial because, in fisheries terms, the FSA is the key document for defining the precautionary principle. Annex II of the FSA specifies the precautionary reference points "as a guide for fishery management", and it is made clear that these are stock-specific. Again, comparison with the Australian *Fisheries Management Act* 1991 is instructive. Under Section 17 (5C), it is a requirement that fishery management plans (FMPs): "for a fishery affecting straddling fish stocks, highly migratory fish stocks or ecologically related fish stocks … must set out stock-specific reference points".

The absence of any mention of reference points in the Fisheries Act 2020, particularly within the sections dealing with management plans – instead the Act only provides, under subsection 6(2)(c) for "*an indicator or indicators to be used for monitoring the effectiveness of the plan*". This is inadequate especially for stocks being managed at MSY.

53 Regulation 1380/2013 of the European Parliament and of Council of 11 December 2013 on the Common Fisheries Policy, amending Council Regulations (EC) No 1954/2003 and (EC) No 1224/2009 and repealing Council Regulations (EC) No 2371/2002 and (EC) No 639/2004 and Council Decision 2004/585/EC, Art. 4(8).

54 Agreement for the Implementation of the Provisions of the United Nations Convention on the Law of the Sea of 10 December 1982 relating to the Conservation and Management of Straddling Fish Stocks and Highly Migratory Fish Stocks (n 25).

Maximum Sustainable Yield

There is insufficient space here to rehearse the arguments against using MSY as the principal management tool.[55] Suffice it to say that the MSY for virtually all the stocks – or straddling or migrating – within the UK EEZ must be entirely theoretical. In any event the prospect of the EU ever choosing to set a total allowable catch (TAC) that would allow these stocks to recover their "natural" MSY is barely within the realms of the possible. Any FMP made under the Fisheries Act 2020 should take a more realistic and ecologically risk-weighted level. I have been developing a new approach that I call *Available Surplus*, which can be defined as the available surplus production of a stock's biomass, without compromising its reproductive capacity, at prevailing environmental conditions, and subject to various caveats, including Art. 6 of the FSA.

In any event, the choice of MSY argues that Defra have not moved their sustainability sympathies in concert with current resource management thinking, let alone with ecosystem-based management.

Final word

The Fisheries Act 2020 is undoubtedly a suitable vehicle for short-term policy statements, but it is not designed, even intended, as a "gold-standard" model for fishery management. It is as functionally a model for the political control of fisheries as the CFP, and as likely to be similarly incapable of sustainable management.

The Act should be seen as an opportunity lost for creating a model for sustainable fisheries management legislation.

Perspectives from Northern Ireland[56]

For the Northern Ireland fishing industry and its dependent coastal communities there are many expected and unexpected consequences emerging from the UK's exit from the EU. A number of these are common to many economic sectors that were highly integrated into European systems, such as access to labour, international collaborations and industry participation in decision-making. Issues of particular importance to the fisheries sector are quota share, access and trade. Below I present a Northern Ireland perspective on these three issues.

55 For a clear explanation of the issues, see B Mesnil, 'The Hesitant Emergence of Maximum Sustainable Yield (MSY) in Fisheries Policies in Europe' 36 (2012) *Marine Policy* 473.

56 This section takes from the speech delivered by Rod Cappell (Poseidon Aquatic Resource Management) in session 2 of the workshop.

Quota

Fish stocks that are managed with quota make up 77% of the total tonnage of landings by the UK fleet and two-thirds of the value.[57] Some commercially important fisheries are not managed by quota, including scallops, the UK's third most valuable fishery, and other important shellfish species like crab and lobster. It is also worth noting that the dependence on quota species differs between the nations of the UK: there is a high dependence on quota species in Scotland and Northern Ireland (NI), but for England it is about 50/50 quota to non-quota and less than that in Wales. The national fleets most dependent on quota were very disappointed by the modest UK quota increases resulting from the TCA, particularly in comparison to the proportion of total catches that are caught in UK waters.

A remaining concern for the Northern Irish industry is how this new UK quota will be allocated between the devolved nations. The allocation between UK nations has only been resolved for 2021, with around 90% of allocation based on the existing quota holdings per nation. Northern Ireland operators hold 8.4% of UK fishing quota. By 2026, when the full agreed transition of EU quota to the UK is made, based on recent values, Northern Ireland could be allowed to catch an extra £20 million worth of fish each year.[58] That is a gain of around 30% in value terms as there are increases in the relatively valuable prawn fishery. But only around half the catch by the Northern Irish fleet is landed into Northern Ireland and that is because only 20% of Northern Ireland's quota holdings comprise fish and shellfish stocks in the Irish Sea. Eighty per cent of the fishing opportunities held by Northern Irish interests is quota for stocks in the West of Scotland, in the North Sea and in the South-West approaches.

Northern Ireland favours continuing the allocation based on existing quota holdings, but other administrations may push for alternatives, particularly if pressured by their industries who are still smarting from the TCA outcome. Any method that apportions additional quota by geographical area will disadvantage Northern Ireland, because it has a relatively small marine zone compared with other nations. There is no certainty of the basis for intra-UK allocation in future years. Beyond 2026, the allocation between the UK and EU is also uncertain as a new deal is to be negotiated.

57 Marine Management Organisation (MMO) 'UK Sea Fisheries Statistics 2019' (2019), <https://assets.publishing.service.gov.uk/government/uploads/system/uploads/attachment_data/file/920679/UK_Sea_Fisheries_Statistics_2019_-_access_checked-002.pdf> accessed 10 April 2021.

58 Northern Ireland Fishermen's Federation submission to the Northern Ireland Assembly, Jan 2021, <http://aims.niassembly.gov.uk/officialreport/reportssearchresultsmoereport.aspx?&eveDate=2021/01/19&rID=322769&hwcID=3221032&aID=25071&pg=3&eveid=12717&sesID=23&dID=0&init=I#3221032> accessed 12 June 2021.

Access

The Northern Irish fleet has experienced the challenges of new access arrangements in terms of both access to fishing grounds and also access to ports to land your catch. Taking the first of these, access to fishing grounds, Northern Irish and Irish vessels have historically fished in each other's waters as part of a *Voisinage* agreement in place since the mid 1960s allowing mutual access out to 6 nm. There was some disruption to this between 2016 and 2019 under legal challenge, but mutual inshore access for smaller vessels remains in place.

Beyond the 6-mile limit, the TCA has attempted to maintain business as usual, at least until 2026, including historic fishing in the 6-to-12-mile zone. But boats now have to be licensed by the respective national authorities and Northern Irish vessels waited months to receive these licences from Irish authorities. Some of the larger potters had to remove gear from Irish waters and such delays could disrupt the usual seasonal fishing patterns.

Northern Irish vessels are also used to landing their catch into Irish ports, either adjacent to Northern Ireland or when they fish further afield. Ports must be officially designated as landing ports with enforcement officers available to carry out the necessary checks on those landings. Northern Ireland had designated seven of its ports to facilitate landings by EU-registered boats. Initially, Ireland had only designated its two largest fishing ports for landings by UK vessels: Killybegs and Castletownbere. The Irish Government has since designated five further ports, but that still doesn't cover all the ports that Northern Irish vessels previously landed to.

Generally, access appears to be moving towards 'business as usual', but there is little incentive for Member State agencies to prioritise the additional administration required for UK vessels and issues resulting from administrative delays may emerge as seasonal fisheries begin. Again, at the end of the adjustment period in 2026, the debate over access will start again.

Trade

The seafood trade has been hit with the double-whammy of Brexit and the Covid-19 pandemic. It's difficult to fully separate the impacts of the two. What we do know to be Brexit-related is the increased paperwork and checks required, which all amount to a cost for operators and administrations.

While not considered as exports or imports for Northern Ireland, the trade route between Northern Ireland and mainland Britain is the main seafood trade route. Fresh whitefish and nephrops are brought in, with landings of various species shipped out to buyers in Great Britain. This Northern Ireland–Great Britain trade was subject to extensive disruption in the first months of 2021 and it still faces additional costs with more paperwork and checks as a result of the Northern Ireland Protocol. Outside this substantial intra-UK trade, Northern Ireland is a net exporter of seafood, exporting £62m of seafood outside the

UK in 2019 and importing half that (£31m).[59] For exports to the EU, Northern Ireland's operators have a slight advantage over other British operators as Northern Ireland remains within the single market under the Northern Ireland Protocol. In practical terms, this means that there is less paperwork without the need for Export Health Certificates and Catch Certificates for landings into Northern Ireland being exported to the EU. However, a catch certificate is still needed if one lands outside of Northern Ireland, and if exporting via Great Britain then an export health certificate will be required.[60] Northern Ireland's operators have not totally avoided the additional administrative burden, but for direct EU exports they do have less paperwork and less risk of rejection or lengthy delays than their counterparts in Great Britain, a critical factor in exporting fresh seafood. A steep rise in shipping costs, which have been further compounded by the Covid-19 crisis and now recovery-fuelled inflation, mean that many input costs have risen significantly and there are also delays in supplies of gear and vessel parts, causing disruption.

Northern Ireland's unique status within the UK could be considered a benefit for an export-orientated seafood sector, but the extra costs for Northern Ireland–Great Britain trade reduces the benefits resulting from the Protocol, and there is mounting political pressure to change or remove the Protocol altogether. As with quota allocations and access, the trade challenges faced by the fisheries sector remain, and the future, even in the short term, is uncertain.

Brexit and Fisheries: An Irish Perspective[61]

Disruptor or partner?

The departure of the UK from the EU throws up many concerns and unknowns around what type of actor the UK will become in relation to fisheries management in the Northeast Atlantic. Will it seek to be a disruptor or pursue a path of being a partner in reaching fishery agreements with its neighbours?

For many coastal States in the Northeast Atlantic, fisheries represent a salient issue politically, economically, culturally and socially. It is a key reason why the Faroe Islands, Iceland and Norway never joined the EU, and why Greenland and the UK, to a lesser extent, left it.

It is this level of saliency, in particular the political perspective, that will likely shape the role the UK will take in the coming years. Like the tides, will the UK push and pull between being a disruptor or a partner?

59 DAERA *Fishing and Seafood Development Programme*, (2021) <https://www.daera-ni.gov.uk/publications/fsdp> accessed 12 June 2021.

60 DAERA, *Direct Landings - Journey Checklists* (2021) <https://www.daera-ni.gov.uk/articles/direct-landings-journey-checklists> accessed 21 June 2021.

61 This section takes from the speech delivered by Ciarán O'Driscoll (European Movement Ireland) in session 2 of the workshop.

However, while the jury is still out on what this role will be at present, the reality is that the UK is now another piece to many more puzzles that need to be solved around securing effective fisheries management. And when puzzles remain unsolved, waters do not settle, and it is fishing communities that suffer, where all too often sea fisheries is the sole economic pillar holding up a community.

For example, the dispute over mackerel in the early 2010s saw more than four years of failed negotiations between the various coastal States over setting TACs, before an agreement was reached. It brought considerable socio-economic instability in the Irish fishing industry due to the importance of the stock.

The Cost of Brexit

However, while many were anticipating losses as a result of Brexit, as by its nature Brexit is the upending of the status quo, they had not expected the level the financial losses in their share of stocks in UK waters.

Even Taoiseach Micheál Martin had admitted in December, after negotiations were concluded, that "there is a significant negative impact, particularly on the mackerel sector and prawns".[62]

One of the Irish fishing industry's leading news publications, the *Marine Times*, carried a by-line in its January 2021 edition that "the government has failed the fishing industry in the Brexit negotiations, leaving it facing a potentially disastrous situation".[63]

The economic cost of Brexit was spelled out in a January 2021 report published by Ireland's Department of Agriculture, Food and the Marine. With the assistance of the Marine Institute and An Bord Iascaigh Mhara, it estimated the losses Ireland would face under Brexit.[64]

It is expected to see a loss of around €42 million by 2026 as a result of losing 15% in the transfer process under the EU–UK Trade and Cooperation Agreement, with mackerel from the West of Scotland, some €27.5m, accounting for bulk of losses.

62 H McGee, V Clarke and M Hilliard, 'Brexit: Taoiseach concedes EU-UK deal will have negative impact on fishing industry' (2020) *The Irish Times*, 28 December 2020, <https://www.irishtimes.com/news/politics/brexit-taoiseach-concedes-eu-uk-deal-will-have-negative-impact-on-fishing-industry-1.4446471> accessed 24 June 2021.

63 M McCarthy and T McSweeney, 'Brexit deal will devastate fishing industry', *Marine Times Newspaper*, January 2021, <https://www.marinetimes.ie/ereader2021/marinetimes_012021.pdf> accessed 24 June 2021, at p. 4.

64 Department of Agriculture, Food and the Marine, *Preliminary Analysis of Reduction of Fisheries Quota Shares under EU/UK Trade and Cooperation Agreement* (2021), <https://www.gov.ie/en/publication/21e48-analysis-of-reduction-of-fisheries-quota-shares-under-euuk-trade-and-cooperation-agreement/> accessed 23 June 2021.

For many in the industry, this is another example of the Irish fishing industry suffering because of Ireland's EU membership. Just as Brexit resulted in a "bad deal" for them, so too did joining the then European Economic Community in 1973.

And perhaps this is the greatest cost of Brexit for Ireland's fishing industry, a deeper sense of trust being lost and eroded between it and EU and Irish State actors, which will only further exacerbate important relations.

Seafood Processing and Brexit: Scottish Perspectives[65]

From a Scottish fishermen and processing point of view, the aspiration has always been to restore the opportunity to grow market share and to re-grow the industry that has over the past four decades gone into decline. Brexit brought along a new vision and a new opportunity. The outcome was not what the fishermen nor what the processing sector had anticipated. There are ongoing debates as to what implications the Brexit outcome will have over the next five years. Much work lies ahead. It is important to remain steadfast while bearing in mind that this is a big political issue. So far what has been brought to our attention is the differing views and standpoints of the various people, depending on where respective folks reside in each of the political sectors. That being said, there has been no argument with regard to the oil and gas that remains in the North Sea to be shared equally across EU nations. This is broadly owing to the fact that oil and gas is far more valuable than fish stocks because the latter are renewable resources and will continue to renew time and time again.

The rules and regulations under the CFP might have looked feasible in theory. However, in practice, fishermen have faced difficulties adhering to those. They can be viewed as counterproductive as they did not deliver on the objectives in a fitting manner. This resulted in fishermen turning against CFP and all that it stood for in so far as it created problems exporting to the EU, which has not been easy to resolve given that no fair and equal political platforms were created on which the fisheries sector could conduct trade and continue business as usual. The sector now has to adhere to the new red tape and bureaucratic system that they are subject to whilst the EU counterparts enjoy the grace and favour of a "free and open market". A more amicable outcome needs to be negotiated to strike a balance that is currently missing. This begs the question: who suffers in all of this? The answer is simple. The folks who are at the front of the industry, the fishermen, the coastal communities and the communities that are entirely dependent on fisheries business.

The other outcome of Brexit was access to a migrant-led labour workforce. Over the years, the fisheries community has relied heavily on migrant labour. That pool is no longer readily available, partly because of Covid-19, and by

65 This section takes from the speech delivered by Jimmy Buchan (Scottish Seafood Association) in session 2 of the workshop.

and large due to Brexit, as it was viewed as diminishing future opportunities. This has certainly led to repatriation whereby migrant workers have repatriated to their native homelands to seek out new career opportunities. Moving forward, this has the potential to create problems. There will certainly be shortages of manpower to process UK catches.

On a positive note, the UK Government has hinted that more investments will be made in the fishing industry with a view to transposing the industry to a more vibrant and green industry. It remains to be seen where the capital investment will go. It is important to focus on the 2025–2026 outcome and whether there will be a continued interest to revisit such a divisive political problem in the future. A sustainable income from a sustainable resource is the backbone of the UK's trade and economy. Realism needs to accompany all future debates, negotiations, actions and delivery on the Government's part. Given the importance of the trade market, politicians ought to consider removing barriers and hurdles for the people engaged in business activities. In terms of fisheries, there is a product for sale, manpower to carry out product marketing and interested clients that are willing to purchase it. What needs to be ensured is that the product can pass through the political bottleneck and enter the market without external interruptions.

10 Conclusions

Jonatan Echebarria Fernández, Tafsir Matin Johansson, Mitchell Lennan and Jon A. Skinner

Chapter 1 contextualised the book by outlining the diversity of the fishing industry across the nations of the UK, and the EU fishing industry as it pertains to fishing in UK waters. It is evident that the EU relies more on access to UK waters than UK vessels in EU waters. However, the UK industry relies on the EU heavily as its key export market. The importance of reciprocal access to both parties' waters and markets is evident, and Brexit has brought about serval difficulties in this regard.

Chapter 2 contains a pertinent contribution by Robin Churchill, setting out the applicable fisheries policy impacting the UK and EU prior to, during and after Brexit. The chapter outlines the fact that, despite now being responsible for managing its fisheries as a so-called "independent coastal state", the UK's (and the EU's, for that matter) fisheries management autonomy is constrained significantly its obligations under the TCA. Those constraints include: i) the adoption of management measures; ii) the allocation of catches; and iii) access to fishing grounds.

Andrew Serdy's detailed critical analysis of the fisheries provisions of the Trade and Cooperation Agreement (TCA) follows in Chapter 3. The UK fell short of achieving its desired aims set out in the fisheries White Paper as a result of fisheries being the final sticking point so late in the TCA negotiation game. The UK was unable to secure catch shares on the basis of zonal attachment, and could not decouple the inexplicable link between trade and fisheries. The result is trade of fisheries and other goods linked in a single instrument, with which the EU can leverage to their advantage. Serdy also highlights that those future adjustments of UK quota shares may come at a price of unpredictable concessions. Importantly, the dispute settlement provisions of the TCA fail to address overexploitation of fish stocks and are "back to front and wide open to abuse".

In the spirit of cooperative fisheries management, Chapter 4 builds on the issue of annual negotiation of fisheries arrangements between the UK and EU highlighted by Serdy and Churchill.. Interestingly both parties must now proactively engage in negotiations for shared stocks in a trilateral format with Norway for the first time. In addition, Norway and the UK, and the EU and the UK have entered negotiations for bilateral fishing arrangements. The mixed

DOI: 10.4324/9781003252481-10

success of these negotiations, analysed within the chapter, raises questions for the future of fisheries cooperation in unpredictable fisheries management regimes in the North-East Atlantic.

Turning to within the UK, Chapter 5 lays out the domestic legislation passed by the UK Parliament to facilitate its departure from the EU. It then introduces the key provisions of the Fisheries Act 2020, and then outlines devolution and evaluates the competency of devolved fisheries policy across the Scottish, Welsh and Northern Irish legislatures as nations within the UK. Arguably, the Fisheries Act facilitates and empowers the devolved administrations with more regulatory authority over their fisheries, with greater control, adaptive capacity and flexibility in fisheries management and conservation than under the EU's common fisheries policy. However, as indicated in the previous four chapters, the present trade and export barriers outweigh the benefits to greater regulatory autonomy in fisheries. This area is still developing.

Chapter 6, co-authored with Mercedes Rosello, explores the legal framework applicable to the UK in exercising sovereignty over its waters with regard to fisheries enforcement through analysis of two pertinent case studies of fisheries conflicts requiring enforcement/exercising of sovereignty by the UK in recent times. The illustrative case study of Rockall provides an interesting contextualisation of fisheries enforcement obligations

Despite Brexit and departure from the common fisheries policy, the UK still has international obligations for the conservation and management of fisheries and the protection and preservation of the marine environment. These are examined in Chapter 7, which makes the point that the UK remains bound by a suite of international environmental obligations that will shape any future fisheries legislation or policy relating to the conservation and sustainable use of the marine environment. This was demonstrated through the inclusion of some, but not all, key fisheries governance elements highlighted in this chapter within the Fisheries Act 2020, as illustrated in Chapter 5.

Chapter 8 turns to another aspect of international fisheries. It outlines the complexities brought about by Brexit with regard to the UK's membership and participation in regional fisheries management organisations (RFMOs) where it was represented by the EU as a member or non-member. Examining five key RFMOs in turn, the chapter illustrates how the Withdrawal Agreement and subsequent approval by the EU facilitated this. However, the UK may face issues with quota allocation, and its membership of the Indian Ocean Tuna Commission remains a contentious issue.

Finally, Chapter 9 presents a synthesis of expertise from across disciplines and stakeholders from both sides of the English Channel and the Irish Sea. This was achieved through the participation of 11 contributors in the "Legal Challenges Faced by Coastal Communities, Brexit and the New British Fishing Policy" workshop held online on 8 June 2021. Evidently, few in industry are satisfied by the outcome of the negotiations between the UK and the EU. For the fishing industry, the annual negotiations for total allowable catches have created a shared feeling of uncertainty.

It is hoped that this book has highlighted the key cross-cutting issues by examining fisheries in a post-Brexit world from an economic, social and environmental, legal and policy perspective – and has been able to provide inferences that will be helpful for academics, policy and decision-makers, and importantly, the UK and EU fishing industries.

Now Brexit is "done", there will continue to be developments, issues and disputes between stakeholders, and while the new legal framework has been negotiated, we are still in the early stages of its implementation, and many provisions of the TCA, for example, have yet to be tried and tested.

Index

Page numbers in *italics* refer to figures, those in **bold** indicate tables.

www.ingramcontent.com/pod-product-compliance
Lightning Source LLC
LaVergne TN
LVHW021109300926
849160LV00009B/663
9781032172507